SOCIALIST INSECURITY

SOCIALIST INSECURITY

PENSIONS AND THE POLITICS OF UNEVEN DEVELOPMENT IN CHINA

MARK W. FRAZIER

Cornell University Press
Ithaca and London

First published 2010 by Cornell University Press

Printed in the United States of America

Library of Congress Cataloging-in-Publication Data
Frazier, Mark W.
    Socialist insecurity : pensions and the politics of uneven
development in China / Mark W. Frazier.
        p. cm.
    Includes bibliographical references and index.
    ISBN 978-0-8014-4822-5 (cloth : alk. paper)
    1. Old age pensions—China.   2. Social security—
China.   3. Public welfare—China.   4. China—Social
policy.   I. Title.
    HD7105.35.C6F73 2010
    331.25'20951—dc22
                                        2009031449

Cornell University Press strives to use environmentally responsible suppliers and materials to the fullest extent possible in
the publishing of its books. Such materials include vegetable-
based, low-VOC inks and acid-free papers that are recycled,
totally chlorine-free, or partly composed of nonwood fibers.
For further information, visit our website at www.cornellpress
.cornell.edu.

Cloth printing   10 9 8 7 6 5 4 3 2 1

Contents

Preface and Acknowledgments

This book reflects my long-standing interest in how the industrial work-force in China experienced the rapid social, political, and economic changes of the second half of the twentieth century. A reviewer of my book *The Making of the Chinese Industrial Workplace* (2002) concluded with the hope that a sequel would bring my detailed discussion of Chinese workers and their state-owned factories of the 1950s and early 1960s up to the present. This book fulfills only part of that ambitious task by examining a crucial element of the unmaking of the socialist work unit and the mass unemployment that followed in the 1990s. To pull this off politically, the Chinese government adopted a pension program that quickly became its most expensive function. Pensions are the most important tool of the Chinese government in building a new welfare state, yet as I note, pensions also reinforce the persistent income inequalities that Chinese leaders profess to resolve.

I first became interested in pensions while conducting research on labor policy and state-owned enterprise reforms in China. Many of the personnel in state-owned enterprises whom I interviewed about labor questions turned immediately to the issue of pensions and the heavy-handed methods that some enterprise managers felt they were experiencing from local government officials. In conversations with retirees and laid-off workers, it became clear that some were receiving pensions and others were not, often depending on how local officials had treated the firm from which they had recently retired. After further investigation, I came to the conclusion that pensions were not so much a program of deferred compensation for Chinese workers as a political tactic by local governments to pay for the mass layoffs from state-owned enterprises by using contributions from local firms and their employees. The literature on the politics of welfare state retrenchment and welfare state expansion made it clear that China was moving in both directions—at the same time that it was dismantling its old welfare state it was also creating a new welfare state. Yet few of the conventional factors that explain welfare state expansion or retrenchment—labor union strength, party structure, economic crises, and so forth—seemed applicable to China.

This book draws on a broad array of sources. Research for this project began in 2001, just after the Chinese government had issued regulations to end the practice in which retirees, especially those from state enterprises, continued to draw pensions from their former places of work. Local governments had only just begun to take full responsibility for the administration of pensions, and local social insurance agencies were asserting their powers to collect pension and other social insurance fees from enterprises in their respective jurisdictions. Pension reform was (and remains) a topic of considerable debate among enterprise managers, officials, workers, and, of course, retirees. Over the course of regular research trips to China, including six months as a Fulbright Research Fellow in 2004–2005, I sought information from official reports and statistics, as well as from interviews and social surveys conducted in cooperation with colleagues in China. Chapters 4–6 describe two primary data sets from which much of the quantitative analysis is drawn: the 2004 Beijing Area Study (carried out in March 2005) and the Chinese Academy of Social Sciences Institute of Economics State-Owned Enterprise Survey (carried out in 2000). Information on the Beijing Area Study can be found in the appendix to chapter 6. The State-Owned Enterprise Survey, containing detailed data on eight hundred state-owned firms as well as other ownership categories of firms, is described in chapter 5. The discussion in chapter 4 also contains statistical analyses of provincial-level data, as reported through the State Statistics Bureau and the Ministry of Labor and Social Security.

The qualitative data (collected during roughly five years of research) consist of interviews with officials, enterprise managers, and urban residents, including focus groups with manufacturing-sector workers, and a wide array of secondary and primary sources. The primary and secondary sources cited throughout the chapters include specialized labor and social insurance journals and publications obtained in China, official and commercial media reporting on pension issues, and the voluminous reports and analyses commissioned or authored by the staff of various international organizations and multilateral banks that offered advice to Chinese officials undertaking pension reforms.

It would have been impossible to collect this information without the steadfast support of colleagues and friends over the years through which this project has evolved. My thanks go to the following for their patience in explaining to a novice all the complexities of the Chinese pension system and its continuing policy changes: Stuart Leckie, Xiulan Zhang, Shi Xiuyin, Zhang Qixin, Yvonne Sin, Hu Angang, along with others who cannot be directly named. For help in arranging research interviews and contacts, I am indebted to K. K. Tse, Dan Wright, Bill McCahill, Sarah Cook, Zhang Ye, and the Shanghai Academy of Social Sciences.

Special thanks go to those whose advice proved so valuable in the design and collection of the public opinion data presented in chapter 6. At the Research Center on Contemporary China, my deepest gratitude goes to Shen Mingming and Wang Yuhua for their advice and support for the inclusion of my questions on pensions in the 2004 Beijing Area Study. At Horizon Research, Victor Yuan, Gloria Zhang, and Marsha Ma provided invaluable suggestions and tremendous effort in conducting the focus groups in 2005. The State-Owned Enterprise Survey discussed in chapter 5 was generously funded by a Henry M. Luce Foundation grant to the National Bureau of Asian Research, with survey design and implementation carried out by the Chinese Academy of Social Sciences, Institute of Economics. My sincere thanks go to respected colleagues Wang Hongling, David Li, Barry Naughton, and Lisa Keister for their many contributions to the 2000 survey.

The following institutions gave me invaluable opportunities to present my research findings at conferences and colloquia: Qinghua University School of Public Policy and Management; Beijing Normal University School of Social Development and Public Policy; the University of Michigan China Colloquium; the University of California, Berkeley, Boalt Hall School of Law; Cornell University School of Industrial Relations; Dickinson College; the University Of Oklahoma Institute for US-China Issues; Bocconi University (Milan); and the University of Toronto Munk Centre.

Financial support for this research came from several institutions. A Fulbright Research Award through the China program provided resources to complete the necessary fieldwork in 2004–2005. The Ford Foundation Beijing Office and the Pension Center at the Industrial and Commercial Bank of China provided necessary support for much of the survey research involved in this project. Institutional research grants from the University of Louisville and from Lawrence University are sincerely acknowledged.

Many colleagues have provided valuable feedback at various stages of the project. Generous comments on the conference papers that eventually became chapters in this book are gratefully acknowledged from Dorothy Solinger, Isabela Mares, and Gregory Kasza. Kevin O'Brien, Elizabeth Perry, and Gregory Noble provided helpful suggestions and statements of support when the project was in its early stages as a research proposal. Comments on early drafts of papers helped me bring all the details of Chinese pensions into broader significance. For these comments, I am indebted to Neil Diamant, Mary Gallagher, William Hurst, Stanley Lubman, Kevin O'Brien, Elizabeth Perry, Jonathan Unger, and Jaeyoon Won. Special thanks go to Ketty Chen and Scott Lawrence for research assistance in the final stages of manuscript preparation.

As I reached the stage at which the project came together as a book, I was fortunate to receive invaluable comments from readers of various draft chapters. I deeply appreciate the many suggestions from Robert Cox, Chong-do Hah, Ben Read, Dorothy Solinger, Mitchell Smith, and Danie Stockmann. At Cornell University Press, two anonymous readers provided detailed comments that have improved the final product considerably, and I am deeply grateful for the time they spent on the manuscript. For expert copy-editing and production, I thank Candace Akins and Julie Nemer of Cornell University Press. A special word of thanks goes to Roger Haydon of Cornell University Press, who has provided expert advice and timely support for this project, from the proposal stages to final production.

Finally and foremost, my deepest thanks go to Karen, Shelby, and Thomas Frazier, who through the years have provided so much support and encouragement for my work as a scholar.

Conversion of Chinese Yuan to U.S. Dollars

EXCHANGE RATES USED IN TEXT (YEAR-END), YUAN PER US$1.00

1990–1991	5.40 yuan
1995–2003	8.28 yuan
2004	8.23 yuan
2005	8.07 yuan
2006	7.81 yuan
2007	7.31 yuan
2008	6.83 yuan

SOCIALIST INSECURITY

SOCIALIST INSECURITY

Introduction

The headlines and news stories from China paint a bleak picture. The "harmonious society" that Hu Jintao and the Chinese Communist Party (CCP) are striving to create appears to be anything but harmonious. Growing inequalities have fueled protests and other mass incidents involving violent clashes between state authorities and aggrieved citizens. Environmental disasters, product and food safety scandals, mining deaths, and other seeming failures in governance provide ample evidence that the CCP either cannot or will not regulate the factories and firms that have fueled the high-growth Chinese economy. In response to the inequities, conflicts, and other negative side effects of China's unbalanced growth, the CCP in the 1990s pushed through a number of significant social policies, such as rural health-care cooperatives, urban minimum income or subsistence allowances, and old-age pensions. These policies have serious flaws, but we should not take for granted what amounts to a transformation in the welfare regime of China over the past two decades.

Welfare regimes are institutions through which states transfer benefits and services to groups of citizens or to the entire population. The recent changes to the welfare regime of China defy easy characterization.[1] They are not simply a transition to a retrenched postsocialist welfare regime. Nor do they easily fit into a narrative of modernization and convergence toward the welfare states of advanced industrialized economies. We must

---

[1] As Dorothy Solinger (2005) demonstrates, welfare policy in China exhibits traits of both transformative institutional change along with crucial continuities.

look elsewhere to explain changes in the Chinese welfare regime. This book does so by examining in detail the most important part of China's new welfare regime—old-age pensions.

It may come as a surprise to many readers that the most expensive function of the Chinese government (including central and local levels) is not urban construction, infrastructure, or even national defense but, instead, the provision of public pensions. The Chinese government spent nearly 600 billion yuan ($82.1 billon) on pensions in 2007 for 49.5 million retirees (Ministry of Human Resources and Social Security [MOHRSS] 2008a). Civil service pensions for 12 million retired civil servants cost another 150 billion yuan ($20.5 billion). Pension expenditures (excluding civil servant pensions) have risen more than threefold from just under 200 billion yuan in 2000 ($24.1 billion, at the year 2000 exchange rate), as shown in figure I.1. Current pension expenditures represent 2.4 percent of the Chinese gross domestic product (GDP).

Public pensions are the costliest component of any welfare regime because pensions provide retirement income for some or all of the elderly population. These costs easily exceed expenses found in other welfare programs, including health care, unemployment, social assistance, and others. China is therefore not unique in having high levels of pension expenditures relative to other programs.[2]

Pension expenditures in China stand out from those of other welfare regimes by virtue of the fact that they arose not through a coherent policy decision by the central government but through the corrupt, rent-seeking behavior of local governments. The governments of Chinese cities and counties, which by the late 1990s operated as many as 3,400 separate pension funds (Ministry of Labor 1997, 167), thwarted central government efforts to standardize and rationalize pensions. A sequence of central government pension regulations between 1991 and 1997 inadvertently created both the costliest program and the most lucrative source of revenue for local officialdom. Whereas the Chinese central government spends very little on pensions, usually through 50 to 100 billion yuan ($6.8 billion to $13.6 billion) in annual subsidies to provincial governments, urban governments (which are with few exceptions subordinate to provincial governments) spend annually over 750 billion yuan ($102.6 billion) on benefits for 51 million retired factory workers and civil servants. This sum, which has risen at rates

---

[2] It is true, as several scholars have pointed out, that pensions in China have until recently ranked among the highest in the world in terms of income replacement, but this measure reflects the low preretirement basic wages of Chinese pensioners, who worked at a time when state-sector wages were held low (Whiteford 2003; Salditt, Whiteford, and Adema 2007).

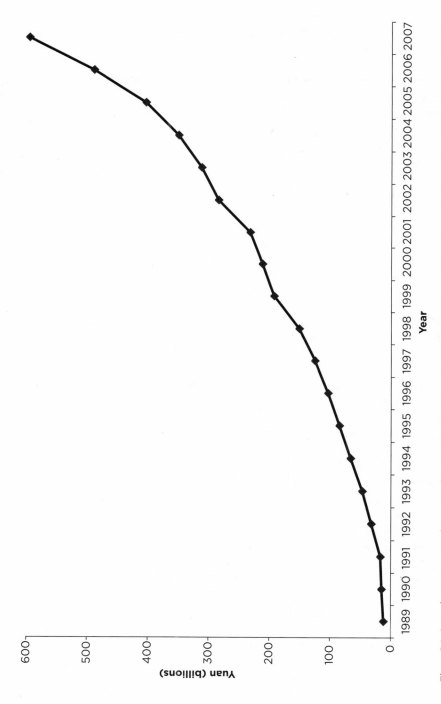

Figure I.1 Annual pension expenditures in China, 1990–2007. Figure includes social insurance pensions only. *Sources:* State Statistics Bureau (2007, table 23-32); Ministry of Human Resources and Social Security (2008a).

over 15 percent per annum, far exceeds what urban and rural local governments spend on education, urban construction, public security, public health, or any other budgetary category.[3] With each city operating its own pension fund, Shanghai and other prosperous cities can accumulate massive sums of pension money in the hands of short-sighted local officials, whereas cities in rust-belt areas fail to collect enough in pension revenues to pay pension benefits for the next month. Moreover, only 51 million retirees have pension rights, and an estimated 80 million people over age sixty in rural areas have access to public pensions. (Approximately 20 million rural residents have coverage under voluntary rural public pension programs.)

The term *pension reform* usually refers to retrenchment or substantial cuts in government expenditures on pensions, but in the case of China, a series of reforms have resulted in rapid increases in pension spending as well as pension debt. Retirement ages, first established in 1951 at age sixty for men and age fifty for women, remain unchanged. Finally, China is distinct from other cases of pension reform for having eschewed the transfer of pension administration to private firms (privatization).

The priority that urban governments place on pensions has arguably come at the neglect of other critical areas of social welfare, including education, environmental protection, consumer safety, and health care. The same incentives that urban officials have to enlarge their pension funds undermine efforts to provide broader public goods. While pensions have become the most expensive function of the Chinese government, health-care expenditures and effectiveness have declined dramatically. The World Health Organization (WHO) ranked the overall Chinese health-care system at 144th out of 188 countries (World Health Organization [WHO] 2000, 152–55). Moreover, health care has undergone de facto privatization. According to a 2008 study by a team of Chinese- and U.S.-based public health experts, the costs of one hospital admission represented 90 percent of average per capita income and the average proportion of an out-of-pocket inpatient visit was over 60 percent (Hu et al. 2008, 1–2). A 2005 report from the Development Research Center of the State Council (the think tank for the premier and cabinet of China) was more blunt: "China's health care reforms have turned hospitals into clubs for the rich" (quoted in *China Daily* 2006).

---

[3] National defense, a central government expenditure, is of course the subject of much scrutiny and debate. But the projections of a Rand study came up with mid- to high-range estimates of 256.6 to 314.5 billion yuan for Chinese defense spending in 2003 (Crane et al. 2005). Pension expenditures that year were 359 billion yuan.

Moreover, the rapid increase in pensions has failed to slow or reduce income inequalities in China. To some extent, this is true anywhere because pensions are more often tied to previous earnings and are not flat-rate benefits. Yet, in China, the expansion of pensions appears to have exacerbated inequality. Eligibility for pensions remains limited largely to urban residents, an exclusion that heightens rural-urban inequalities. Even within urban areas, household surveys have shown that the poorest households are the least likely to have pension income. The China Household Income Project (CHIP) survey shows that pensions made up 6 percent of urban household income in 1988, and this figure rose to 14 percent in 2002. As Qin Gao notes in her analysis of the CHIP data from 1995 to 2002, "In both urban and rural China, social benefits, particularly pensions and health care, were distributed increasingly unequally over time" (2008, 346). Official statistics show that the increase in pension expenditures has failed to keep up with rising average wage levels, even though pension benefits are calculated on the basis of local average wages rather than local prices. Average annual pensions rose from 1,713 yuan ($317) in 1990 (representing approximately 80 percent of average wages) to 9,715 yuan in 2004 (falling to approximately 61 percent of average wages)(State Statisics Bureau [SSB] and Ministry of Labor and Social Security [MOLSS] 2005, table 11-10; SSB 2007, table 5-22). By 2007, annual pensions were at 11,100 yuan ($1,518), whereas average urban wages were 24,932 yuan, or 44.5 percent of average wages (SSB 2007; MOHRSS 2008b). Pensions have also done little to relieve urban poverty. Urban governments established a form of transfer payments to the poor with the minimum income guarantee program (*dibao*) in the late 1990s. The number of recipients of the *dibao* reached 22.7 million in 2007, and according to official statistics, they received an average payment of 102 yuan per person per month (1,224 yuan per year, or $167). This represented a little more than one-tenth of the average pension. Rural residents also were eligible for minimum income payments, and in 2007 this program covered 34.5 million people, an increase of 18.6 million from the preceding year (SSB 2008). They received 37 yuan per person per month (444 yuan per year, or $61) (Ministry of Civil Affairs 2008). Together, these figures highlight a paradox: the impressive number of new welfare programs and increases in welfare spending have not reduced but reproduced economic inequalities in China. This book addresses this paradox by analyzing the political agents that were responsible for the evolution of pensions in China.

It is important to note that the increase in China's pension and other social expenditures over the past two decades reflects in part the fact that urban governments have taken over responsibilities that were once borne by state-owned enterprises (SOEs) and urban collectives (usually smaller firms operated by basic-level urban officials). In the past, welfare expenses for pensions and other programs appeared on the books of enterprises in the command economy; they now appear on the budgetary records of urban governments. Yet it would be wrong to view rising social expenditures in China as merely an artifact of a shift in welfare responsibilities from SOEs to urban governments. The very fact that urban governments have assumed responsibilities for social expenditures is significant. Urban governments, which some scholars have identified as important entrepreneurial actors in the economic growth of China (Segal and Thun 2001), are also, for better and worse, the catalysts that transformed the welfare regime in China. Several studies have looked at the social and economic consequences of pension reforms in China, but few analysts have closely examined the political dynamics driving pension reforms and the broader evolution of the Chinese welfare regime.[4]

Positive or negative assessments of recent changes in welfare policies in China depend on the baseline or comparison group selected to examine social conditions and welfare programs. Some observers compare the welfare policies of contemporary China with those of the Maoist period (1949–1976) or the pre-reform era (prior to 1979); others select a comparable set of countries for measuring progress or setbacks in Chinese health care, pensions, education, and so on. For example, as noted above, most observers argue that primary health care was broadly available in urban and rural areas during the Maoist period, and policy changes under the reforms have left much of rural China without access to basic health care facilities. Urban residents have also faced rising health care costs (Wang 2004; Hu et al. 2008).

But a more positive interpretation of welfare policy changes is also possible when contrasted with the Maoist period. As I will show in the chapters that follow, the new Chinese welfare regime represents a fundamental change in relations between state and society. At the end of the Maoist era, the Chinese welfare regime was egalitarian in name but highly stratified in practice. An individual's benefits depended largely on his or her status in the hierarchy of the urban workforce, with full-time employees in SOEs at

---

[4] Exceptions to this pattern in the study of pension reforms in China include Hurst and O'Brien (2002), Zhao and Xu (2002), and Béland and Yu (2004). The voluminous studies on pension reforms in China, published in English alone, can be grouped into those that primarily emphasize legal-regulatory (Chow 2001; Frazier 2004b; Kwong and Qui 2003), demographic (West 1999; Jackson and Howe 2004), financial (Wang et al. 2000; Sin 2005), and policy prescriptive (Salditt, Whiteford, and Adema 2007; Dunaway and Arora 2007; James 2002; World Bank 1997) aspects.

the top in terms of benefits and farmers at the bottom. As recently as a decade ago, welfare provision as it existed came from urban work units (factories, offices, etc.) and neighborhood committees. Rural residents held on to the remnants of health-care cooperatives, and the vast majority received no old-age pensions. Today, the changes to the welfare regime in China have flattened the employment status hierarchies so that, in theory, all urban workers (including migrant workers) have equal rights to welfare provision through social insurance. The number of urban workers covered by social insurance for pensions stood at 141.3 million in 2006 (SSB 2007, table 23-33). This was only half of the 283.1 million workers in the urban workforce reported in official statistics for that year, but it was a significant rise from the 52.0 million workers who had social insurance pension coverage in 1990 (when urban employment stood at 170.4 million). For other forms of social insurance, the National Bureau of Statistics in 2006 reported that 111.9 million workers had unemployment insurance, 115.8 million workers had health-care insurance, 102.7 million had workplace injury insurance, and 64.6 million had maternity leave insurance (SSB 2007, tables 5-1, 5-2, and 23-34). By 2007, health care coverage for urban workers had risen to 134.2 million (MOHRSS 2008). An estimated 720 million rural residents (or 86 percent of the rural population) had joined rural health-care cooperatives (Hu et al. 2008).

When China's welfare regime is examined from an international perspective, the picture is somewhat mixed. Differences in national accounting standards make direct comparisons of social spending figures difficult across countries. According to World Bank data, Chinese expenditures on health care in 2003 were 2.0 percent of GDP, compared with an average of 2.5 percent for low-middle-income countries and 1.3 percent for low-income countries. The average for the East Asian–Pacific region was 1.9 percent of GDP (World Bank 2006, 102). Pension spending has remained at between 2.1 and 2.4 percent of GDP since 2000 (Salditt, Whiteford, and Adema 2007, 25). This figure is also not large by the standards of transitional or middle-income developing countries. According to the 2008 World Bank Development Indicators (reported in table I.1), Brazil had among the highest pension expenditures in the world, with 12.6 percent of GDP in 2004. The pension expenditures of China are closest to those found in Peru (2.6 percent of GDP in 2000) and Ecuador (2.5 percent of GDP in 2002). Mexico spent 1.3 percent of its 2003 GDP on pensions. The same report shows Russia spending 5.8 percent of GDP (in 2004) on pensions and Poland spending 13.9 percent of GDP (in 2003). But the share of the workforce covered by pensions was only 20.5 percent in China (as of 2005). More important in terms of spending is the fact that in China approximately

TABLE I.1
Pension spending and coverage in advanced, transition, and developing countries

Country	Pension expenditures as percentage of GDP (%)	Percentage of formal-sector labor force covered (%)
Poland	13.9 (2003)	84.9 (2005)
Brazil	12.6 (2004)	52.6 (2004)
Japan	8.9 (2005)	95.3 (2003)
United States	7.5 (2003)	92.5 (2005)
Russia	5.8 (2004)	a
China	2.7 (1996)[b]	20.5 (2005)
Peru	2.6 (2000)	16.3 (2003)
Ecuador	2.5 (2002)	27.0 (2004)
Vietnam	1.6 (1998)	13.2 (2005)
Mexico	1.3 (2003)	34.5 (2002)
Iran	1.1 (2000)	35.0 (2001)
India	a	9.0 (2004)
Nigeria	0.1	1.7 (2005)

Source: World Bank (2008, 72–74).
[a] No information provided in World Bank (2008).
[b] More recent estimates put Chinese pension spending at 2.4 percent of GDP in 2006 (Salditt, Whiteford, and Adema 2007, 25).

one-third of the 150 million people over age sixty receive pensions. As pension rights expand in China and as the population ages, pension spending will continue to grow much faster than the growth rates of China's GDP.[5]

For some, the appropriate peer group for assessing Chinese welfare policies (or any other policy measure) is the postsocialist transition economies, especially Russia. For those who identify the Chinese growth pattern with those of the East Asian developmental states, the welfare policies of China are more sensibly compared with those of Japan, South Korea, Taiwan, and others during their high-growth decades of the twentieth century. As I argue in chapter 1, China's welfare regime can be most fairly and usefully analyzed if we compare it with those of other countries with large populations, which by their very size and distribution of capital and other resource endowments are likely to face built-in income inequalities. Political

[5] Measuring the welfare commitment of a state in terms of spending as a share of GDP can pose several problems. As Gregory Kasza (2006, 74–75) shows, expressing expenditures in terms of GDP underestimates the welfare effort of countries that are undergoing rapid GDP growth. If we compare welfare spending in a high-growth economy (such as Japan between 1950 and 1992 or China since 1979) with that of a developed or slower-growth economy, it is easy to infer that the government is a "welfare laggard." In fact, as Kasza shows of postwar Japan, governments that appear to have low social expenditures relative to GDP could be crafting policies that deliver high levels of welfare spending on a per capita basis.

leaders in China, like those in other large uneven developers such as India, Brazil, and Indonesia, have had to make difficult choices at critical junctures about how to distribute wealth more evenly without undermining policies and coalitions that have supported generally successful but uneven economic growth.

This book is not explicitly comparative in the sense that it covers a discrete set of country cases, but it places the Chinese welfare regime and its public pension system in an implicitly comparative framework. Chapter 1 and the conclusion make reference to the experiences of other large uneven developers that created welfare policies as they faced, like China, fewer resources and less stable labor market institutions than those found in rich countries. Quite clearly, China is unique among large uneven developers for having experienced a socialist revolution and nearly three decades of state socialism. Whether this legacy matters, and how it matters, in the welfare regime of contemporary China will be assessed in the chapters that follow. In addition to its revolutionary past, China is exceptional for its high levels of foreign investment and trade. There are good reasons to expect that such international transactions could influence the design and development of the Chinese welfare regime.

The empirical chapters in this book (chapters 2–6) discuss the institutional legacies, political actors, economic forces, and public pressures that gave rise to the dramatic changes in the welfare regime of China. Welfare regimes anywhere begin as responses to the demands from social forces for protection from the risks associated with industrialization, urbanization, and other social transformations. The histories of welfare regime development in Western Europe, Japan, and elsewhere chronicle the efforts of social affairs or labor ministry bureaucrats to persuade government leaders to create labor and welfare legislation as a preemptive move against more radical redistributive solutions promoted by socialists and some trade unions. Yet, in China, the sequencing was obviously different; socialist revolution, rapid industrialization, and urbanization in the 1950s created a distinct pattern of socialist welfare provision. The gradual introduction by the Chinese state of market forces into the industrial sector in the 1980s, followed by the rapid dismantling of unprofitable state enterprises in the 1990s, set in motion political debates over what to dismantle of the old welfare regime and what to create as part of the new welfare regime. Because local governments promoted and carried out industrialization and the privatization of state enterprises, the process of welfare-regime formation also reflected local, especially urban, government preferences. Urban officials benefited greatly from the creation of social insurance programs that allowed them to collect fees from local firms. Because of the nature of the funding requirements, pensions became the most lucrative source of social insurance revenue for urban governments. Through their individual actions at urban levels to administer pensions and distribute benefits to re-tirees, urban governments created a large transfer program that extended benefits to jobless state-owned workers but did little to resolve issues such as health-care costs or urban poverty.

In this book, I use pensions to make two central arguments about the Chinese welfare regime and its political consequences. First, the contem-porary welfare regime in China has emerged from political conflict on two fronts: the debates over dismantling the socialist welfare regime of the past and the debates over the creation of the new welfare regime. The vast ma-jority of scholarly work conducted on welfare policies around the world examines either the expansion or the reduction of the welfare state. The chapters to come explore the politics of *both* welfare retrenchment and wel-fare expansion in contemporary China. Second, the emergence of a new welfare regime in China has occurred together with new forms of political demands and attitudes toward government. In terms of policy as well as practice, urban workers and others are no longer "subjects" who receive benefits from a paternalistic state but "taxpayers" or contributors who have rights to accumulated premiums for programs such as health care and, most important, pensions. The creation of social insurance–based welfare policies such as pensions shows that the Chinese government can be re-sponsive to social forces even without formal institutions of representative government. Moreover, in creating such welfare policies, the Leninist politi-cal regime in China will be challenged throughout its future to make good on the promises that it has enshrined in rights and policies.

Pensions and welfare policy more broadly are certain to loom large in Chinese politics in the twenty-first century. The CCP pledged at its Seven-teenth Party Congress in 2007, and at a subsequent Central Committee Plenum in October 2008, to address income inequalities and other press-ing social problems under what Hu Jintao termed the "scientific develop-ment outlook." This concept, which the CCP enshrined in its Party Consti-tution in 2007, suggests that the CCP is attempting to remedy the widening gaps in Chinese society by crafting policies that can bring about continued growth while also attending to the numerous problems in health care, edu-cation, environmental standards, and other areas. *Scientific development* refers to having both the rapid economic growth of the past along with scientific approaches to the provision of public goods that the CCP has clearly failed to create in sufficient amounts. Others have noted that attach-ing the word *scientific* to *development* is a political choice by Hu Jintao to implicitly criticize the approach of his predecessor Jiang Zemin, who is associated with the unplanned or inequitable growth policies of the 1990s (Fewsmith 2008, 252–53).

One of the most critical areas that the CCP scientific development strategy will address is the vast divide in health-care and pension coverage between urban and rural citizens. The former are nominally covered by regulations that call for "employees of urban enterprises" to participate in medical and retirement programs. For rural residents, however, health care and pensions are available only if their villages provide such coverage as part of a voluntary program. One telling measure of CCP progress in its scientific development outlook will be the ability of the CCP to create a welfare regime that is capable of supporting the poor with transfer payments and is financially sustainable through a mix of government and individual contributions. If the Hu-Wen administration aspires to deliver benefits to those left behind by the reforms, it could do so by expanding pension rights to most of the working-age population, in effect giving rights to migrant workers and farmers.

New labor legislation passed in 2007 reflects what some have called the populist orientation of the Hu-Wen leadership team. The Labor Contract Law enacted in 2007 remains controversial, largely because it imposes unprecedented obligations on employers regarding the duration of labor contracts, overtime, work rules, and the termination of employment. When the National People's Congress (NPC) posted a draft of the Labor Contract Law in 2006 for public comment, the draft legislation drew broad and heated public response. In late 2008, the NPC took similar steps by posting for public comment a draft of the Social Insurance Law (SIL), which promised to provide universal coverage for pensions and other forms of social insurance. The SIL draft received 70,501 responses (largely through the Internet) from across a broad range of the public during the fifty-day comment period that ended in February 2009 (NPC 2009).

The SIL as of mid-2009 seemed to be headed for formal enactment by the NPC within the next year. Chinese policymakers and international experts have discussed drafts of the SIL since 1994, and the potential costs associated with expanded or universal coverage were largely responsible for the long delay in moving toward final passage (National People's Congress [NPC] 2008). For good reason, Chinese policymakers remain wary of making financial promises to provide coverage for rural residents after having seen the escalating costs associated with pensions in urban areas. When or if the Chinese government expands pension coverage to rural areas and to those urban workers not yet covered (such as migrants, the self-employed, and the unemployed), the costs will be enormous. Raising the payroll tax to finance an expansion in pensions and medical insurance would probably lead to further evasion on the part of employers and, consequently, a surge in informal employment. Employers and workers in China already pay in comparative terms very large social insurance fees, ranging from 30 to 50 percent of the wage bill when health care, injury, and other forms of social insurance are added to pensions.

The findings presented in this book can also contribute to the debate among China specialists over the ability of the CCP to respond to an increasingly complex set of social problems. Are state institutions in China being eroded by corruption at various levels of government, or are new legal and administrative institutions promoting improved governance? Recent publications from China scholars have made strong assertions on both sides of this question (Gilley 2004; Yang 2004; Pei 2006). The example of pensions, and the broader social insurance project of which pensions are the most important part, offers important evidence in this debate.

On the one hand, it is a sign of the substantial expansion in the capabilities of the Chinese state that its officials have created a pension and social insurance system that requires sophisticated monitoring of payrolls and the contributions of each worker over time. On the other hand, the Chinese state has acquired these capabilities at considerable expense in terms of its control over the thousands of social insurance agencies that collect revenues from local firms. The lack of effective controls has led to widespread diversion of pension funds by local governments. The most infamous case was revealed in 2006, when investigators found that the Shanghai government had for more than a decade used its social insurance funds to make an estimated 33 billion yuan ($4.2 billion) in loans to local developers. This case, and the emergence of public pensions in China more generally, reveals a paradox in the expansion of state capacity in China. As the Chinese government enhances its broad capabilities through new welfare programs such as pensions, it loses its ability to monitor the agents running these programs. State capacity expands in terms of the scope of functions that the Chinese state performs, but, at the same time, the lack of central control over local state agents can eventually lead to a dispersion or dilution of state capacity, if not its erosion (Pei 2006). The most direct manifestation of such inadequate monitoring of local officials is the escalating hidden pension debt that local officials have created.

If there is one simple fact in the complex world of pensions, it is that they are explicit promises to pay beneficiaries in the future. Such promises require funding in the present in order to make payments in the future. In

China, the public pension commitment remains unfunded because urban governments have spent virtually every yuan that workers have contributed to individual retirement accounts. Urban governments—aside from the corrupt practice of diverting money from pension funds—have "borrowed" money from individual retirement accounts to pay benefits to current retirees. The lack of adequately funded retirement accounts for future use means that the Chinese government, at all levels, has an extremely large hidden debt.

The practice of borrowing pension revenues and accruing debt to future generations of retirees is certainly not limited to China. The present value of the money that a government owes to future generations of retirees is known as the implicit pension debt (IPD). Measures of IPD vary based on the assumptions that are used for estimating life expectancy, retirement age, and average benefits. The Chinese IPD rose from virtually zero in the 1980s to an estimated 6.33 trillion yuan ($765 billion) in 2000, or 71 percent of the GDP (Wang et al. 2000, 26). This figure was estimated during the late 1990s, in a period of exceptionally low interest rates and deflation. More recent projections by a World Bank study have put the Chinese IPD at 141 percent of GDP for 2001, or 13.23 trillion yuan ($1.6 trillion) in future obligations to pensioners. IPD is projected to remain above 100 percent of GDP for most of this century (Sin 2005, 30–31). These staggering amounts do not include pensions for civil servants or for the few million rural residents who are in voluntary pension schemes. When and if pension coverage expands, this debt will certainly rise. With each new eligible citizen covered by pensions will come another guarantee by the state to pay for that citizen's retirement benefits.

When analysts projected what Chinese social spending would include if pensions were expanded to provide universal coverage, the estimated government expenditures as a percentage of GDP roughly doubled. A 2005 Rand study estimated that government expenditures on pensions, education, health, and interest costs on government debt will rise from 7.5 percent of GDP in 2000 to 15.5 percent in 2025 (Crane et al. 2005, 215). This estimate was based on the assumption that the Chinese government will provide a small universal pension of 20 percent of basic wages to all citizens (urban and rural) over 65.[6]

The many predictions that experts make about the future of China are usually based on debatable assumptions about the continuation of recent trends. One lesser acknowledged trend, however, is certain to persist for

---

[6] The Rand estimate does not include the costs of making up for large deficits in the current pension system.

the foreseeable future: population aging. The share of the Chinese population over age sixty is predicted to triple between 1990 and 2030, by which time the elderly will make up 24 percent of the population of China; the elderly population is projected to increase from 130 million in 2005 to 397 million in 2040 (Jackson and Howe 2004, 2). With declining fertility rates, the ratio of the Chinese working-age population to the elderly will fall from 6.4 to 1 in 2000 to 2 to 1 in 2040 (Jackson and Howe 2004, 6). By 2030, the age structure in China will resemble that of contemporary Japan but with a per capita income of only 20 percent of industrialized countries today (World Bank 1997, 14). But the expansion in pension spending noted here has come *before* the demographic consequences of the one-child policy begin to take their most serious effect, around 2015. Pension spending in China accelerated beginning in the 1980s and has continued to grow rapidly since then, well before demographic pressures made their mark on welfare policy decisions.

We can question the claim, usually attributed to Auguste Comte, that "demography is destiny," but demographic changes do bring predictable challenges. For example, population aging requires higher taxes, much higher government debt, or rapid productivity increases to finance the retirement and health-care needs of the expanded elderly population. Population aging is not exclusive to nation-states; many large firms face the same problem if they have made past assurances to provide company-sponsored pensions and health-care expenses for their workers. A "demography is destiny" analyst might therefore explain the demise of the U.S. automobile industry as the result of past promises and demographic shifts within the workforce as much as poor management. How politicians (or business owners) respond to population aging is less predictable, and this is where the determinism of the demographers has to be pushed aside in favor of politics. Social scientists (or historians, for that matter) have scarcely scratched the surface in addressing patterns of political conflict in countries undergoing population aging. For China, this much can be said: the promises made under pension policies adopted in the 1990s mean that the Chinese government and a shrinking workforce will be asked to finance the heavy pension costs for an aging Chinese society. China may not go the way of General Motors, but population aging will compel China to replace its successful but now outdated economic model with something new. The political conflict over that replacement process is just beginning. As the global financial crisis deepened in late 2008, with tens of thousands of factories in the Pearl River Delta closing their doors, the stakes rose considerably in the search for a new growth model—and for welfare polices to go with it.

CHAPTER 1

Local Coalitions, Uneven Growth, and National Welfare Politics

During summer 2006, more than one hundred investigators and auditors from central government ministries descended on Shanghai to piece together a vast network of loans and bribes among leading Shanghai officials and entrepreneurs. The investigation team members sequestered themselves behind the gates of a local hotel, and police had to be called out to disperse scattered protests (Areddy 2006). At the center of the loan scandal was the Shanghai Social Insurance Agency (SIA), whose pension fund had become the chief source of financing for at least a dozen of the property developers in the city and their high-profile real estate projects. According to subsequent reports and evidence presented at trial, Zhu Junyi, the head of the Labor and Social Security Bureau, had taken bribes of 1.6 million yuan in exchange for loaning out 3.7 billion yuan ($474 million) of the pension fund to local real estate developers, a toll-road operator, and other local businesses.[1] An investigation completed in 2007 by the National Audit Office revealed that the Shanghai SIA had illegally diverted as loans and other investments a total of 32.9 billion yuan ($4.2 billion). The Shanghai pension fund had financed many of the landmark real estate developments and commercial plazas in the city (Chen 2008; Wang, Zhao, and Ji 2008). The Shanghai pension scandal also brought down Chen Liangyu,

---

[1] At Zhu's trial in December 2007, prosecutors said that Zhu had turned over 2.65 billion yuan in loans to Zhang Rongkun, who rewarded Zhu with a 1.32 million yuan bribe, including half a kilogram of gold bullion. Zhang also provided Zhu's wife with a job at his company and gave Zhu's daughter a diamond necklace, a digital camera, and funds for overseas travel and study (Chen 2007).

who was the most powerful Shanghai politician and both the party secretary of Shanghai and a member of the CCP Politburo when the scandal broke out. Chen was expelled from his party and government posts in July 2007. In addition, dozens of Shanghai's leading politicians, top managers of SOEs and private business magnates were implicated in the case.

The Shanghai pension scandal is arguably the most dramatic corruption case in the history of the People's Republic of China (PRC), given the amount of money and the ranks of the officials charged with various crimes. The scandal will probably go down in history as CCP Party Secretary Hu Jintao's decisive move against the "Shanghai faction" of CCP officials— Chen and others deemed to be overly loyal to Hu's predecessor and the leading light of the Shanghai faction, ex-party chief Jiang Zemin (1989–2002). Yet the Shanghai pension scandal is more than a story of how factional politics brought down the Shanghai leadership. The scandal also revealed the extremes to which urban officials could go in fulfilling the ambiguous and largely unfunded mandates handed down by the central government in the 1990s to enact social welfare measures. These unfunded mandates, found largely in the Labor Law of 1994 and in subsequent regulations, required that local governments set up social insurance programs that could provide pensions, unemployment payments, reimbursements for medical expenses, compensation for workplace injuries, and maternity leave payments. Because coverage for these programs was limited to employees of urban enterprises, city officials bore the direct responsibility for administering them.

Urban officials used these unfunded mandates as the basis of their authority to collect social insurance fees, at rates they set themselves, from technically all urban employers and their workers. Social insurance revenues for pensions alone quickly exceeded the amounts local governments collected in actual tax revenues (see chapter 4). Without adequate oversight, pensions and other social insurance funds were easily diverted for other uses. In the city of Guangzhou (where two officials allegedly diverted 600 million yuan in pension funds), in Hunan province (71 million yuan), in Liaoning province (11.5 million yuan), and in Zhejiang province ("hundreds of million yuan"), the general pattern was consistent with what occurred in Shanghai (National Audit Office 2006). Local officials in charge of the funds collaborated with local business owners, who promised high rates of return on investments or high interest payments on loans. A former SIA official in Guangzhou went on trial in late 2007 for allowing some 520 million yuan to disappear after having loaned out 750 million yuan during the 1990s. Prosecutors were pursuing another seventeen criminal cases related to the diversion of Guangzhou pension funds (Xinhua 2007).

An official report in 2006 from the National Audit Office estimates that local governments in China—excluding Shanghai—had loaned and/or embezzled 7.1 billion yuan ($857 million) in pension, medical, and unemployment insurance funds, including 4.8 billion yuan ($580 billion) after the year 2000. The placement of pension funds in special accounts to be used by various entities, including local enterprises, accounted for 2.3 billion of the 4.8 billion yuan in misused funds (National Audit Office 2006).

For its part, the Shanghai SIA managed to collect over 10 billion yuan from the largest employers in the city by operating a "supplemental pension fund" in exchange for tax deductions. It had been a well-known fact among observers of pension policy in China throughout the late 1990s and early 2000s that the Shanghai SIA had sought higher returns on its 10 billion yuan ($1.2 billion) supplemental pension fund by making loans to various financial and real estate companies that promised an attractive rate of return on the borrowed SIA funds. The Shanghai SIA also participated in initial public offerings, acquiring shares of blue-chip SOEs that were listed on the Shanghai Stock Exchange in the early 2000s (Xinhuanet 2002). It was only in 2006, after what must have been approval from the highest levels, that the supplemental pension fund of the Shanghai SIA was regarded as illegal in the eyes of the CCP anticorruption monitor, the Central Disciplinary Inspection Commission.

The Shanghai SIA also operated what was, ironically in retrospect, the most successfully developed social insurance program in the country. In addition to collecting supplemental pension funds that could be provided as extra pension benefits to high-income earners who worked in the thriving commercial and financial sectors, Shanghai SIA officials had also established pioneering programs in health insurance for migrants and for rural residents in surrounding counties (see chapter 4). The Shanghai Labor and Social Security Bureau also had received plaudits for its reemployment programs for laid-off workers (Lee and Warner 2004). As subsequent events revealed, the paragons of welfare regime development in Shanghai were in many ways the victims of their own success.

THE ARGUMENT

The Chinese welfare regime expanded rapidly but erratically in the 1990s as local politicians sought to continue economic growth without further widening existing inequalities. The Chinese experience with welfare development is best understood not as a retrenchment but as a response to uneven growth. Whereas many scholars compare the political economy of China with those found in transition economies or in the East Asian developmental states, in this book I propose an alternative grouping to understand the political economy of welfare in China. Like other large-population states with diverse regional economies, China faces built-in inequalities by virtue of its size and geographical expanse. Not all such states have managed to achieve sustained growth, but those that have—such as Brazil, Indonesia, India, and South Africa (at different times)—are comparably analyzed as large uneven developers. The large uneven developers commonly face a political choice after years of rapid growth. That choice comes down to whether the governments will adopt welfare policies to redistribute wealth from the beneficiaries of the growth to those left behind by otherwise generally successful growth policies. Proposals to establish new welfare programs to compensate these lagging sectors create political opposition from most employers and from other beneficiaries of the status quo. Public pensions represent an attractive solution to the political conflict over uneven growth. Pensions transfer wealth primarily across generations rather than across income groups, which makes pensions less likely to face opposition than other, more explicitly redistributive programs that transfer wealth from rich to poor. Among the large uneven developers, Brazil and South Africa (discussed in the conclusion) adopted what turned out to be extremely costly pension programs. India, by contrast (as of 2009) retained its outdated provident model that relies unrealistically on individual savings. In all three of these cases, however, politicians retained somewhat rigid labor market institutions. China (as discussed in the next chapter in some detail) took a distinct path among large uneven developers by achieving the introduction of public pensions based on social insurance together with the liberalization of labor markets.

The reasons that China took this path toward social insurance pensions with labor market liberalization are somewhat puzzling when we examine the situation from the perspective of urban governments and state enterprises.[2] In the 1990s, the last thing that an urban government would have

---

[2] In this book, the term *urban governments* refers to the 283 administrative units classified as municipal governments (*dijishi*) and the 369 administrative units classified as county-level governments (*xianjishi*) (State Statistics Bureau [SSB] 2007, table 1-1). *Urban governments* also refers to Shanghai, Beijing, Tianjin, and Chongqing, which are provincial-level cities (*zhixiashi*) that oversee eighteen to nineteen (forty in the case of Chongqing) district governments classified as *dijishi*. As noted in chapters 2 and 4, pension administration is concentrated at the top levels of these provincial-level cities (e.g., district governments do not operate their own pension funds).

desired would be to assume the potentially very large costs posed by pensions. Fiscal reforms in 1994 drastically reduced local revenues by turning sizable shares of revenue over to the central government coffers. While local revenues declined, the fiscal responsibilities of urban governments remained the same (Organisation for Economic Cooperation and Development [OECD] 2006). Urban governments should have preferred to let state enterprises continue to make payments to their retirees, and many cities did in fact maintain this stance. Yet, by the early 2000s, urban governments had taken over the administration of pensions and the expensive promises that came with such a program. By 2006, they were responsible for providing pension benefits to 46.3 million pensioners (not including civil servants) by drawing up social insurance fees collected from 141.3 million urban workers and their employers (State Statistics Bureau [SSB] 2007). The sources of this transformation are explored in subsequent chapters, and here I offer a preview of the argument in theoretical and empirical terms.

The theoretical basis for understanding the rapid adoption of pension funds by urban governments lies with what comparative political scientists call historical institutionalism. This concept (discussed in greater detail in chapter 3) essentially boils down to the notion that political preferences do not create institutions but are, instead, created by them (Thelen and Steinmo 1992; Pierson and Skocpol 2002; Thelen 2003). For historical institutionalists, groupings such as classes, factions, or cultures do not explain patterns of political conflict and policy outcomes as well as the rules and norms (i.e., the institutions) that people use to interpret problems and pursue their resolution. The power of existing institutions to influence preferences constrains the possibilities of radical policy changes and creates a pattern of path-dependent or incremental change. In the terms discussed here, to explain a welfare regime transformation such as that which occurred in China during the 1990s requires paying close attention to how individuals and groups within state and society—urban officials, SOE managers, SOE workers, SOE retirees, and others—defined their interests and mobilized resources to defend the policy status quo in the face of calls for rapid policy change.

In empirical terms, the argument found in subsequent chapters can be summarized as follows. Pensions rose to prominence in the new Chinese welfare regime because of the conflict over how to distribute the social costs of SOE reforms in the 1990s. SOE reforms led to the reduction of state-sector employment from 109.5 million employed in 1996 to 69.2 million employed in 2002. Employment in urban collectives declined even more drastically in percentage terms over the same period, falling from

29.5 million to 10.7 million by 2002.[3] Urban officials, in collusion with state enterprise managers, used local pension funds to shift many of these 40 million workers from ailing enterprises to the pension registers. Urban officials and state enterprise managers thus gained access to valuable state assets through privatization while successfully externalizing the social costs of those made jobless in SOE reform. The central government, as well as urban workers who kept their jobs, indirectly assumed most of these costs, which largely took the form of an exploding pension debt. Moreover, urban officials managed to retain administrative control over the Chinese public pension system by operating local pension funds. Governments in rich areas, such as Shanghai, created a massive extra-budgetary source of revenue (and investment capital). Governments in poor areas had a more complicated task of externalizing the social costs of SOE reform through pensions, but even in these cases they eventually coaxed large amounts of subsidies from the Ministry of Finance to cover pension costs. In short, the Chinese pension-dominant welfare regime emerged from a coalition of local cadres and crony capitalists who overcame resistance from reform-minded bureaucrats in Beijing and from the urban public.

The power of this coalition of local cadres and crony capitalists helps to account for the specific designs and limitations of the new Chinese welfare regime: the preference for social insurance over direct transfers, the increasing levels of social expenditures dominated by pensions, and the persistent inability of the central government to redistribute welfare spending across localities. This outcome has compromised the capacity of the central government to use the impressive accumulation of wealth in Chinese society for new welfare programs, but at the same time the central government and CCP leadership have escaped blame for the many welfare policy failures. Urban governments defend the highly fragmented nature of pensions because pension funds have become an important resource for politicians to deliver selective benefits to specific constituencies. Fiscal relations within the multilevel governance structure of China give urban politicians powerful incentives to oppose a nationalized universal pension scheme, which would deprive them of a valuable political resource.

---

[3] Only some of these lost 60 million jobs can be accounted for by the conversion of SOE ownership into limited-liability, joint-stock, and other corporate forms. Firms in this ownership category are grouped as "other" forms of ownership, along with foreign-invested firms, in Chinese national statistical reporting. The number of jobs reported in the "other" ownership category rose from 9.4 million in 1996 to 25.6 million in 2002 (SSB and Ministry of Labor and Social Security [MOLSS] 2005, 24).

MULTILEVEL GOVERNANCE IN CHINA

China is constitutionally a unitary state in which subnational governments are stratified across multiple layers (provinces, counties and cities, townships, and villages). Although the CCP possesses the all-important powers of personnel appointments and promotions, local governments at lower levels retain considerable powers of implementation, especially following administrative reforms beginning in 1980. These reforms altered fiscal arrangements to give local governments greater incentives and responsibilities to provide local public goods such as economic growth, infrastructure, and social services (Shue 1988; Shirk 1993; Oi 1999; Whiting 2001). With this fiscal decentralization has come a crucial transformation in property rights. Local authorities at basic levels (cities, counties, and townships) possess rights to revenue from local economic activity and, therefore, have strong incentives to create and sustain revenue-generating firms (Montinola, Qian, and Weingast 1995; Oi 1999). Local officials also have political incentives to invest these revenues in local infrastructure and related projects because their promotions within the CCP hierarchy are tied explicitly to local growth rates (Whiting 2001; Landry 2008).

Fiscal and administrative decentralization created overlapping regulatory authority in many policy areas (Lieberthal and Oksenberg 1988; Lieberthal 1992). Because local territorial governments usually have to fund the operations of local agencies belonging to the central government with budgeting, staff, and other resources, policy implementation is dependent on local governments and their priorities. As a result, the central government can find it very difficult to implement policies if it is not in the interests of local officials to do so (Mertha 2005). Kevin O'Brien and Lianjiang Li (1999) argue that reforms gave local rural officials a greater degree of autonomy from central policymakers above and from social forces below, resulting in "selective implementation" by rural officials. Andrew Wedeman (2001) shows that policy noncompliance is virtually guaranteed by the time a central directive passes down through and is altered by agents found in the five separate levels of government: the center, provinces (in some areas, prefectures), counties, townships, and villages. To date, very few studies of China have looked at local government behavior in terms of its influence on social policy.[4]

The same pattern of intragovernmental conflict that others have identified in the Chinese policymaking process has also prevailed in the case of

[4] An exception is Huang (2004).

Chinese attempts to reform pensions and other social insurance programs.[5] The Ministry of Labor and Social Security (MOLSS; renamed in 2008 the Ministry of Human Resources and Social Security, MOHRSS), the Ministry of Finance, and the Ministry of Civil Affairs (MCA) have long engaged in turf battles over the design and implementation of rules related to pension and other social insurance matters. Each of these ministries had regulatory control over pensions for particular groups. The Ministry of Personnel handled pensions for civil servants and employees of public-sector units (*shiye danwei*), the Ministry of Labor managed pensions for state enterprise employees, and the MCA provided pensions to eligible military veterans and, until the late 1990s, to those in rural areas that had established pensions (Leckie and Pai 2005, 35). This diffusion of authority over pensions also meant that reforms to consolidate pensions would create bureaucratic winners and losers. For example, in 1998, the MCA waged an unsuccessful battle to retain regulatory control over the voluntary pension programs in rural areas. Rural pensions, which according to MCA figures covered 82.8 million participants and nearly 558,000 pension recipients, were handed over to the newly named MOLSS (Leisering, Gong, and Hussain 2002, 18). A subsequent study of rural social policy sponsored by the Asian Development Bank offered rare criticism of the transfer of rural pensions to MOLSS. Once MCA knew that it was turning over rural pensions to MOLSS, the program stagnated considerably (Leisering, Gong, and Hussain 2002, 24–26). Whereas the number of those receiving rural pensions reached 3.9 million in 2007, the number of contributors had fallen drastically to 51.7 million from the 82.8 million a decade earlier (Ministry of Human Resources and Social Security [MOHRSS] 2008a).

In addition to horizontal or interministerial fragmentation, the central government faces numerous obstacles in gaining adequate compliance and in monitoring the behavior of local government officials to comply with pension and other social insurance regulations. The MOHRSS, despite its 2008 upgrade to a super-ministry, remains limited in its ability to influence policy implementation at subprovincial levels. City and county governments hold sway over the allocation of personnel and budgeting for SIAs, which are charged with the critical task of collecting pension contributions and distributing them to pensioners. But the fact that pensions involve the potential collection of large amounts of money from local sources is crucial.

As I discuss in subsequent chapters, social insurance agencies have emerged as powerful players in local finance and welfare provision in China.

---

[5] Duckett (2003) describes the bureaucratic competition and intragovernmental conflicts over the introduction of health policy reforms during the 1990s.

SIAs are responsible for all revenues and benefits related to five forms of social insurance: pensions, health care, unemployment, workplace injuries, and maternity leave. Central government efforts to merge SIAs and their social insurance funds at higher levels of administration, such as the provincial level, have met with fierce resistance. Social insurance funds and SIAs represent the money and power behind the new Chinese welfare regime.

Some have challenged the relationship between decentralization and reforms (Cai and Treisman 2006), arguing that the center directed and coordinated decentralization, and that the real key to effective growth in China lies in the ability of the center to maintain effective controls over local officials. Thus, one interpretation of pension reforms in China is that the central government successfully created a public pension system by creating the right incentives for local officials. Provisions for local governments to establish social insurance measures are spelled out in the 1994 Labor Law and in subsequent regulations on social insurance. This line of argument asserts that the central government effectively turned over the financing of retirement pensions from state budgets (channeled through state enterprises) to local governments. As a result, the Chinese state (including local levels) took on a new role in regulating a complex social insurance scheme based on mandatory contributions. Indeed, for some observers, the very large amounts of money (more than 649 billion yuan, or $88.8 billion, in 2007) that urban governments collect for social insurance pensions could be construed as evidence of expanded central government power because local agents did the bidding of the center to establish a new and very costly welfare program.

I argue otherwise in the chapters to come. The evolution of a new welfare regime in China created a highly fragmented system in which each city and county operates its own pension and other social insurance funds. This structural fragmentation is a major constraint on building a national pension system. More broadly, the fragmented, localized nature of the Chinese welfare regime has created serious obstacles to redistribution across regions.

China scholars and the China-watching community in general disagree on the extent to which Chinese officials have been able to come up with effective reforms to cope with various crises in health care, environmental degradation, and corruption, among others (Gilley 2004; Yang 2004; Pei 2006; Peerenboom 2007). Much of this debate depends on an assessment of the extent to which the central government can discipline its local agents. For skeptics, the ability of local officials to ignore or evade central government directives means that decentralization has undermined state capacity. For optimists, the same central government that decentralized administration to local officials can also revoke this authority as it wishes by recentralizing control over areas deemed sufficiently important. At the very least, the central government can come up with the right incentive structure if it wishes to get local officials to comply with policy goals (Huang 1996; Landry 2008).

My analysis of the emergence of social insurance agencies and the pre-eminence of pensions in the new Chinese welfare regime follows from some of the assumptions found in the literature on predatory states. Scholars who have applied this label to the actions of state officials usually do so on the basis of their rent-seeking behavior, in which officials take bribes from firms in exchange for exclusive rights over some economic activity (Shliefer and Vishny 1993). Recent studies using statistical analyses of different data sets have examined the effects of federalism and decentralization on corruption and have found that multiple levels of government and decen-tralized fiscal powers are associated with greater levels of corruption (Fan, Lin, and Treisman 2009). China presents a classic case for studying how fiscal and administrative decentralization generate corruption. Minxin Pei (2006) uses the concept predatory local states to emphasize how corrup-tion occurs among local Chinese governments, whose rent-seeking has eroded overall state capacity.

As illustrated in the Shanghai pension scandal, local state predation was not the classic case of government officials taking bribes in exchange for rents but, instead, was a matter of public officials abusing their legal author-ity to provide public goods. The problem was not that local governments such as those in Shanghai arbitrarily gave out old-age pensions to favored clienteles. Consistent with Pei's concept of decentralized predation, urban governments enjoyed a new source of extra-budgetary revenue when they levied social insurance fees on local firms and then spent this money on projects entirely unrelated to providing old-age pensions. During the 1990s, urban governments facilitated deals in collusion with SOE managers to sell off state enterprises and use pension funds to compensate those made jobless in the process. Following the completion of the SOE sell-offs, ur-ban governments used collected pension revenues as the basis for loans to real estate developers and other favored clients. Also consistent with de-centralized predation, the central state was deprived of access to these revenues and could exert only limited controls over local officials.

Despite its utility in explaining corruption and governance failures, the concept of local predatory states has some important limitations. First, the theory does not make clear what happens to the revenues that local offi-cials extract from society. Pei (2006, 135–39) presents convincing evidence that local predatory states spent considerable sums of money on themselves, in the form of enlarged budgets and personal bank accounts (domestic and foreign). Yet there is nothing in the theory of predatory states that identifies the conditions under which the predators might squander the extracted surpluses on personal consumption, when they might reinvest the funds in improving their extractive capacities, or when they might choose to put some money toward broader collective purposes, including investment in public goods or even redistribution through payments to the poor.

Second, the discussion of predatory states has little to say about the response of society or of the groups within society who are victims of local predation. The theory does not specify the conditions under which social forces might resist the levies of local predators and what form such resistance might take. Presumably local state predation represents some equilibrium condition in which state agents and the social groups from which they extract revenue have reached an accommodation. But this raises the question of how long such predation can occur without the depletion of the predator's tax base. Moreover, how can the public or groups within it curb the grabbing hand of local state predators or at least persuade them to redistribute some of their revenues? Political institutions such as legislatures, public auditors, and an open media could curb the personal consumption habits of local predators, but they could also prevent local predation in the first place.

A third problem with the assumed consequences of predatory states is that their rent-seeking does not *ipso facto* result in the erosion of state capacity and governance capabilities. Pei and others point to the corruption and rent-seeking found in China and then link this behavior to the poor governance and social welfare indicators found in various cross-national rankings and measurements (Pei 2006, 168–81). Clearly much of the poor performance, in terms of both social spending and performance on measures such as public health, can be attributed to the distorted incentives of local officials to spend the revenues from their tax collections on goods and projects that serve their personal and career interests over those of the public. (For example, buildings that house local government offices in China are notorious for being oversized relative to their assigned functions and ostentatious relative to their surrounding communities.) On the other hand, it is plausible that local officials could face strong incentives to redistribute their revenues. Two such redistributional incentives are identified in this book: (1) the threat of public protest and social unrest and (2) a credible threat of disciplinary action from the central government. The case of the Shanghai pension scandal and the central government investigations that followed demonstrate the ability of the central government to pursue the punishment of local officials engaged in the corrupt use of pension funds. As discussed in chapter 3, the outbreak of protests over unpaid pensions compelled local governments to spend their social insurance funds on pension benefits and to increase them over time.

Although the studies of local predation serve as a much-needed corrective to the overly optimistic developmental state arguments found in earlier accounts, both sides in this debate assume that local officials—and, by extension, the Chinese state—pursue economic development as a strategy solely for the purpose of accumulating wealth and power. Others have critiqued this functionalist logic for overlooking what they consider to be the essence of state-building—the process of acquiring legitimacy (Shue 2004; Lee 2008, 16–19). Just as states must devise strategies to accumulate wealth from the populations that they aspire to govern, they must also justify their right to rule over these populations. Indeed, the latter may be a necessary condition for successfully achieving the former. State claims to legitimacy can draw on multiple sources and can vary across time, as is obvious in the case of China. Welfare policy as analyzed here and in the chapters that follow lies at the intersection of these twin imperatives of accumulation and legitimation. Modern states that base part of their legitimacy on improving the well-being of the people must appear to be responsive to those who suffer declining living standards, and they must remain attentive to inequalities more generally. To finance welfare programs that can enhance or renew declining legitimacy, state officials must raise revenues. At this point, local state agents charged with accumulating revenues can quickly undermine the claims of legitimacy by the central state. Legitimation and accumulation thus take place concurrently and in contradiction with one another. As Ching Kwan Lee writes of China, "local officials see their abiding interest in accumulation while they scorn welfare reforms as unfunded mandates thrust upon the localities by the center. . . . The pursuit of local accumulation without a corresponding emphasis on welfare and equity has begun to chip away at the regime's legitimacy" (2008, 19).

Yet local accumulation does not have to work at cross-purposes with the provision of welfare and, by extension, the renewal of legitimacy. By collecting social insurance revenues from society, local states in China deploy their well-worn strategies of accumulation. By spending social insurance funds on pensions and other programs, the local state demonstrates or aligns itself with the central state's strategy of legitimation. The logic of accumulation is clear—local states want more money. The logic of legitimation is less clear. It is understandable that local states want to preserve their monopoly on political power, but it is more difficult to explain why they wish to comply with unfunded mandates from the central state. Do they merely pay lip service to central government mandates? Do they provide minimal funding to certain welfare programs while neglecting others? Are they more responsive to certain social forces that demand welfare provision than others? In this book, I identify conditions under which local states engage in the redistribution of revenues and thereby deploy legitimation strategies in addition to their accumulation strategies. In so doing, I address the issue of how politicians in an authoritarian regime respond to public preferences and to public opinion more generally.

The secrecy surrounding the way that the CCP reaches decisions on policy and other issues makes it difficult to determine how or even if public preferences influence policymaking in China. Although it would be going too far to say that the CCP or government decision-making bodies are responsive to public opinion, leaders at various levels often make reference to the public as a potential constraint on policy choices, and the discussion of pensions is no exception. Chinese politicians and policy analysts routinely associate pensions and other social welfare policies with the maintenance of social stability. A CCP secretary of Liaoning province opened a 2003 report in the influential CCP journal *Qiushi* with the remark: "Establishing and improving the social security system is a matter concerning social stability and national long-term peace and stability" (British Broadcasting Corporation [BBC] 2003). During interviews for this book and at a 2004 central government policy conference on pensions that I attended as an observer, officials frequently ruled out policy options such as raising retirement ages because they felt that the public reaction would be too strong. "We Chinese officials fear the public" (*pa laobaixing*) was a frequent comment over the course of my interviews with officials handling pensions. Such putative awareness of anticipated public reaction does not of course rule out repression of public opinion, as shown in the case of Di Tiangui, the retired SOE worker in Taiyuan who openly called for an independent pensioners' association for SOE retirees in 2002 and who was quickly charged with subverting the state and jailed for nearly one year (China Labor Watch 2003). Some informants traced the intense focus of the central government on the living standards of the elderly to the shocking display of collective action in May 1999 by Falungong, when adherents peacefully surrounded the main gate of the compound housing top CCP officials in Beijing.[6] The membership of Falungong, at that time at least, came largely from the ranks of urban retirees. A decade later, the

---

[6] This can be found in documents such as National Committee on Aging (2002).

Seventeenth Party Congress in 2007 stressed the CCP commitment to providing social welfare to those left behind by the Chinese reforms. The CCP emphasis on "scientific development" represented an implicit criticism of the unpopular and inequitable development approach of Jiang Zemin's leadership in the 1990s.

During the 1990s, the political challenge to the CCP from urban workers arose less from their ability to mobilize as organized opponents of state enterprise reforms than from their ability to voice grievances that called into question the ideological and economic rationale of state enterprise reforms. Urban state-sector workers who lost their jobs and benefits during SOE reforms used public protests to highlight the broken promises of the CCP and the hypocrisy of a nominally socialist regime abandoning the core principles of socialism (Hurst and O'Brien 2002; Won 2004; Cai 2005; Lee 2008). They could also point to the massive corruption in the transfer of state assets to officials who enriched themselves through the sale of state enterprises. Protests by jobless SOE workers, many of whom had been designated by state policy as "pensioners" or "laid-off workers," became a commonplace occurrence in many Chinese cities in the 1990s and early 2000s, especially in rust-belt areas or older industrial centers. Such protests were not expressions of resistance against pension reforms but expressions of grievances against factory managers and city officials for their failure to compensate those left jobless by SOE restructuring. Pension protests subsided in the early 2000s. This decline in protest activity can largely be attributed to the increase in pension spending by urban governments and to the provision of central government subsidies to rust-belt areas in which local governments encountered difficulties in paying pensions on time.[7] Urban officials increased pension benefits by taking funds from the newly established retirement savings accounts of workers and using them to pay pension benefits to contentious SOE retirees. Urban governments used pensions to undermine the original intent of pension reforms—whose goal had been to reduce, not increase, future pension burdens for the Chinese government.

My analysis in the chapters to come examines pensions in the new Chinese welfare regime from the perspective of accumulation and legitimation, and shows how the cooperation of social forces in both processes is cru-

---

[7] Sporadic protests were reported when the Shanghai pension scandal was announced in summer 2006. A handful of retirees were said to have gathered outside the compound of the Shanghai SIA in reaction to the news that authorities had diverted billions of yuan from the city pension fund (Areddy 2006).

cial. My account also suggests the need for new lines of theoretical inquiry in comparative studies of how welfare regimes form and develop.

CHINA AND WELFARE REGIMES

The abundant literature on the differences and similarities among welfare regimes provides plenty of clues for analyzing the case of welfare policy development in contemporary China. Those who emphasize the similarities among welfare regimes argue that they evolve in a linear and largely convergent process of modernization, whereas those who stress the differences among welfare regimes point to variations in patterns of political conflict among classes, interest groups, bureaucratic agencies, or levels of government. As I show in the discussion that follows, the Chinese welfare regime cannot be adequately explained as the product of structural changes associated with urbanization and modernization. The Chinese welfare regime is also difficult to explain, as most accounts do, solely in terms of national-level political conflict and compromise that brings forth national legislation. Finally, the Chinese welfare regime challenges explanations that view international economic forces and other external linkages as the primary sources of welfare regime development.

The Timing of Welfare Regimes

The story of welfare regime emergence and development, as derived from studies of the first welfare regimes in the West and in Japan, is in many respects a story of industrialization, urbanization, and modernization. As economies industrialize, fiscal surpluses are available for states to spend on welfare programs for the population. As societies urbanize, interest groups and political parties mobilize as potential constituencies for new welfare programs or for the expansion of existing programs. As states modernize, by adopting professional civil service bureaucracies, they acquire the capabilities to operate complex welfare programs. Such programs require specialized government functions in order to collect the necessary revenues, verify eligible beneficiaries, and administer programs that involve potentially very large transfer payments from one class or social group to another. By this logic, the emerging economies of today will also face pressures to create welfare policies aimed at the ranks of their expanding industrial workforces.

There is good reason to view modernization as a necessary condition for welfare regime development. The history of mature welfare states shows that industrialization and urbanization made it fiscally possible and politically necessary for governments to initiate welfare policies such as social assistance, unemployment payments, old-age pensions, and medical insurance. Changes in social structure associated with the rise of factories and cities and the emergence of unions and political parties seeking to incorporate workers eventually compelled Western and Japanese governments in the late nineteenth and early decades of the twentieth century to bring forth social legislation.

Yet there is a problem in grafting this evolutionary approach on to developing countries. That is because many of these countries adopted welfare regimes far earlier than we might predict based on their levels of urbanization and other socioeconomic indicators. What might be called "precocious welfare regimes" emerged from socialist revolutions in the mid-twentieth century in China, Vietnam, and Cuba; from populist and nationalist movements in the 1920s in Latin America; and in Africa and South Asia following independence. Although these welfare regimes were never broad in scope and were often hierarchical in the benefits that they extended to certain groups in the population, they proved to be costly for many governments. Faced with pressures to reduce public debt, many governments turned the budget-cutting axe to their welfare regimes by the 1980s and 1990s. Yet such pressures to retrench the old welfare regime came just as governments also faced demands to create welfare policies that would deal with the dislocations and risks associated with urbanization and industrialization. In China and other countries with growing economies, the liberalization of state-owned and other protected sectors set in motion the dismantling of old welfare regimes while structural changes associated with industrialization catalyzed political forces that created new welfare regimes. In short, welfare expansion and welfare retrenchment occurred together. Paul Pierson (1994) rightly notes that political forces and strategies differ considerably under welfare regime retrenchment. What we see going on in China and in many other developing countries is a convergence of the politics of welfare expansion with the politics of welfare retrenchment. This makes the task of explaining welfare politics more complex but crucial nonetheless.

The Chinese example, and that of most other developing countries, shows that governments did not wait until the pivotal transition from a rural-agrarian to an urban-industrial economy to initiate welfare legislation. Welfare policy diffused rapidly regardless of level of modernization (Collier and Messick 1975). Governments adopted welfare policies at very early stages of economic development largely to gain the support of key constituencies, such as the military or labor unions. Generally speaking, the interests of state-sector managers and workers, especially within the firm, were closely aligned (Waterbury 1993). This coalition consisted of businesses in the formal sector (including state enterprises) and state officials (including unions) that defended policies that served the interests of both firms and workers in them. Business owners or state officials running the enterprises wanted to continue subsidies and protection from foreign and private-sector competition. Workers and their unions sought to preserve relatively rigid labor market policies that provided job security and wide-ranging benefits.

The established linkage between employment in the "commanding heights" sectors of the economy and access to various social policy programs leads to a critical political choice regarding how social policy and labor market liberalization proceed. All else being equal, the introduction of policies to liberalize or dismantle the public sector and to create more flexible labor markets directly influences the scope and content of welfare provision. For example, the absorption of rural labor into labor-intensive export-based firms could extend coverage because these workers are joining the formal sector. At the same time, the dismantling of public-sector firms, or economic and fiscal crises that impact formal-sector employment, creates a spike in informal employment, and these workers often fall outside the scope of welfare coverage. Regardless of whether employers are private investors or state officials, whether labor unions are corporatist or Leninist in their organization and ideology, they share a strong interest in the defense of the policy status quo and oppose the expansion of welfare provision (Haggard and Kaufman 2008, 6–10). The introduction of new welfare programs or the expansion of benefits could occur either through the weakening of this opposition, via the dismantling of the core industrial sectors, or through the (less likely) decline in their political influence.

This is where public pensions, and the strong public support that usually comes with pensions, can serve as the grounds for compromise. The parameters of this compromise can be seen in the way pensions were used in countries that undertook economic transitions from a planned to a market economy. These countries created welfare policies that simultaneously pursued two goals. The first was to compensate workers in the state sector for the withering away or at least the downsizing of that sector after the introduction of competing nonstate firms. The second was to shift responsibility for financing welfare measures from the state to a combination of state, employer, and individual contributions. In these transitions, politicians faced something of a dilemma in that social benefits were vital in order to sustain political support for the economic transition but overly costly benefits would undermine an important goal of the transition to remedy fiscal imbalances. Moreover, in moving away from the zero-unemployment policy of state socialism to far less rigid labor policies, governments had to come up with measures to cope with the new phenomenon of unemployment (Mandelbaum 1996, 5; Haggard and Kaufman 2008, 341–45).

Because of rapid privatization, the problems of high inflation, and the need to sustain regime legitimacy, governments in transition economies increased social spending—primarily pension expenditures—during the 1990s. Pensions rose rapidly in nominal terms through indexation and other measures aimed at protecting retirees. Whereas workers in transition economies suffered dramatic declines in purchasing power, retirees generally fared much better than workers in terms of changes in real income (Kramer 1996; Rutkowski 1998; Inglot 2003, 222–25). These policies aimed at pensioners came at the expense of social protections accorded to the poorest and most needy citizens in these countries (Inglot 2003, 241). State-sector workers threatened to disrupt the political transition as well as the economic reform policies of the fledgling democratic regimes. Politicians in these regimes engaged in compensatory policies at the same time that they invoked broader macroeconomic reforms. Both compensation and macroeconomic adjustment were usually focused on the two costliest welfare programs: health care and pensions (Nelson 2001).

Although China and other transitional economies engaged in a simultaneous dismantling of state socialism and the construction of new welfare state institutions, China differed from the other postsocialist cases in important respects. First, as a result of their high levels of urbanization, the Eastern European and many ex-Soviet governments faced vastly greater social commitments than those that China encountered in the 1990s. Eastern Europeans and Russians enjoyed universal coverage for health care and pensions, but with aging populations and large government deficits, public pensions and health-care programs had to be scaled back after the initial surge in these expenditures that came with state-sector privatization (Kramer 1996; Kornai, Haggard, and Kaufman 2001; Inglot 2003). Second, and as a consequence of the potential fiscal crises imposed by welfare expenditures, governments in Eastern Europe and in some former Soviet states tended to undertake radical versions of reform, such as pension privatization (Müller 1999). China, by contrast, transferred the welfare functions once performed by state enterprises to local governments and set up a social insurance system, but it did not engage in privatization. Third, the social policy reforms in Eastern Europe and the former Soviet Union took place in the context of the early years of newly installed democratic regimes. Because most of these economies were also operating under transitional democracies, the observed changes in social policy might easily be attributed to traits associated with new democracies and not to the politics of economic transitions per se. Finally, with the exception of a few cases such as Yugoslavia, China was unlike the other socialist planned economies in having established a decentralized administration of industry and commerce prior to the reforms. Even at the height of Russian regionalism in the 1990s, pension administration was centralized within the federal government Pension Fund (Chandler 2004, 84–85). The relative flexibility that local officials in China enjoyed in implementing central directives and economic plans were a crucial factor in the success of the Chinese economic reforms. This decentralized administration meant that local officials in China, unlike in other postsocialist transitions, were also crucial in shaping changes to welfare policy.

National and Local Politics

The second problem with most scholarly accounts of welfare regime formation relates to the unit or level of analysis. Simply put, in most studies of welfare regimes, all politics is national. Politicians form national coalitions that push for national policies and legislation to redistribute wealth or channel funds on a national scale. Many explanations of welfare state development and retrenchment tend to assume that political and economic pressures operate on a national legislature or central government and that, in response to these pressures, the national government comes up with new welfare policies. Yet in the case of China, national politicians did not simply translate competing preferences into policy. There is good reason to use the passage of national welfare laws as a landmark in the account of welfare state development. But there is also good reason to bring into the study of national welfare legislation the behavior of local governments and their preferences. Depending on the fiscal relationships between the central governments and local administrations, the latter can be asked to administer or even to finance costly welfare programs. This is especially true in the case of China, where local governments are required to fund the operations of virtually all government agencies and the services they are supposed to provide. Just as the social affairs bureaucracies and their civil servants are an area of focus for the historical accounts of modern welfare regimes in the West and Japan, local governments can be seen as vital agents in contemporary welfare politics, especially in developing countries.

According to several studies of social policy, decentralized administration strongly influences the outcome of national-level social policy. This is true of both formally federal systems, in which central and subnational governments possess explicit powers, and of multitiered governments, in which subnational units exercise influence over policy implementation. For China and other large uneven developers, the capacity of local governments is a crucial influence on social policy. This simple point regarding the influence of local governments on the design and implementation of welfare programs has gone missing in most discussions to date of welfare policy in developing countries. As a broad literature on welfare policy in the West has shown, multilevel governance issues directly influence welfare policy outcomes.

For example, subnational governments that first establish a policy or program can later constrain efforts by the central government to make changes in social policy (Pierson and Leibfried 1995, 16). As Keith Banting notes, "The first level to establish significant social programs has the strategic advantage with affected social interests and the wider public, and captures for itself the political support inherent in social policy" (1995, 297–98). This aspect of shared policymaking between central and local governments, in a more optimistic view, leads to successful experiments at local levels that are then adopted as policy at the national level and implemented nationwide.[8] Yet it is also true that when local governments preemptively adopt social policy, they can impose constraints on the subsequent designs for national social policy, especially if this takes place in federal systems that provide local governments with strong representation in the national legislature.

In addition, the resources and identities of political actors in federal or multitiered governments can pull social policy in different directions (Pierson 1995). In some federal systems, local governments are highly reluctant to impose costly social wages on firms that can move to another jurisdiction that will not impose such costs. For example, to the extent that regional governments and businesses seek to attract foreign investment or to engage in international markets, they will oppose social policy proposals that might undermine their objective of attracting foreign capital. Firms in low-wage regions, even though they may stand to gain from redistributive welfare policies, will oppose the nationalization (or centralization) of welfare policies because they wish to maintain their low-wage advantage in

---

[8] In fact, two scholars have argued that strong local state capacities actually preceded and were necessary conditions for the emergence of social democratic welfare states in northern Europe (Sellers and Lidström 2007). Yet, in these cases, centralized institutions found in political parties or peak associations of labor and business were necessary to "both empower local governments to carry out policies and furnish higher-level governments with the means to assure that local governments maintain the pursuit of egalitarian ends" (Sellers and Lidström 2007, 612).

attracting mobile capital away from higher-wage regions. By contrast, social policy in some federal systems can set off a competitive process in which politicians seek to bolster their political standing and legitimacy by bettering the central government in the level of social provision that they can make available to local residents. Paul Pierson (1995, 453–54) also notes that locally based coalitions can supersede class-based cleavages. For example, businesses in one region may join labor unions in support of a national social policy that will raise the costs for rival businesses in a low-wage region.

Finally, and perhaps most crucially, the social policy preferences of subnational governments depend in large part on whether multilevel systems have rules to enhance the fiscal capacity of subnational units by equalizing or sharing social policy revenues among them (Pierson 1995, 466–67). In federal systems that provide localities with very few fiscal transfers from the central government, such as the United States, local governments are reluctant to engage in redistributive policies that may scare off their tax base. On the other hand, if subnational governments enjoy some measure of revenue sharing or fiscal equalization, such as the German *Länder*, they are less reliant on mobile sources of taxation and more willing to experiment with social policy designs that can address local problems. In general, and especially without revenue sharing, the shared policymaking found in multilevel or federal systems leads to what Fritz Scharpf (1988) calls "joint decision traps," in which social policies are vulnerable to the power and interests of different coalitions of subnational units. The idea of local interests superseding the development of national social policy is especially relevant in the politics of pensions in China (see chapters 2 and 3).

Relative to other countries, local governments in China have very broad responsibilities for spending. Subnational governments in China account for 75 percent of total government spending, a figure that includes both on-budget and extra-budgetary expenditures such as social insurance fund payments. Chinese subnational government spending exceeds that of even more explicitly decentralized and formally federal systems such as Russia, where subnational government spending amounted to 55.4 percent of total public expenditure in 2002, or Mexico, where the comparable figure is less than 40 percent (OECD 2006, 27–28). Christine Wong and Richard Bird (2008) estimate that subnational spending in China was concentrated at levels below the provincial governments—prefectures, counties, and townships. These levels accounted for 55 percent of total government spending, compared (albeit roughly, given cross-national public finance statistics) to 13 percent for developing countries and 35 percent for developed countries.

Despite their heavy expenditure assignments, local Chinese governments receive very little assistance in the way of fiscal equalization or sharing of revenues across provinces and counties. Subnational governments lack incentives to share revenues and have strong incentives to attract outside capital (foreign and domestic). This general pattern pertains to social insurance revenues as well. The introduction of social insurance in China coincided with an overhaul in fiscal relationships between the central and local governments in the 1990s. Once dependent on SOEs for local revenues, local governments had to share revenues with the central government after the enactment of fiscal reforms in 1994. Since that time, central tax agencies collected some revenues that were once retained locally. Moreover, the revenue base of state enterprises shrank in the 1990s as most of these firms changed their corporate identity, filed for bankruptcy, or otherwise disappeared.

As suggested by the empirical work cited in the preceding discussion, virtually all this literature on social policy and multilevel governance is derived from the study of democracies in North America and Europe. Several important recent studies of federalism in developing countries do not directly address how federal structures influence social policy, but explain differences in economic reforms (Wibbels 2001, 2005). Local governments in developing countries have asserted a much stronger role in social policy, in part because of the manner in which economic responses to globalization have eroded national welfare policies.

International Influences

The third problem with current explanations of welfare regimes lies with the role of international or external sources of welfare politics. No one doubts that international actors, including international organizations and multinational corporations, are important influences on domestic-level welfare politics. The problems are how to specify the conditions under which external or international forces matter and which ones matter most. For example, are welfare regimes more influenced by international trade or by capital flows? Are such forces more applicable for large or small economies? What about the influence of ideas and international organizations that promote what they regard as best-practices to a government considering welfare policy reforms?

The deepening of external economic linkages has the potential to alter the relative power and authority between central and subnational governments. The adoption of neoliberal policies can put constraints on central governments by encouraging the dismantling of the central regulatory structures and the devolution of policy to subnational governments (Kahler and Lake 2003). We might therefore expect that economic reforms emphasizing international openness would give local governments greater responsibilities over revenues and expenditures. The question is, what sort of welfare policies will subnational governments invoke in response to global economic forces? Some local governments might seek to impose new taxes on producers to pay for expanded safety nets, whereas others might do just the opposite to attract foreign investors seeking low taxes and production costs.

As a large body of work in trade economics and international political economy has shown, the movement of production factors associated with international trade exerts a strong impact on welfare policy outcomes. Opening to international trade distributes gains or losses to either capital-intensive or labor-intensive sectors (depending on factor endowments). These sectors respond by opposing or trying to push for further liberalization (Frieden and Rogowski 1996). The shift in production factors that accompanies trade and foreign direct investment (FDI) liberalization tends to weaken some sectors at the expense of others. When relatively labor-abundant countries such as China trade with relatively capital-abundant countries such as the United States, sectors in China that produce capital-intensive goods will suffer. Capital-intensive firms will mobilize to roll back or thwart the further opening of trade. They might also seek compensation in the form of subsidies. Job losses and firm bankruptcies associated with import competition create pressures for states to compensate the losers of trade liberalization.

Some scholars have found that trade liberalization and capital flows can exert a powerful influence on welfare policy by generating demands from import-competing sectors to receive social protections. The most open economies in Europe developed some of the most extensive levels of welfare protection and expenditures as part of a political bargain in which labor unions accepted the pursuit of open trade in exchange for business associations' acceding to heavily redistributive welfare policies (Katzenstein 1985).

But this political bargain has not obtained in most developing countries, even those with democratic regimes. Given the increased mobility of capital relative to the earlier era of post–World War II social bargains, firms in at least some sectors can credibly threaten to move abroad to avoid high labor costs. Inflows of capital and goods still generate movements in production factors, but governments respond by cutting, not increasing, social expenditures. Governments do so for two main reasons: to attract foreign investment by lowering production costs and taxes on joint ventures and foreign-owned firms, and to present a more disciplined fiscal policy to global investors and international financial institutions. The incentives to reduce social expenditures and to loosen labor standards to lure outside capital is also sometimes labeled the "race to the bottom" argument. As Nita Rudra (2002, 419–20) has argued, in developing countries that host foreign investment numerous obstacles to collective action—authoritarian governments, large informal sectors, and others—prevent labor from organizing and participating in politics as it does in industrialized countries.

The links between globalization and social policy can also have a broader impact on national politics and regimes. Rudra (2005) has shown using a statistical analysis of developing countries that increases in national social spending in response to globalization are associated with the subsequent expansion of political rights. Faced with social unrest and other regime-threatening reactions to the effects of greater openness to trade and capital flows, elites can either crack down or use social spending as an instrument for pacifying disaffected social groups. According to Rudra's model, if the costs of repression are greater than the costs of increased social spending, then elites will choose to expand social safety nets. Welfare expansion has the effect of assuring political elites that the threats to their assets and interests can be thwarted by social spending. Authoritarian regimes thus become more willing to expand political rights after increases in social spending.[9] The critical unanswered question is whether governments will respond to unrest with social spending or with more repression.

If global economic linkages such as trade and foreign investment influence the welfare policies of the countries that engage with the global economy, then high levels of international trade and FDI in China would lead us to suspect that, if globalization affects welfare policies anywhere, it should do so in China. The influence of globalization on welfare policy, however, is indeterminate—it can lead to the shrinkage or the expansion of welfare programs.

For this reason, some scholars emphasize transnational ideologies and normative currents in social policy (Orenstein 2005) rather than specific economic forces. Scholars have used the wave of pension reforms that swept through Latin America, Eastern Europe, and the former Soviet States during the 1980s and 1990s to analyze the influence of international organizations and other external actors on domestic policymaking (Madrid 2003; Müller 2003; Brooks 2005; Orenstein 2005; Weyland 2005). The

---

[9] In a concluding section, Rudra suggests that the Chinese government has responded to ongoing social unrest by announcing its intention to address chronic social welfare problems.

puzzle is driven largely by the observation that so many economies of disparate demographic and economic conditions nonetheless adopted a rather uniform set of regulations on pensions, generally involving privatization. Given that the World Bank promoted a template for pension reforms beginning in the early 1990s, the scholarly debate has centered on the extent to which the influence of the World Bank explains the pension privatization wave.

Raúl Madrid (2003) and Mitchell Orenstein (2000, 2008) have argued that the influence of the World Bank was substantial. Using different cases and methods, Madrid and Orenstein demonstrate that linkages between the World Bank staff and reform-minded technocrats created the momentum that placed pension reform on the policy agenda. Although the actual technical designs varied depending on domestic-level institutions and other factors, the common outcome in pension privatization, these scholars argue, cannot be explained without reference to the influence of the World Bank and its policy networks. By contrast, Kurt Weyland (2005) argues that the diffusion of pension reforms is better understood as a mimetic process in which governments sought to emulate the apparent success of the Chilean model of pension privatization in 1981. The World Bank influence was, therefore, simply an artifact of the decision by governments to draw in international expertise. According to Weyland, governments exercised considerable autonomy in adopting some World Bank policy suggestions and rejecting others.

Despite their differing interpretations, these discussions of the role of international financial institutions (IFIs) in the pension reform wave make a number of implicit assumptions that deserve further scrutiny. First, policy adoption is the end point of analysis, the observation to be explained. Policy implementation, along with the potential role of IFIs in implementation, is left out of the discussion. Pension reform as such has an identifiable year or date of enactment, after which the influence of the international agents promoting reform declines. Second, the direction and locus of influence is assumed to be from the IFIs to the central government. Under this perspective, analysts look for evidence that agencies and actors in the central government held meetings with IFI officials and evaluated options that the latter presented for policy reforms. Third, because the World Bank promoted broad structural reforms rather than incremental or parametric pension reforms, analysts associate radical or discontinuous reforms with strong IFI influence and gradual marginal reforms with weak IFI influence.

This conventional model of international influence on social policy, including pensions, disregards or deemphasizes a number of important facts about policy reforms, especially in developing countries. Policy adoption or enactment is not readily distinguished from implementation, but there are sound reasons to treat reform as encompassing *both* enactment and implementation. It is possible that a policy measure deemed radical in its regulatory and legal clauses might be far less so in its implementation. Moreover, as illustrated in the case of China, the adoption of central policy can sometimes represent the ratification or endorsement of successful local polices and experiments. This means that if analysts wish to measure the effects of the international-level variables on policymaking, they should look at subnational governments in addition to the agencies at the central level.

This discussion of China in the context of existing arguments for welfare regime development suggests the need for a middle-range theory rather than universal laws. Causes that brought about the first wave of welfare regime development in the late nineteenth and early twentieth centuries differ considerably from the causes of welfare regime development in the late twentieth and early twenty-first centuries. Welfare regime formation in China has taken place in the absence of what many take to be a necessary condition for the deepening of welfare regimes—powerful labor organizations and/or electoral competition with viable social democratic parties. Nor have progressive bureaucratic agents among relevant ministries succeeded in pushing social legislation forward, as occurred in many incipient welfare regimes. In the concluding chapter of this book, I argue that welfare policy in China is best understood using a comparison group of large uneven developers that, having achieved rapid growth, faced pressures to expand existing welfare programs or to create new ones. Such cases (Brazil and South Africa) have inequalities that arise from geographical as well as historical causes, and during periods of rapid economic growth, these inequalities generally intensified. As social divisions widened, governments of large uneven developers adopted pensions as the centerpiece of their social policies.

OUTLINE OF CHAPTERS 2-6

Chapter 2 provides the details of the evolution of pension policy in China since 1949, with particular attention paid to the reforms of the 1990s. Conflicting preferences among urban governments and among central government ministries meant that pension reform did not come as a landmark piece of legislation but took shape with a sequence of vague central government regulations. For example, 1995 pension regulations gave provinces and urban governments wide latitude in designing pension revenue and benefit calculations. After the State Council issued stricter regulations to unify local pension designs in 1997, urban governments stubbornly and successfully resisted measures that would have pooled pensions at provincial levels. The details of these State Council pension regulations undermine those interpretations that see local agents complying with central government edicts.

Chapter 3 examines the preferences and behavior of urban governments and workers in the process of pension reform. Fiscal decentralization gave urban governments partial property rights over SOEs. The control rights that urban governments had over locally generated revenues meant that they had incentives to dismantle money-losing SOEs and to take over the welfare functions of these SOEs. For those left jobless by the closing of SOEs, the institution of workplace welfare and the broader socialist social contract gave them collective claims to compensation from SOE managers and local officials.

The three subsequent chapters examine in greater detail and with more specific evidence how these institutions defined the preferences and strategies of local governments, firms, and the urban public toward pensions. Chapter 4 examines the channels of revenue collection for social insurance and identifies how urban governments administered and spent pension funds. In some areas of China, social insurance coverage expanded rapidly. Expansion varied greatly depending on available resources (e.g., firms and their workers) and on the concentration of pensioners with claims on local pension funds. Differences in the flows of labor and capital (both foreign and domestic) created incentives and disincentives for local SIAs to collect revenues. Pensions represented by far the largest share of this revenue, which local SIAs fiercely resisted redistributing outside their jurisdiction. Thus, as Chapter 4 also shows, areas that lacked a social insurance revenue base and also had large concentrations of pensioners, such as the northeast, had to rely on pension subsidies from the central government. They did so against the steadfast opposition from Ministry of Finance officials, who were concerned about the fiscal consequences of having the central government take on the role of financing pensions for the entire country.

Chapter 5 identifies the sectors or types of firms that most influenced the development of social insurance in China and its heavy emphasis on pensions. Recent scholarship on the development of welfare states in Western Europe and the United States makes the important point that employers differed sharply over the expansion of social policies (Gordon 1991; Mares 2003). Chapter 5 shows how local SIAs engaged in conflict with the large SOEs under central government administration over the collection of pension revenues. These firms were highly reluctant to join local pension funds because of the higher levies and reduced pension benefits they would receive. Local SIAs were much less confrontational with local SOEs that were under municipal administration. For private and foreign-owned firms, SIAs adopted different strategies depending on their scale. Although the divergent preferences within the business or capitalist class are useful in explaining outcomes in welfare policy in China and elsewhere, it is important to remember that business-government collaboration on welfare policy was conducted in the shadow of both the anticipated reaction of and actual resistance from specific groups in society. If local cadres and crony capitalists laid the groundwork for the Chinese welfare regime, they did so in response to the looming threat of labor unrest and in anticipation of popular protest.

Chapter 6 uses public opinion data to compare the outlooks of pensioners, workers, and the unemployed across a range of questions dealing with expectations and attitudes toward pensions. The discussion is centered around the question of whether the attitudes of urban Chinese workers reflect a lingering support for welfare provision through work-unit socialism or whether workers accept, as some studies suggest, the notion of market hegemony (Blecher 2002), in which employment and benefits are determined by market forces of supply and demand. The results show that the preference for state provision of pensions among urban workers is less a legacy of state socialism and more a result of their experience in the uncertainties of the labor market. Urban workers want the state to provide protections against the risks that they face in the labor market.

CHAPTER 2

Pathways to Pensions

Many governments adopted their first old-age pension laws during the early phases of industrialization, in part to cultivate a loyal if small working class. The initial policy decisions about who gained pension rights and how they would be financed carried important long-term consequences. The choice of initial design was crucial because pensions are potentially very costly and, once governments make the initial commitment to provide pension benefits to some or all of the population, such promises are extremely difficult for even authoritarian governments to modify or revoke. The choice to cover some workers and not others, the choice to finance pensions from current workers or from funded accounts, and many other design questions reflect political choices made during the initial adoption of pension legislation. These options of pension design are laid out in this chapter to place the pension regulations of China in the context of other large developing countries and to further suggest why it may be less useful to group China with other postsocialist countries when discussing welfare politics.

One option, found in the early stages of capitalism, is the provision of pensions through the operating budgets of enterprises. Many U.S. firms practiced welfare capitalism in the early twentieth century (Brandes 1976). Large firms, especially those in monopolistic industries, have an interest in intrafirm welfare provision because it can enable firms to reduce labor turnover and can give firms the ability to manage the sizable funds needed to operate pensions and other programs. Such intrafirm welfare provision obviously excludes those outside the firm. Under the state socialist labor practices in pre-reform China, SOEs paid for pensions and other welfare benefits out of their operating budgets. The provision of pensions from within the firm was mandatory, for SOEs at least, in sharp contrast to firms in market economies, which voluntarily choose to provide pensions to workers. Still, the problem of socializing such costs—of shifting what had once been intrafirm pension costs into a social cost to be funded by taxpayers and corporations—can create political conflict. Firms with large pension costs have an incentive to dump these costs on to society.

At the other extreme in terms of pension coverage are noncontributory universal or citizenship-based pensions, which are often financed out of general tax revenues. These exist in a few small economies such as New Zealand, but also in South Africa and in Brazil (for rural pensions). Benefits vary widely depending on occupation, but all citizens are nonetheless eligible for pensions. In Brazil and South Africa, which have some of the largest income inequality measures in the world, household surveys suggest that non-contributory pensions have served as a vital source of income for the poor (Seekings and Nattrass 2005, 211–19; Barrientos 2006, 377).

A third policy choice for pensions is privatization, or turning over the administration of pensions to private commercial institutions. At least twenty-nine countries adopted some form of privatization between 1993 and 2004, with many persuaded by the apparent success of the 1981 pension privatization in Chile (Madrid 2003; Brooks 2005; Orenstein 2008). In many of these cases, policymakers determined that existing pension arrangements would be too costly to continue. Under this design, workers and employers make contributions to designated pension fund managers such as banks or insurance companies, who then administer the funds by investing them and distributing benefits to retirees. As critics of pension privatization have noted, such arrangements transfer large amounts of risk to the individual and reduce the commitment of the state to providing only a subsistence pension, if even that (Orszag and Stiglitz 1999).

A fourth option for pension policy design is the provident fund model, in which contributions from an employee and an employer accumulate in a fund that is paid out as a lump sum when the worker retires. Unlike privatization, provident funds are often placed under government control, and the accumulated capital can be managed as part of the state industrial development strategy. Provident funds are commonly found among the former British colonies, such as India. In East Asia, the Central Provident Fund of Singapore is widely hailed as the vehicle that financed the successful industrial development of this city-state since the 1960s.

A fifth option, and the one found most commonly among advanced industrial countries, is social insurance. Like provident funds, social insurance programs require contributions from employees and employers, but they also include some mix of accumulated savings and government-guaranteed benefits. Benefits are not paid out in a lump sum but as an annuity. Social insurance is based on the principle of workers' and employers' making contributions to various funds for health care, pensions, unemployment, and workplace injury, among others, with contributions being pooled so that the risks or costs are distributed across the broad population. Social insurance models are most commonly linked with employment and serve to cushion the risks of the labor market. One of the crucial decisions in social insurance is who manages social insurance funds. In some cases, labor unions administer the funds, and in other cases, government agencies perform this function. In any event, the regulatory and legal provisions that exist to ensure the sound management of such funds are crucial.

The variations in pension policy are summarized in table 2.1, which displays the pension policy designs found in China, two large uneven developers (India and Brazil), and a classic postsocialist case (Russia). As table 2.1 shows, there is no clear pattern in terms of pension rights, benefits, relative share of contributions by workers and employers, or the type of pension system (e.g., provident fund or social insurance). China, like Brazil and Russia, uses a social insurance model. China also shares with Brazil and Russia the presence of flat-rate benefits combined with earnings-related benefits. All three countries use pay-as-you-go financing (China does so in practice), and the retirement ages and years of eligibility threshold (fifteen years) for China are not substantially at variance with those found in Russia and Brazil. If anything, India is the outlier in table 2.1 because of its provident fund model. Nevertheless, China is distinct from Brazil and Russia, and more like India, in lacking universal coverage for pensions. In further contrast to Brazil, China lacks noncontributory pensions.

The distinction between universal pension coverage for all citizens and exclusive or occupation-based pension coverage carries crucial political implications. As Julia Lynch (2006) notes in her study of pensions among advanced welfare states, the fragmentation found in company- or occupation-based welfare programs (including pensions) gives politicians a crucial, divisible resource to gain support from selected constituencies. In fragmented pension systems, politicians can increase pension benefits to targeted groups, but under universal coverage, pension and other welfare benefits resemble more of a public good, and "a raise for one is a raise for all" (Lynch 2006, 65). Lynch (2006, 65–67) argues that fragmented welfare

TABLE 2.1
Varieties of pensions

Trait	China	India	Brazil	Russia
Main source of financing	Social insurance	Provident fund	Social insurance	Social insurance
Universal coverage?	No (only for urban workers)	No	Yes	Yes
Noncontributory pension for poor?	No	Yes	Yes	No
Flat-rate pension and earnings-related benefit?	Yes	No	Yes	Yes
Pay-as-you-go financing?	Yes, de facto	No	Yes	Yes
Employer vs. worker contributions (% of wages)	Employers pay larger share	Workers pay larger share	Employers pay larger share	Employers pay all
Retirement age (years)	60 (men); 50 or 55 (women)	55	65 (men); 60 (women)	60 (men); 55 (women)
Period of contributions for pension eligibility (years)	15	None	13–15	5

Source: U.S. Social Security Administration (2008).

programs are often found among countries in which the dominant mode of political competition is marked by patronage or particularism, in which politicians deliver concrete benefits to narrow groups in exchange for votes. Universal or citizenship-based welfare programs have emerged in countries in which politicians and political parties seek to deliver much broader programs to large groups of voters. Lynch's hypothesis provides a useful starting point to understand the apparent reluctance or inability of the Chinese government to introduce universal social insurance coverage, for pensions and other programs. While clearly the nature of political competition was not based on appeals to voters, urban governments in China fiercely defended their authority to administer pension funds and to deliver benefits to local pensioners.

Pension reforms in China over the course of the 1990s brought about rapid increases in pension spending and pension financing through new channels, but the reforms left many areas unchanged. For example, retirement ages, set in 1951, continue to be age sixty for men, age fifty for women, and age fifty-five for women in clerical occupations. Urban governments undermined the original objective of policymakers in Beijing to reduce future pension burdens for the Chinese government by having workers establish funded personal retirement accounts. Instead, urban governments used nearly all the money in these nominally funded accounts to pay benefits for current retirees. Thus, unlike pension reforms elsewhere in the world, the Chinese government has not really retreated from or abandoned its role in providing pensions. Instead, it has shifted the administrative responsibilities for pensions from SOEs to urban governments. Even though some commercial insurance firms and banks in China are involved in the handling of nonpublic or voluntary supplementary pensions, no one would call this pension privatization. It is even difficult to identify a specific date or law ushering in pension reform in China, as we can do for landmark cases of pension reform or privatization in Latin America and Eastern Europe.

Pension reforms in China took place over an extended period and involved multiple competing preferences and policy designs from different actors. The details of pension reforms contained in this chapter confirm other accounts of policymaking in China as fragmented and constrained by the competing interests within the Chinese bureaucracy at both the central and local levels (Lieberthal 1992). Pension reforms also demonstrate a familiar pattern of conflict between local government preferences and central government edicts and the consequences that result from local implementation of the policies of the center (Mertha 2005). Yet the protracted nature of pension reforms cannot be explained solely by the fragmented Chinese policy process. The behavior of urban governments made pension reforms look incremental and disjointed, but urban governments were also active supporters of pension reforms.[1] Why they pushed for changes rather than supporting the status quo is the subject of chapter 3.

PENSIONS AFTER 1949

During the planned economy period (1952–1979), the primary access points for social welfare provision were the production unit, urban residence committee, and rural collective. Eligibility for welfare was tied to employment and to residency. Full-time workers in state enterprises and urban collectives received the most comprehensive welfare benefits, including housing,

---

[1] In this sense, pension reform in China represents the sort of gradual institutional change that is nonetheless dramatic in its content and consequences. As Thelen notes, "there are many political institutions that are interesting precisely because if we look at them today we are struck, simultaneously, by how little *and* how much they have changed over time" (2003, 211). Emphasis in original.

whereas urban residents without such employment ties to state enterprises relied on their residence committees and received much less in the way of welfare provision. Peasants had basic but generally limited access to health care and other welfare programs through their rural collectives. Gordon White characterizes the planned economy era of China as a "communist developmental state aiming at high levels of accumulation and unwilling to spend large amounts of funds on welfare benefits which were not directly productive" (1998, 178). It is important to remember that for all of its commitment to socialism, the CCP has never espoused universal welfare coverage based on citizenship. (Details of 1950s pension regulations and subsequent pension regulations during the reform period are summarized in table 2.2.)

The most important pension policies of this period were contained in the 1951 Labor Insurance Regulations of the People's Republic of China. These regulations were the commitment of the new regime to the small but politically influential urban working class. In these regulations, the state provided assurances against the enduring threats to workers' livelihoods: workplace injuries, illnesses, and the onset of old age (Han and Jiao 1997, 4–7; Xie and Ba 1999, 119–33). The 1951 regulations covered employees in public and private factories and mines that had one hundred or more employees, as well as various branches of railroad, shipping, postal and telecommunication, and state-owned construction companies with over one hundred employees (Xie and Ba 1999, 119–20). Although the number of actual retirees at that point was only approximately 20,000 (Han and Jiao 1997, 5), the regulations were pathbreaking because they provided the first assurance by the Chinese state of old-age income to any group. Some workers were said to have considered the 1951 regulations to be the urban equivalent of land reform, in that the CCP had provided them with a financial asset with a reliable supply of future income, not unlike the distribution of land to peasants (Yuan 1990, 197).

Whereas the 1951 Labor Insurance Regulations laid out broad policies on pensions and other forms of insurance, the regulations that followed in 1953 and 1958, and again in 1978, were more explicit in delineating coverage and the distribution of pension benefits. Because the 1951 and 1953 Labor Insurance Regulations applied only to firms with one hundred or more employees, those who worked in smaller private firms, cooperatives, and other nonstate firms were excluded from these provisions. In 1953, those without labor insurance included all the estimated 7.8 million handicraft workers, the majority of the 1.3 million workers in cooperatives, and most of the 3.7 million workers in private enterprises. Despite the lack of precision in these estimates, they do represent a significant portion of

TABLE 2.2
Summary of pension policy and reforms in China

Years	Coverage	Benefits	Eligibility for pensions after	Contribution	Level of administration	Pooling
1951–1969	After 1958, full-time state and urban collective workers	50–70% of preretirement wages, linked to years of service	25 years (1951)	3% of wage bill, paid by employers	Enterprise unions and local unions	70% pooled locally; 30% pooled nationally
1969–1986	Full-time state and urban collective workers	60–90% of preretirement wages, linked to years of service	10 years (1978)	Determined by enterprise	Enterprise management	None
1986–1991	State and urban collective workers, including contract labor	60–90% of preretirement wages, linked to years of service	10 years	Varies; contract laborers have wage deductions of 3%	Urban (experimental)	By ownership sector (state, collective, foreign-invested, etc.)
1991–1995	Employees of urban enterprises	60–75% of preretirement wages, linked to: years of service and accumulations in individual account	15 years	15% of wage bill paid by employers; 3% of wage paid by workers	Urban governments	At city level; calls for provincial level
1995–1997	Employees of urban enterprises	60–75% of preretirement wages, linked to: years of service, accumulations in individual account, and local average wages	15 years	Wide local variation; 11% of wage bill paid by employers; 3–5% of wage paid by workers	Urban governments and some industrial ministries	At city level; calls for provincial level
1997–present	Employees of urban enterprises	58% of preretirement wages, linked to: accumulations in individual account and local average wages	15 years	20% of wage bill paid by employers; 4–8% of wage paid by workers	Urban governments	At city level; calls for provincial level

the approximately 26 million urban workers classified as enterprise employees and handicraft producers in 1953 (State Statistics Bureau [SSB] 1985, 83–86).

Even with the collectivization of industry and the consolidation of private firms into large SOEs, the workers in firms with fewer than one hundred employees in 1957 (and thus ineligible for labor insurance) included 6.5 million handicraft workers, most of the 1.8 million workers in cooperatives, and a large share of the 3.4 million workers in jointly owned public-private enterprises (*gongsi heying qiye*), out of a total of 31 million enterprise employees and handicraft producers in 1957 (SSB 1985, 83, 86). Subsequent regulations in 1958 eliminated the one hundred–employee threshold and gave all full-time SOE and urban collective workers pension coverage. After the completion of the socialist transformation of industry in 1957, not many urban firms remained with fewer than one hundred employees. Still, the 1958 regulations explicitly excluded from pension coverage workers in handicraft cooperatives, transport cooperatives, and workers in certain joint state-private enterprises (article 13). The Chinese state had thus created administrative status groups and extended highly inequitable benefits to them.

The 1951 and 1953 regulations also stipulated retirement ages that limited women's participation in the workforce. Men were to receive pensions starting at age sixty and women at age fifty. The likely reason for this difference in retirement ages stemmed from the desire by the new regime to resolve the urban unemployment problem by reducing the participation of older women in the workforce and opening positions for younger workforce entrants. Regulations in 1953 made adjustments to the retirement ages, but with the same gender-based distinctions. These regulations called for workers subject to physically demanding work conditions, such as mines, steel mills, and others, or high-temperature working conditions to have retirement ages of fifty-five for men and forty-five for women. These younger retirement ages have proved remarkably resistant to change during the reform era. (The population-wide life expectancy in 1950 was fifty years, compared with seventy-one years in 1997; World Bank 1997, 28.)

Under the 1953 regulations, pensioners could expect an income replacement rate of 50–70 percent of their preretirement wages, with higher replacement rates tied to the length of their participation in the workforce and number of years at a particular enterprise. (These two measures were often the same under lifetime employment in the same work unit.) At a minimum, twenty-five years of employment were needed before a worker was eligible for pension benefits. The 1950s regulations established a precedent of linking postretirement income to two variables: the base wage in the final year and the length of service at the enterprise. Under the command economy, these two criteria were closely related because base wages were themselves tied to length of service.

The calculation of a worker's length of service was heavily laden with political criteria. For example, the 1951 regulations excluded from labor insurance benefits those who had been "deprived of their political rights" and imprisoned as counterrevolutionaries or other enemies of the new regime. The 1953 regulations further stipulated several restrictions on how the twenty-five-year length of service requirement was calculated for various politically undesirable categories of employees. Article 41 essentially eliminated from the years-of-service calculations the time that shop floor bosses, supervisors, factory police, and military personnel had been employed at enterprises during the Japanese Occupation and the postwar Nationalist regime.[2]

The 1950s regulations called for pensions and other labor insurance programs to be financed by enterprise contributions to union committees within the enterprise and to the relevant local or industrial union. Firms were to submit 3 percent of the enterprise wage bill for such purposes (Xie and Ba 1999, 120). Local branches of the All-China Federation of Trade Unions (ACFTU) pooled these funds at city levels so that pensions could be distributed from newer SOEs to older SOEs that had large numbers of retirees. The ACFTU even channeled 30 percent of local collections to the national level, where the funds were to be redistributed from cities with few retirees to cities with larger retiree populations.

The dismantling of the ACFTU and purging of its officials during the Cultural Revolution destroyed whatever pension funds the union had managed at the city and national levels. In 1969, a crucial policy change made enterprises solely responsible for financing and distributing pension benefits to all retired workers. As legal commentators have noted, these provisions "turned social insurance into enterprise insurance" (Xie and Ba 1999, 125). After 1969, Chinese pension financing was in practice no longer a pay-as-you-go intergenerational transfer from the earnings of current workers to retirees. Instead, pensions were a type of operating expense that enterprises were to distribute to retirees according to national regulations. This dependency on the enterprise left older workers vulnerable to ruses by enterprise management to prevent them from retiring. By 1978, as many as 2 million workers and 600,000 state officials who were supposed to be

---

[2] Employees who had been members of various Nationalist Party committees and branches or members of the Huidaomen religious sect could not count their pre-1949 work toward their years of service for pension eligibility.

receiving pensions had been denied them by their work units (Xie and Ba 1999, 123).

For all the problems of fragmented programs of social insurance in China today, it is important to keep in mind that before the local governments took over the administration of social insurance benefits in the 1990s, welfare administration was even more decentralized. Welfare provision by the work unit, including retirement benefits administered by SOEs after 1969, gave enterprise managers and shop floor supervisors wide discretion to distribute favorable rulings and classifications for certain employees over others. Although Maoist ideology stressed egalitarian wage distribution and equal access to welfare provisions within the work unit, the bureaucratic rank of an individual's work unit and his or her classification as a full-time or temporary employee meant substantially different treatment for workers in terms of the scope and benefit levels of various welfare programs.[3]

New pension regulations issued in 1978, the year usually designated as the beginning of the economic reforms, were as generous as any pension policies since 1951. The 1978 regulations were designed in large part to relieve unemployment pressures arising from the return to cities by educated youth who had been sent to the countryside in the years following 1968. The most important modification to existing pension rules lay in the reduction of the number of years needed to become eligible for pensions. The years-of-employment requirement was lowered from twenty-five years to only ten years. These regulations calculated benefits at 80 percent of basic wages if an employee had participated in "revolutionary work" (i.e., was active in the CCP or its underground unions before 1949) (Han and Jiao 1997, 6; Xie and Ba 1999, 124). For those who joined the workforce after 1949, the income replacement rates ranged from 60 to 75 percent.[4] Income replacement rates continued to be linked to years of service, but in effect someone with only ten years of work in an SOE could retire with a pension that amounted to 60 percent of his or her preretirement wages. As a further incentive, SOE workers who chose to take what amounted to early retirement could also designate a son or daughter of working age to replace them at their SOE.

---

[3] Maoist China was not unique among state socialist economies in creating a stratification of welfare benefits. As Chandler notes, "The Soviet social welfare system . . . never lived up to its substantial claims of generous benefits and accessibility to all" (2004, 19).

[4] In 1978, most of these post-1949 workforce entrants would have remained under retirement age. Assuming that the oldest of this group started working at ages fifteen to eighteen in 1950, they would have been forty-three to forty-six by 1979.

The 1978 regulations had the intended effect of moving large numbers of workers out of jobs in SOEs. The number of retirees receiving pensions from SOEs rose from 3.1 million in 1978 to 21.2 million in 1988, and expenditures rose from 1.7 billion yuan to 32.3 billion yuan. In the year before the first national pension reform regulations were issued in 1991, SOEs were paying 46.6 billion yuan ($8.63 billion) in pensions to 23 million retirees (Xie and Ba 1999, 126).

Industrial-sector reforms beginning in the 1980s permitted SOEs to retain profits, but firm managers also retained their obligations to provide welfare to employees, including pensions for retirees. The legacy of the 1969 regulations to end pooling and make individual SOEs responsible for the costly financing of pensions was felt most heavily by the 1980s as the combination of soaring number of retirees and fiscal reforms wreaked havoc on the production costs of SOEs, especially those that were established early enough to now be responsible for large numbers of retirees. In some older industrial sectors such as textiles, pension expenditures could make up 50 percent of the wage bill or even exceed the wage bill; by contrast, in sectors with relatively younger firms and workforces, such as electronics, SOEs spent less than 5 percent of their wage bill on pensions (Han and Jiao 1997, 13). A publication authored by Ministry of Labor officials mentions in passing that in the 1980s, when some SOEs with large retiree populations suspended payments to pensioners, the retirees responded with petition marches. In a few cases, unpaid pensioners committed suicide (Han and Jiao 1997, 13–14). Although no other open sources mention such protests in the 1980s, it is safe to assume that the onset of local experiments in pension reforms in the 1980s and early 1990s arose from the pressing need to spread the costs of pensions more evenly across SOEs.

PENSION REFORM MEASURES

Local pension funds emerged around the mid-1980s as cities and counties persuaded SOEs to contribute payroll deductions to local pension pools so that the responsibility for paying benefits to SOE retirees could be more evenly spread (Whiteford 2003, 48). Because enterprises had been completely responsible for all pensions, health care, and other costs for their current workers and retirees, the older and larger SOEs were enthusiastic about the cost-sharing involved in local pools. With such locally run social pools (*shehui tongchou*), larger and older SOEs with many workers at or near retirement age could draw some money from the local fund rather than paying all pension costs from their own operating budgets. Initially, only SOEs and urban collectives participated in the pools because their workers were the only ones eligible for pensions. Workers outside the state sector generally had little if any labor insurance, including pensions. In addition, as contract labor became more prevalent among state enterprises in the 1980s, these workers also lacked pension coverage (Xie and Ba 1999, 126). Regulations in 1986 brought SOE contract workers under pension coverage by calling for 3 percent of their wages to be deducted and contributed to pension pools.

In 1991, the State Council issued regulations on the basis of what were thought to be successful local experiments in the pooling of pension funds by state enterprises (State Council 1991). The regulations made a critical change in the calculation of pension benefits. Rather than calculating pension benefits as a fixed percentage of preretirement wages (with years of service the key variable in benefit calculations), the 1991 regulations introduced the idea of basing pension benefits on a combination of three sources, or "pillars." Subsequent local experiments and national regulations elaborated on the principles of this three-pillar pension model. First, a basic or defined benefit was tied to preretirement wages and paid out of the local social pool. In contrast to the prereform pension benefit calculations, which provided between 60 and 80 percent of preretirement wages, local social pools now provided benefits amounting to 20 percent of the officially determined local average wages of the city. This amounted to a subsistence pension, or a minimum amount that workers could expect in retirement. The second source of pension benefits was the accumulated funds in a worker's individual account and was thus a defined contribution benefit that placed much greater responsibility on the worker to accumulate the necessary funds. The third pillar of pension benefits called for by the 1991 regulations lay outside the public pension system; it was simply the personal funds that a worker had accumulated through individual savings, private insurance, and other vehicles (Chow 2001; Leckie and Pai 2005, 29–30).

The 1991 regulations faced a problem that would hamper future pension reform measures. Because local practices varied so widely, it was impossible to make specific provisions in the national regulations. For example, national regulations could not impose a standard payroll tax on employers or a standard contribution rate for workers' individual accounts because each locality had its own mix of retirees and SOE payrolls from which pension benefits would be paid. Moreover, because basic pensions were now to be linked to local average wages (the determination of which was up to local governments), the national regulations could not specify with much detail how local governments determined the pension benefit levels. As a result, urban governments were told to set their own contribution rates and to ensure that these rates would generate enough in pension benefits so that local retirees received a monthly amount equivalent to a certain percentage of the average wage in a given city. When urban governments made their calculations, the amount of contributions from employers and workers needed to fund local retirees and future beneficiaries resulted in large levies that commonly exceeded 20 percent of the enterprise wage bill.

The 1991 regulations also failed to create larger pension pools by having local pension funds come under the administrative control of the provincial governments. The regulations stated that "those areas that have not yet implemented provincial-level pools for basic pension insurance funds must actively create conditions for them, and current city- and county-level pools must gradually be transferred into provincial pools" (Han and Jiao 1999, 82). Because cities had already established their local pension funds, local authorities resisted national regulations that called for pooling at higher levels. Unless the provincial governments (or even the central government) were also going to take over responsibilities for distributing pension benefits, there would be little that the provincial governments could do to compel urban governments to turn over their local pension funds.

Another significant area of fragmentation at this time came from the fact that local pension pools were divided among those for SOEs, urban collective enterprises, and foreign-invested enterprises. By the mid-1990s, in addition to having pension pools for state enterprises in 3,423 city- and county-level governments (Ministry of Labor 1997, 167), there were also 2,219 separate pools for urban collectives and 764 pools for foreign-invested enterprises (Han and Jiao 1997, 15). In actual fact, even for the thirteen provinces that reported having "provincial wide pooling" in line with the 1991 regulations, only some SOEs were involved in sharing pension revenues across a province.

Finally, the 1991 regulations did not alter the retirement ages, which remained at sixty for men, fifty for women, and fifty-five for women in clerical positions or white-collar jobs, even though life expectancies had lengthened considerably since the early 1950s when these regulations had been put in place. The basic problem was that those who were at or near retirement age had no opportunity to accumulate funds in individual accounts. Their benefits had to come almost entirely from pooled funds. But because local social pools were stretched thin and because the number of retirees in most urban areas was rising quickly, urban governments simply "borrowed" the money from the individual accounts of current workers to pay pension benefits to new retirees. The central government objective of introducing a defined contribution pension using mandatory individual retirement accounts with real funds had failed. Urban governments maintained a de facto pay-as-you-go pension system in which the earnings of workers went to pay benefits to local retirees.

This shift in pension reform from a stance emphasizing mandatory savings to one that transferred pension contributions across generations reflects very well the cross-currents of pension retrenchment and pension expansion that made up Chinese pension reforms. The central government issued regulations that cut back on the use of state finances to provide public pensions. Yet the same regulations also expanded the role of the state in administering and distributing pensions by extracting pension revenues from, in theory, all urban employers and workers. The opportunity to reduce the amount that local SOEs had to pay in pension benefits to their retirees and the chance to raise pension contributions from all local enterprises were attractive to urban governments. Moreover, in the absence of explicit national regulations on how to determine pension revenues and benefits, or even for how pension surpluses could be invested, local governments enjoyed considerable leeway.

Pension policy became an agenda item at one of the crucial policymaking enclaves of the Central Committee of the CCP in 1993, when the Fourteenth Central Committee's Third Plenum endorsed the principle of "integrating social pools and individual accounts" practiced in many urban governments by that time (Jiao 2001, 33). The plenum statement supported the idea that future pension benefits should be drawn from both urban pension funds and mandatory individual accounts. The stated intention of the document was that pensions should no longer be paid solely from public funds but should also be paid from what a worker had saved in a mandatory (publicly managed) individual retirement account. In practice, the Third Plenum document gave urban governments a crucial loophole to integrate social pools and individual accounts by using money from both of these coffers to deliver pension benefits to current retirees (Jiao 2001, 48).

According to the published account of a vice minister in charge of social insurance at the Ministry of Labor and Social Security (Jiao 2001), local governments in China by the mid-1990s were using three quite different pension policy designs. One, promoted by what was then called the Ministry of Labor, was based on local experiments in two cities in Jiangxi and Liaoning provinces. Under this model, pension benefits were calculated based on prior wages and the number of years a worker had made contributions. Benefits were also linked to local wage levels. By contrast,

Shanghai and Shenzhen, notable for their high levels of FDI and rapid growth, had developed pension schemes in which benefits were based heavily on accumulations in individual accounts, in close imitation of the Central Provident Fund in Singapore and the privatized pension system in Chile. The Shanghai pension regulations, issued by its local government in 1994, also compelled officials and public-service workers to pay into the city pension fund. Benefits were linked not to local wages, as in the Ministry of Labor model, but to local prices (Jiao 2001, 30). The third design, found in Guangdong province (excluding Shenzhen) with provincial regulations in 1993, combined the individual accounts and defined contributions of the Shanghai model with the pay-as-you-go defined benefits model promoted by the Ministry of Labor. It indexed pension benefits to wages and guaranteed a minimum pension based on a percentage of local average wages. The Guangdong regulations also sought to cover all enterprises and public-service units, as well as small and medium enterprises (Jiao 2001, 31–32).

The vastly different approaches to pensions that emerged across Chinese cities—especially in terms of defined benefit versus defined contributions—made it extremely difficult to adopt a national policy on pensions. It is not unusual for national policy to draw on locally successful experiments in China or elsewhere, but when regional policies vary as widely as they did in Chinese cities, national policy, if it ever gets adopted, can reflect these divisions. This is just what occurred with the 1995 pension regulations.

The 1995 regulations were driven by the need to spell out provisions for the "integration of pooling and individual accounts" endorsed at the Third Plenum of the Fourteenth Central Committee in 1993. The Ministry of Labor pushed for its defined benefits model to be incorporated in the national regulations. The State Structural Reform Commission promoted the Shanghai model of defined contribution pensions. These differences were never resolved; the 1995 State Council regulations allowed the thirty-one provinces, as well as the eleven funds run by the industrial ministries for the SOEs that they managed, to select from three choices (State Council 1995), which were in essence based on the State Structural Reform Commission model and the Ministry of Labor model. In trying to effect a compromise solution, the State Council triggered deeper fragmentation and divisions in pension programs. Jiao Kaiping later likened the effects of the 1995 regulations to the "hundred schools of thought" era of the Warring States (2001, 38). The authors of a World Bank (1997) study on pension reforms in China called this policy the opening of a Pandora's box of unstandardized regulations and unintended consequences.

By 1996, official statistics put the number of SIAs operating at provincial, city, and county levels at 3,422 (Ministry of Labor 1997, 167). Each of these SIAs did not operate its own pension fund—an unknown number of the 2,926 SIAs at county levels were aggregrated into urban SIAs if they were located next to cities of sufficient size and administrative status. On the other hand, many of these 3,422 local SIA offices operated more than one pension fund; separate pension funds for state enterprises, urban collectives, and foreign-invested and private enterprises existed up until the late 1990s. Moreover, these funds operated under widely different rules for financing and benefits, with each resembling either more or less the Shanghai model or one of two variants of the Ministry of Labor model.

Against this backdrop of pension fragmentation, pension benefits actually increased as urban governments in charge of financing and managing their own pension funds took over the responsibilities of paying pension benefits to local retirees. Average pensions (in nominal yuan) rose from 1,330 yuan in 1989 to 6,674 yuan in 2000. In 1999, average pensions represented 90 percent of per capita GDP and 75.5 percent of average SOE wages (Salditt, Whiteford, and Adema 2007, 28). Pension reforms had brought pension benefit increases, for current retirees at least. It is important to emphasize that despite these increases in pension benefits—and more likely because of them—an estimated 3.8 million pensioners encountered delayed pension payments by the year 2000 (All-China Federation of Trade Unions [ACFTU] 2002, 90). With rising fragmentation and with deepening financial commitments to pensioners that local governments apparently could not meet, the central government moved in the late 1990s to bring greater unity to the Chinese pension system.

CENTRAL GOVERNMENT MEASURES TO UNIFY PENSION ADMINISTRATION

It is difficult to say with confidence how political divisions within the CCP during the 1990s translated into policy preferences for pension reforms. Regarding labor policy broadly, one study identifies substantial policy divisions between "statist marketeers" and "pragmatic planners," who fought over the speed of state enterprise restructuring and the relative importance of first establishing a means of welfare support for those left jobless by SOE restructuring (Johnson 2002). One example of this policy dispute is reflected in the fate of the Ministry of Labor—which the statist marketeers, among them Zhu Rongji, wanted to eliminate and replace with a ministry that would serve the function of a national social security agency. The change in name and function would replace a labor ministry that had once been in charge of job allocation in a planned economy with an agency that would serve to cushion workers from risks in the newly liberalized labor market. The eventual outcome was a defeat for Zhu and the statist marketers and a victory for the pragmatic planners. The statist marketeers got their social security agency, but it was embedded within the Ministry of Labor and in 1998 was renamed the Ministry of Labor and Social Security (MOLSS) (Johnson 2002, 165–66). In 2008, this ministry was renamed the Ministry of Human Resources and Social Security (MOHRSS).

Despite the apparent setback for the statist marketers over the disposition of the Ministry of Labor, it is clear that, beginning in 1998 with Zhu Rongji's ascension to premier, the Chinese government took aggressive measures to dismantle SOEs and to invoke labor policies that would trigger mass layoffs and early retirements. The strategy behind SOE reform was not to eliminate public ownership but to make large SOEs profitable by shedding their responsibilities for paying pensions and other welfare costs to their retirees.

Zhu also had his cabinet take aggressive moves to unify the serious fragmentation in pensions. First, the Ministry of Finance and MOLSS, after heated negotiations in which the fiscally conservative views of the former yielded to those of the latter, agreed that central government finances had to be transferred to the provincial governments to make up for the gaping deficits in pension funds. In September 1999, twenty-four provinces received 6.4 billion yuan ($773 million) in subsidies from the Ministry of Finance (Ministry of Labor and Social Security [MOLSS] 2001, 243). In 2000, the following year, pension subsidies increased to 33.7 billion yuan ($4.1 billion) (MOLSS 2002, 272). According to Minister of Finance Xiang Huaicheng, pension subsidies between 1998 and 2001 "at all levels" (including those from the central government and from the provincial governments to cities) totaled 83.9 billion yuan ($10.1 billion), in addition to 43.4 billion yuan for subsidies for laid-off workers. Central government pension subsidies for 2002 were estimated to reach 41 billion yuan (Xiang 2002). Such subsidies were not large for a central government budget that was approaching 1 trillion yuan ($121 billion) by the year 2000. Still, the central government could no longer expect to have a viable public pension system without contributing some of its own finances.

Second, central government officials rapidly used the technical capacity and expertise of pension experts from multilateral banks and global financial corporations. Among the most significant of the linkages of the central government with foreign entities was its involvement with the World Bank in pension reform design during the 1990s. In 1996, a joint research group of seven central government commissions and ministries launched an investigation into the persistent problem of the broad disparities in pension pooling (Han and Jiao 1997, 60). At the invitation of the Chinese government, World Bank staff compiled a report in 1996 and presented it to the State Council ministers. The following year, this report was published under the title of *Old Age Security: Pension Reform in China*. According to one informant, the report was widely read at the highest levels of the CCP, including by Jiang Zemin himself (Interview #102604).[5] The report was critical of Chinese pension measures to date and warned of a looming pension crisis, but it also argued that there was sufficient time to address the problem by funding the individual accounts of current workers.

The World Bank authors delivered some uncharacteristically candid criticism of how the Chinese government had handled pension reforms to date. The essence of the World Bank authors' criticism came down to the fragmentation in pension regulations, benefits, and contributions and the inability of the central government to consolidate the management of locally based pension funds (World Bank 1997, 17–23). The World Bank authors were especially critical of the 1995 regulations that allowed local governments to select one of two pension financing and benefits arrangements. "Each municipality is attempting to differentiate its scheme from that of others to retain control over the pension system and pension funds," the report notes (World Bank 1997, 17).

Third, the central government issued regulations in 1997 that, in theory at least, brought unity to the design of pensions by compelling local governments to follow certain parameters for calculating revenues and benefits, administering pension funds, and so on. The 1997 regulations attempted to standardize contribution rates—the percentage of the wage bill that enterprises would remit as fees to local pension pools. They gave provincial-level authorities the administrative powers to set the contribution rates, but placed a ceiling on employee contributions and a floor on individual contributions. The former could not exceed 20 percent of the wage bill, and the latter could not go below 4 percent of the individual's basic wage. The individual contribution rate would rise 1 percentage point per year until it reached 8 percent in 2001. A portion of these contributions was to be put aside for funding individual accounts that were to make up an important component of pension income for future retirees (State Council 1997).

The 1997 regulations also called for the gradual transfer of county-level pools to the provincial government or to "prefectures that receive authority from the provincial government." This demand went unmet, and MOLSS

---

[5] The interviews are listed in the appendix at the end of the book.

and the Ministry of Finance issued a subsequent notice in late 1999 in which they demanded the abolition of county-level pools and their transfer to prefectural or municipal pools. This notice set a deadline of year-end 2000 for this transfer to be carried out (MOLSS and Ministry of Finance 1999). In actual practice, only three provincial-level governments still administered their own pools by that year. Not coincidentally, these were urban governments with provincial-level rank (Shanghai, Beijing, and Tianjin), and these cities had maintained their own pools since the late 1980s. Eight other provincial-level governments organized redistribution funds (*tiaojijin*) that were simply redistributive mechanisms that channeled small portions of funds from urban government-run pools that were in surplus to those that were in deficit. So, although pension policy was unified in 1997, pension administration remained highly fragmented. The collection of pension fees and the distribution of benefits to retirees were left largely to local governments. Pensioners became heavily dependent on the efforts of local SIAs to collect sufficient revenues from firms within their jurisdiction. The direction of money flowing from firms to local pension funds and from the latter to pensioners is depicted in figure 2.1.

Because local SOEs remained largely responsible for paying pensions to their retirees, unpaid pensions accumulated rapidly. (In terms of figure 2.1, more money was going out on the right side in the form of benefits than was coming in from the left side in the form of pension fees levied on wage bills.) Between late 1997 and May 1998, the amount of money that pensioners were owed in delayed pension payments rose from 3.75 billion to 8.7 billion yuan (Hu 1999, 14). Between the first half of 1998 and the third quarter of that year, the number of provinces whose local pools paid out more in pensions than they collected in contributions rose from seventeen to twenty-five (Hu 1999, 15). By year-end 2000, according to an ACFTU publication, accumulated pension arrears totaled 7.1 billion yuan owed to 3.8 million pensioners. This represented 13.9 percent of 27.2 million retirees nationwide, according to the ACFTU calculations. Of the 43,617 firms that owed unpaid pensions to retirees, 21.7 percent were located in the northeast provinces of Liaoning, Jilin, and Heilongjiang (ACFTU 2002, 90). Although central government regulations in 1999 and 2000 compelled local SIAs to take over responsibilities for the payment of pensions from SOEs (see chapter 3), this transfer did not absolve SOEs of their delinquent payments to retirees. As the bankruptcies of money-losing SOEs accelerated in the late 1990s, the problem of unpaid pensions grew more severe. Pension protests (see chapter 3) targeted SOEs as well as local government officials who had invoked mass layoffs without providing adequate funding for jobless SOE workers.

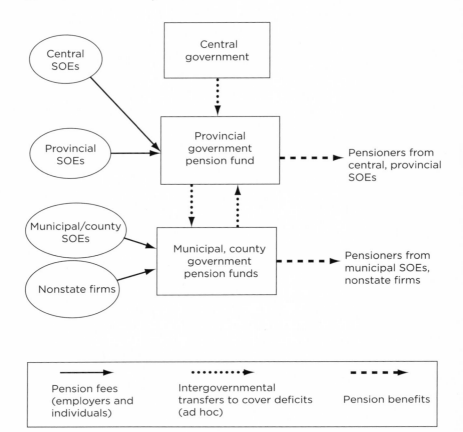

Figure 2.1 Administrative structure and pension pooling in China following the 1990s reforms. SOE, state-owned enterprise.

In May 2000, Premier Zhu Rongji convened a conference on "Unifying, Standardizing, and Perfecting" the social security system. The conference title belied the urgency with which Zhu and the relevant ministries (including the newly established MOLSS in 1998) regarded the failings of local pension and unemployment programs to provide safety nets for the victims of SOE closings. Zhu stressed linkages between the social security system and overall state enterprise reform and warned that delayed payments of pension and unemployment benefits increased the risk of economic and political crises (Xinhua 2000b). In late December 2000, Zhu chaired a national work conference in Beijing on social security. At the meeting, which also was attended by vice premiers Wen Jiabao and Wu Bangguo, Zhu said that "governments at all levels should implement and carry out to the letter the central authorities' present policy measures on social security" (Xinhua 2000c). This and subsequent policy meetings saw different proposals for reform hotly debated (Interview #062802A). The biggest problem was that urban SIAs could not collect enough in pension contributions from employers to cover payments to local retirees. The central government could resolve this problem by reasserting controls over pension administration, but in so doing it would probably also assume the financial responsibility for providing pensions to some 38 million retirees nationwide.

MEASURES TO CONSTRAIN LOCAL CONTROL

By the early 2000s, it was apparent that no amount of threats and strong talk from the blunt-speaking premier would solve the problem that many provinces faced in assuring that cities paid pension benefits on time and in full to retirees. A public pension system fragmented into so many local funds could not be unified at the wave of a hand from Beijing.

As already noted, the central government, despite assurances that it would not subsidize pensions from its budget, reluctantly began to make transfers to the provincial governments in 1999. Provincial governments then passed these subsidies on to urban pension funds that had been unable to provide timely payments of pensions to local SOE retirees. In 2002, central government subsidies to provinces totaled 41 billion yuan (Xiang 2002) and rose to 46.6 billion yuan ($5.6 billion) in 2003 (Wang and Yang 2004, 105).

To escape what they saw as a trap of escalating commitments to pensions, Ministry of Finance officials promoted three further regulatory changes that had the effect of establishing pension funds that were out of the reach of local SIAs. These measures included an experiment in 2001 in Liaoning province to fund individual accounts, the establishment of the National Social Security Fund (NSSF) in 2000, and the introduction of enterprise annuities (essentially corporate pensions) in 2004. Although these pension policy initiatives put constraints on urban governments and their local SIAs, these regulations did not succeed in moving pension administration above city levels. In fact, by creating alternative pension funds separate from those under the control of urban governments, these measures made pension administration even more fragmented.

The National Social Security Fund

The central government established the NSSF in 2000 as a kind of firewall against the pleas of the provincial governments for pension subsidies. In this sense, the NSSF is considered a fund of last resort (*China Economic Review* 2005). The NSSF 2006 annual report states that its assets had grown to 282 billion yuan ($36.1 billion), up from 211 billion yuan at the end of 2005. These assets were invested by ten fund management companies (one of which was a joint venture) that acted as trustees on the board of the National Council of the Social Security Fund ([NCSSF] 2006). The central government enlisted foreign advice in selecting the fund managers in a careful screening process. The NSSF policy guidance and administration comes from the MOHRSS and Ministry of Finance. As of 2006, regulations permitted 30 percent of NSSF assets to be invested in the stock market, leaving the majority to be invested in government bonds and bank deposits.

The NSSF drew its funds from three sources: an unknown amount of transfers from the Ministry of Finance, the sale of social security lottery tickets to consumers, and, most significantly, the revenues from sales of SOE stock and from the initial public offerings (IPOs) of Chinese firms on domestic and international exchanges. The Ministry of Finance allocations to the NSSF declined from 47 billion yuan in 2001 to 36 billion yuan in 2002, and they ceased in 2003 (Interview #110904). A sizable 10 percent of the money raised in domestic and international IPOs beginning in 2001 went to the NSSF. This practice was halted in 2003 for domestic IPOs, but it continues for international IPOs. As one informant noted, "I wonder if New York and Hong Kong investors who bought shares of China Life when it listed [in 2004] realized that ten percent of their money was going into the National Social Security Fund" (Interview #110904).

The conflict between central policymakers and local governments came into stark relief in 2000 with a proposal to transfer 10 percent of all non-tradable shares in listed SOEs to the NSSF. The proposal was fiercely opposed by provincial and urban governments that held the controlling rights over SOEs and feared having shares in their SOEs turned over to NSSF ownership. This proposal led to large sell-offs in the stock exchanges because investors feared that the sale of government-held shares (amounting to over half of the US$500 billion in the domestic market as of 2002) would flood the market and drive down share prices. Opponents of the transfer of SOE shares to the NSSF gained a victory in 2002 when the proposal was put on hold, despite the support of Zhu Rongji and Zhou Xiaochuan, the head of the China Securities Regulatory Commission (Kynge and Leahy 2002; Anderlini 2006). When the transfer of SOE shares to the NSSF was revived in 2006, it mobilized opposition from the State-Owned Asset Supervision and Administration Commission (SASAC) as well. SASAC oversees the largest 156 SOEs by holding a controlling stake in the firms and exerting regulatory authority and managerial appointment powers. Li Rongrong, the chair of SASAC, openly announced his opposition to the transfer of SOE shares and was willing to transfer cash to the NSSF rather than shares (Xinhua Economic News Service 2006). The proposal stalled once again in 2007 despite the support of the China Securities Regulatory Commission (CSRC), Ministry of Finance, People's Bank of China, and MOLSS.

The NSSF thus represented a political compromise between the fiscally conservative central government and provincial governments that were pleading for further pension subsidies that they could transfer to cities that had deficits between pension expenditures and revenues. In the NSSF, the central government created an autonomous source of pension revenues, but the assets under NSSF management will always be vulnerable to political demands from provinces whose urban governments face continuing pressures to cover pension expenditures.

Enterprise Annuities

The central government also used foreign expertise and capital to develop what became known as enterprise annuities (*qiye nianjin*). This policy led indirectly to the revelation of the Shanghai pension scandal in 2006 and to the toppling of the Shanghai party secretary and several of his cronies. In 2004, the State Council issued regulations that essentially permitted enterprises, after they had fulfilled their obligations to remit social insurance, to set up pension plans with financial institutions, much like 401(k)s in the United States. This policy was seen as largely an attempt to mollify large SOEs in sectors such as telecommunications, utilities, airlines, railroads, and petrochemicals that been compelled in 1998 to turn over their own sectorwide pension funds to the control of provincial social insurance agencies. SOEs in these sectors generally enjoy stable, steady profit streams because of limited competition and therefore have an incentive to lower their taxes by setting up pension accounts for their employees. As one expert on this investment vehicle explained, "Everyone knows that officials who run the firms in these sectors want to retire with generous pensions" (Interview #012505). Nevertheless, because the contributions to enterprise annuity funds are in part tax deductible (although this is up to provincial governments to decide), the policy represented a potentially heavy loss of revenue for the large SOEs and foreign firms that contributed large shares to local tax collections.

In their legal conception, enterprise annuities closely followed the trustee models found in the United States, in which a trustee selects a custodian bank or asset manager and assumes legal liability for the funds. This model has much higher transaction costs than other models and has been criticized as not being appropriate for the Chinese context. But it was pushed vigorously by a MOLSS department head who had engaged in extensive travel and research in the United States and was convinced about the merits of the trustee model (Interview #012505). According to another source, the fund management regulations for enterprise annuities closely resembled those of the Hong Kong Provident Fund (Interview #032105A).

Provincial governments, especially Shanghai, were said to be strongly opposed to the introduction of enterprise annuities because the regulations called for local governments to turn over any supplemental pension funds to banks or other trustees of enterprise annuities (Interview #012505). The 2006 scandal that took down Party Secretary Chen Liangyu arose over the use of the Shanghai SIA supplemental fund. This 10 billion yuan ($1.2 billion) fund was collected largely from the high-wage firms of the city. In the early 2000s, the Shanghai SIA hired about a dozen investment advisors and a few custodian banks to help them manage the pension assets (Interview #032105; Interview #012505). As long-standing proponents of the Chilean model of funded individual accounts and pension privatization, Shanghai social insurance officials I interviewed in 2005 talked openly about their strategy of pension "privatization" (Interview #040605). As noted at the opening of chapter 1, the Shanghai privatization came to an abrupt end in August 2006 when the CCP launched an anticorruption drive that led to the dismissal of Party Secretary Chen and other high-ranking officials in connection with the questionable management of the city supplemental pension fund.

The Liaoning Pilot

In 2001, the State Council selected the rust-belt northeastern province of Liaoning as the place to make a stand against the pay-as-you-go practices of local governments and the ensuing pension deficits that they created. In choosing Liaoning, central officials made the case that, if an experiment in funding individual accounts could work there given the high unemployment, severe pension deficits, and ongoing pension protests in Liaoning, it could work anywhere. The MOLSS received project advice from the Asian Development Bank (ADB) on the technical aspects of the administration, investment, and actuarial analysis that were involved in establishing bona fide–funded individual accounts. The ADB, according to an informant, offered a range of best-practices suggestions, but it did not help with the actual implementation (Interview #032105). Liaoning is now the only province in which individual accounts are pooled at the provincial level, although the accounts started accruing returns only as of 2001. By April 2005, the province managed 13.8 billion yuan in individual account funds, but this was well short of the estimated 50 billion yuan ($6.2 billion) that the province needs to have by 2010 to meet the "high tide" of retirements and claims to the individual accounts. The Liaoning SIA was also under pressure to seek far higher returns than it received from deposits in the Chinese state banks. These were hardly risk-free investments, as one official noted (Interview #040405A).

The Liaoning pilot was hailed as a success, but it came at a cost of central government subsidies of 3.7 billion yuan in 2002 and between 5 and 6 billion yuan in the following two years. The central government announced plans in 2005 to extend the same practices of funding individual accounts to the two other northeastern provinces and possibly to the rest of country. In so doing, the central government was anticipating that large subsidy payments made now could fund individual accounts that could be used in the future. In the long run, this would lower the massive implicit central government pension debt of 80–90 percent of GDP, or approximately 10 trillion yuan ($1.3 trillion) (Interview #032105). As noted in the introduction to the book, the IPD is an attempt to measure the total liabilities associated with pension payments to future generations of retirees.

Although the Chinese central government at the start of the 2000s initiated new pension policies using international connections and expertise, these initiatives did not succeed in bringing unity to the Chinese pension system and, more broadly, its welfare regime. These measures were attempts by the central government to use a tried and true method of bringing foreign pressure or the promise of foreign capital to bear on an obstreperous domestic political coalition of local governments and local state enterprises. Enterprise annuities, for example, gave financial institutions the ability to move in on the turf of the local SIAs. The Liaoning pilot and its diffusion to other provinces essentially walled off funds in individual accounts from predation by local government agencies. Finally, the NSSF gave the central government its own war chest of pension funds, with the ability to invest them in areas that SIAs could not, such as domestic and international stock markets. In short, the new policies were supplements to, not substitutes for, a clearly flawed public pension system tied to local governments and local interests.

THE SOCIAL INSURANCE LAW AND ITS OPPONENTS

The tension between the central and local Chinese governments over pensions is further evidenced in the failure by policymakers and legislators in Beijing to craft an acceptable SIL. Drafts of the SIL date back to the mid-1990s, but until 2009 at least, disagreement among ministries over the provisions in the draft law kept it stalled within the NPC (Interview #070202). The MOLSS generally supported the passage of the SIL, although with some reservations if it meant that the MOLSS would lose regulatory authority over social insurance fee collections (Interview #062802A). The Ministry of Finance was concerned about the fiscal implications of providing universal coverage or of expanding pension coverage to peasants. The MCA, which had regulated rural pensions until this function was transferred to MOLSS in 1998, had an enduring interest in regaining social security provision in rural areas. Such bureaucratic infighting within the Beijing ministries was sufficient to stall the passage of the SIL until late 2008, when the NPC released the draft SIL for public comment. The legislation appeared headed for passage in 2009 or in 2010.

During the 2007 NPC deliberations over the draft SIL, several NPC Standing Committee members as well as policy specialists voiced concern that the SIL did not go far enough in establishing a provincial or national fund that could better redistribute pension fund money across cities. Several commentators also noted the urgent need to create provincial pension funds, or even a national pension fund, so that labor mobility could be facilitated and the retirement accounts of migrant workers who paid into pension funds where they worked could be protected (National People's Congress [NPC] 2008). It is difficult to discern from the NPC's summary account of the debate why the SIL authors did not attempt to create broader provincial or national pension funds. Yet it is clear that the urban governments and local SIAs would stand to lose a great deal of authority and revenues if they were compelled to turn over their local pension funds to a provincial or national pension administration.

In the absence of laws from the central government, provincial and city governments during the 1990s and 2000s passed a range of local laws. The Hunan provincial People's Congress in the late 1990s issued legislation that established a Social Insurance Tribunal (Song 1999, 12). The establishment of the tribunal reportedly increased compliance among firms that were accused by SIAs of evading their pension obligations. The city of Qingdao passed "provisional methods" and "provisional regulations" covering pension, unemployment, medical, workplace injury, and maternity insurance in 1998 (Xinhua 1999c). The Standing Committee of the Shanghai

People's Congress passed a regulation (*guizhang*) in 1998 that gave the Shanghai SIA the power to apply to courts to seize property or use the sale of enterprise assets to compel firms to pay what they owed in delinquent pension contributions (Xinhua 1999a). Liaoning Province also issued a local regulation (*difang fagui*) on pension insurance in July 1999 (Xinhua 1999b). One commentator noted that the lack of national legislation on social security, including pensions, produced an "abnormal flourishing of local social insurance legislation" (Xie 2002, 209).

Many policy analysts and officials argued that the SIL would improve pension administration whose many flaws were attributable to multiple local regulations and the absence of a national law. Commentators who advocated the SIL noted that, except for a 1953 revision to the 1951 Labor Insurance Regulations, there had been no social security legislation in China (Feng 2001, 205). In part, pension protests took place because workers had no legal channels through which to pursue claims for unpaid pensions (Hurst and O'Brien 2002; Frazier 2004b; Lee 2007). One specialist argued that the effects of evading social insurance fees were no less harmful to the society than tax evasion. Unlike the latter, however, there were no specific legal statutes if an employer did not remit social insurance fees (Xie 2002, 209). One local labor and social security (LSS) official from the city of Qingdao noted that the State Council regulations issued to date still lack the coercive measures that other parts of the Chinese bureaucracy enjoy. This official cited specifically the fact that Tax Bureau officials can arrest and jail a person who refuses to pay taxes and that the State Administration of Industry and Commerce (SAIC) can revoke the business license of a firm that refuses to comply with any number of regulations that SAIC oversees (H. Chen 2002, 174).

It remains to be seen whether the increasing number of disputes over social insurance will persuade enough top CCP leaders to insist on the passage of the SIL, but even if this happens, local government and business interests would remain strongly aligned against its successful implementation. Despite the merit of the arguments for the SIL, from the perspective of urban governments there is an equally sound reason to oppose or resist a strict implementation of the SIL. Were the SIL to contain detailed provisions about the payment of social insurance fees and to expand coverage to all citizens, it would become difficult for local governments to disaggregate pension policy into measures that give them considerable flexibility in dealing with pensioners, enterprises, and others.

In a candid assessment of Chinese pension reform policies of the 1990s, researchers at the State Council Development Research Center (DRC) observed: "Looking at the implementation of these measures, problems arose, reform objectives were not achieved, and the pension security system faced a crisis. It had generated a negative impact on reforms in other aspects and [on] social stability. Such a situation has nothing to do with the objectives of reform, but resulted from deviations in implementation" (State Council Development Research Center, Research Group 2001, 10).

"Good policies, poor implementation" is a common refrain in assessments of policy shortcomings in China. Yet, in the case of Chinese pension reforms, we could easily turn this argument on its head. The policies themselves were flawed, in part because they vaguely summarized and synthesized lessons from local pension administration and grafted these on best-practices advice from international institutions. The policies were also flawed because they attempted to achieve two competing aims: to pay for the transition or legacy costs associated with layoffs in the state sector and, at the same time, to introduce a new norm of individual responsibility for accumulating one's own savings for retirement. Local governments took the politically expedient route of paying SOE legacy costs (i.e., pensions) with money from individual accounts of current employees (from SOEs and non-SOEs).

CHAPTER 3

Resolving the Puzzles of China's Pension Reforms

The considerable amount of scholarly work done in recent years on pension and other social policy reforms adopts the metaphor of the veto to explain the substance and eventual fate of policy outcomes. The logic is that policy proposals are more likely to go down to defeat, or at least be substantially diluted, as the number of veto points increases. Thus, Raúl Madrid (2003, 149–51) shows that Brazil, unlike Argentina and Mexico, failed to enact pension privatization in part because it would have required a constitutional amendment supported by three-fifths of both houses in the legislature. Linda Cook (2007) shows that substantial variation in social policy emerged in three transition economies because of the different veto points within them and different levels of access that interest groups had to key political institutions. Stephen Kay (1999) makes a similar argument for the pension privatizations in the southern cone (Chile, Argentina, and Uruguay). The number of veto points is often determined by constitutional design and by the rules of party competition. Fewer veto points increase the chances of pension reforms passing, and the greater the number of veto points, the less the likelihood of deep pension reforms such as privatization.

The dominance of the CCP over political institutions in China suggests that once a consensus is reached within the uppermost ranks of the CCP (e.g., the Standing Committee of the Politburo) the opponents of new policies will lack access points at which they can block reforms. Yet, as students of Chinese politics have long been aware, policy is susceptible to a large number of veto points across territorial and functional bureaucracies. Even if a law is enacted by the NPC, the implementation of its provisions falls heavily on the willingness and incentives of the implementing agencies at the national, provincial, city, county, and other local levels (below the level of the county). The presence of what might be called post hoc veto points across local governments at various levels might explain the inability of the center to carry out its reform objectives. In the case of the Chinese pension reforms, urban governments were both active agents of policy change and veto players in the central government attempts to standardize and nationalize pension policy and administration.

As discussed in chapter 2, the initiative for pension reforms came not from central bureaucracies but from urban governments, in collaboration with state enterprises. The momentum for pension reforms originated in the efforts to pool the pension funds of ailing SOEs within an urban area and thereby share or externalize the costs of financing local pensioners from state enterprises. As much as central government policymakers tried to enact reforms that would channel pension funds across broader levels of administration beyond the cities, these efforts failed as municipal governments resisted demands to pool their pension funds. Despite the steadfast efforts of leaders such as Zhu Rongji and the technical expertise of the World Bank and other international agencies, further pension reforms were constrained by the institutional structure of decentralized and fiscally self-reliant Chinese local administrations. Why did urban governments choose to take on the responsibility of managing pensions themselves instead of allowing higher levels, such as provincial governments (and, indirectly, the central government) to do so?

The theoretical framework known as historical institutionalism can help resolve this question. Historical institutionalist accounts stress that preferences vary depending on the institutional context in which political agents find themselves. Preferences do not precede and therefore lead to the formation of institutions, as rational choice theorists have it; instead, institutions shape preferences and political conflict over policy (Thelen 1999). Indeed, institutions persist for long periods of time because political agents mobilize to defend them in periods when such institutions are under pressure. The welfare state as a durable institution has been the empirical focus of some of the most influential works in the historical institutionalist literature. Specific programs found in advanced welfare states have strengthened bureaucratic agencies and mobilized interest groups. Policy feedback and policy learning influence the cognitive process and strategies that political actors adopt (Pierson 1994). As Hugh Heclo notes for pensions in late-nineteenth-century Britain, "pensions helped advance the organization of the British labor movement as much as the reverse" (1974, 165). Businesses and their associations have also mobilized to support welfare policies and proposals such as national health insurance, whereas other business sectors have opposed them (Mares 2003). Some business owners support and others resist welfare policies for what appear to be rational or self-interested motivations, but their diametrically opposed stances can be explained by seeing how institutions shape preferences.

Turning to the case of Chinese pension reforms, the preferences and behavior of urban officials seem surprising at first. Why would urban officials push for taking on the responsibility of financing the benefits of local retirees rather than defending the status quo in which SOEs bore the costs of their retirees? At the very least, why would urban officials not choose to subsidize the costs of continuing enterprise-based welfare through bank loans or other means? Why would urban governments, even though they quickly ran up sizable pension deficits by assuming responsibilities for local retirees, so stubbornly oppose the nationalization or centralization of pension funds at higher levels? For their part, why would local SOEs, whose distribution of retirees varied considerably depending on the age of the firm, agree to contribute to local social insurance funds for pensions and other welfare programs? Some firms, including non-SOEs with few if any retirees to support, had an interest in evading social insurance regulations. (The stances of private and foreign-invested enterprises are discussed in chapter 4.) But even large SOEs that enjoyed relatively steady revenue streams from a monopoly or duopoly of their sector also had an interest in avoiding social insurance. For example, managers in such SOEs might try to avoid the leveling effect of joining a local urban pension pool when doing so would lower benefits for their workers and managers, as was frequently true of large SOEs in heavily protected sectors such as energy and finance.

The reaction of the urban public, especially the SOE workers who lost jobs over the course of SOE reforms, also poses a puzzle. Several studies on the plight of the laid-off Chinese proletariat have noted that responses to the broken promises of lifetime employment and secure welfare benefits were rather muted. At best, such reactions saw only limited appeals to classwide mobilization against the policies of SOE reform and labor market liberalization (Lee 2008; Gold et al. 2009). The message from these studies is that, although workers' resistance varied considerably, at the end of the day it was entirely unsuccessful in checking the pace of SOE reform and the job losses in the state sector. This is a valid point, but it overlooks the surprising success of jobless SOE workers in having certain claims met by local officials and by the Chinese state more broadly. Street protests and other forms of resistance by jobless SOE workers invoked the symbols of state socialism and Maoist egalitarian political culture, but their demands were often highly specific and centered on the provision of unpaid pensions or other forms of severance pay.

If historical institutionalist accounts are valid in explaining the preferences and behavior of urban officials, local enterprise managers, and SOE workers, then there should be preexisting institutions that influenced such preferences and behavior. The point of this chapter is to identify institutions that may have influenced the preferences of particular agents and to begin to put a historical institution-based argument to the test using the evidence. In chapters 4–6, I turn to closer empirical tests of the preferences and behaviors of local officials, firms, and urban residents regarding pension policy.

The ambiguous property rights regime that emerged under the Chinese transition from state socialism allowed urban officials and local state enterprise managers to sell off state assets in the form of SOEs for lucrative private gains, despite the political risks posed by the ensuing mass layoffs of state workers. Furthermore, the institutional practices that permitted municipalities to retain locally raised revenue gave strong incentives for them to set up social insurance agencies that could collect pension and other social insurance revenue from all local employers, not simply SOEs. The property rights claims that urban governments had over SOEs and the rights of urban governments to locally raised revenue are the two institutions that best account for the preferences and behaviors of otherwise reluctant urban officials and local SOEs in carrying out experiments in local pension reforms. Such institutions also explain the resistance of urban governments to the pooling of pension funds at higher levels of administration. The preferences and behavior of jobless SOE workers, their localized patterns of protest, and their demands for justice, can be explained as a consequence of the institutional legacies of the work unit (*danwei*).

WHY URBAN GOVERNMENTS DISMANTLED ENTERPRISE WELFARE

By the mid-1990s, the competition from foreign-invested enterprises and quasi-private township and village enterprises made most SOEs unprofitable and deeply indebted to state-owned banks. Local governments that had once drawn on SOEs as a main source of revenue now had incentives to sell off the assets to foreign and private investors *if* workers in SOEs were provided with some form of compensation. But giving appropriate severance payments and pensions to those who were to be retired, laid-off, or otherwise transferred out of SOE jobs was not so easily accomplished. SOE employees had been promised lifelong jobs and extensive nonwage benefits in exchange for low wages and restricted consumption choices. Faced with this challenge, most local governments continued to pressure banks to loan to SOEs to cover their operating costs, including employee benefits (Steinfeld 1998).

By the mid-1990s, the conjunction of a foreign investment boom and the growth of sizable local pension pools made it possible to invoke a massive restructuring of the state sector. According to OECD data, 60 percent of Chinese FDI in 1999 was in the form of foreign capital merging with state enterprises (Gallagher 2005, 49). Local governments sold their firms, foreign investors got their discounted state assets, and state workers got something resembling compensatory payments, most commonly in the form of buyouts that were labeled "pensions." As local governments and central government ministries that ran the largest enterprises sought to prepare them for stock listings on foreign exchanges, the balance sheets had to be improved by transferring the legacy costs of health care and pensions out of the listed entity.

With de facto privatization and restructuring of the state sector, the SOE workforce declined from 109 million in the mid-1990s to 69 million by 2002. The work-unit system essentially dissolved as state enterprises turned over functions of health care, pensions, housing, and other once-free welfare provisions to the urban governments (Cook and Maurer-Fazio 1999; Solinger 2002; Duckett 2004). Contract labor, introduced in the mid-1980s, ended the institution of lifelong employment and with it access to enterprise-financed welfare measures (Gallagher 2005). In its place, the Chinese government instituted a system of social insurance in which urban governments collected fees from local firms and pooled the funds to pay for retirement benefits, health care, unemployment, workplace injury, and maternity leave. Government policies took away the state-financed cradle-to-grave welfare benefits enjoyed by some 100 million state-sector workers and replaced them with benefits financed largely from payroll taxes paid by workers and employers. Minimum income payments for the urban poor (*dibao*) were initiated in national regulations in the 1990s and financed through government expenditures rather than social insurance. In some regions, especially the northeast, the layoff process was highly contentious, given the severe lack of funding for pensions (Hurst 2004). Still, as a general rule, local governments desperate to sell off assets to foreign and private investors successfully did so by transferring the legacy costs to local pension funds.

The adoption of the 1997 national pension regulations (see chapter 2) came amid preparations for the Fifteenth Party Congress in October 1997. Party congresses, held once every five years, release the newly appointed Politburo and Central Committee membership lists and issue major policy directives that the government will pursue for the next several years. The Fifteenth Party Congress promoted SOE reforms with policies that encouraged local governments to shed all but the largest SOEs. As many studies have pointed out, the reform of SOEs promoted at the Fifteenth Party Congress, through the slogan of "release the small [SOEs], retain the large," only gave voice to what had been happening for at least the previous five years (Lin and Zhu 2001; Gallagher 2005). The strategy of reform explicitly avoided the term *privatization* and called for the state to retain ownership of large SOEs. But throughout the country, local governments were engaged in de facto privatization of all but the largest SOEs, which were usually under the control of the central ministries. Local officials in some cases took "road shows" to Europe and the United States to market local SOEs to foreign investors through outright sales and through the grafting of SOEs to foreign joint-venture partners (Gallagher 2005). One of the biggest obstacles to such sales was the cost of providing compensation to those left jobless by the mergers and sales, but the prospect of retiring large numbers of workers by providing them with early pensions proved to be an attractive solution to the problem.

When local governments received the signal from the central government that SOE privatization was now accepted policy, they quickly moved to transfer the legacy costs to pension funds. A massive wave of retirements swept through China, and many of these were early retirements. According to official statistics, the number of pensioners from enterprises (most of which were SOEs and urban collectives) rose from 23.7 million in 1995 to 32.6 million in 2002 (State Statistics Bureau [SSB] and Ministry of Labor and Social Security [MOLSS] 2003, 530), a 37.5 percent increase. More serious was the rise in pension expenditures, which for enterprise retirees rose from 91.5 billion yuan in 1995 to 241.7 billion yuan ($29.2 billion) in 2002, that is, at a pace at which pension expenditures doubled approximately every five years (SSB and MOLSS 2003, 530).

A sizable number of these pensioners who were added during the 1990s were young even by relatively early Chinese retirement ages. A survey conducted by MOLSS scholars in 2000 (involving a very large sample size of 7.7 million workers in forty-two cities) found that 25 percent of all retirements occurred before the comparatively early legal retirement ages of sixty for men and fifty for women (fifty-five for women in clerical positions) (Wang 2004). A subsequent World Bank study based on a sample from seven cities found that the *average* retirement age was fifty-six for men and fifty for women, indicating that sizable portions of pensioners were under the legal retirement age (Sin 2005, 10).

In large part, the retirement wave was fueled by the outcome of negotiations between local governments and private investors over the mergers and sales of SOEs. To make SOEs competitive, local governments sought outside capital and in exchange gave the investors considerable autonomy over internal labor practices (Gallagher 2005). In most instances, as Mary Gallagher relates, the grafting of ailing local SOEs to, or their merger with, foreign capital invariably brought layoffs and retirements, including negotiations over how welfare benefits for the redundant workers would be financed (Gallagher 2005, 51, 143). The enterprises most likely to have been merged, sold off, or otherwise shut down were those that had higher levels of retirees in 1995 (see chapter 5).

Workers who lost jobs from the dismantling of SOEs did also receive as compensation from their employers access to housing at highly favorable prices. Yet, according to household surveys, the implementation of housing reform, which in many cases distributed enterprise-owned apartment units and provided housing subsidies for SOE workers, was quite unequal. Because housing subsidies made up for the gap between the rental value and actual rent paid by residents, those who received the most valuable housing allotments also received the highest subsidies. Surveys in 1995 found that 60 percent of housing subsidies went to the wealthiest 10 percent of the population. This imbalance had improved substantially by 2002, but housing subsidies remained concentrated among those at the higher income levels (Khan and Riskin 2005, 371–72).

In invoking a mass retirement wave and paying for it with pensions, urban governments openly defied many provisions of the 1997 pension regulations and subsequent measures of the central government. According to several informants, Zhu Rongji was deeply concerned at the rising expenditures on pensions and expressed his outrage at how local governments, especially Shanghai, acted as if central regulations never existed (Interview #062802A). Zhu's concerns were warranted, given what was happening as SOE reform accelerated. As local governments and SOEs collaborated to get desperately needed foreign capital, they were happy to shed as many workers as possible by promising to pay higher pension benefits. They assumed that money for these benefits would come from somewhere else, in the form of subsidies. Local governments approved retirements for practically any reason, on the assumption that the next highest level would take care of transferring the necessary pension money.

The initial conflict between urban officials and local SOEs over pension policy can be seen in the struggle, beginning in 1998, over central government orders that freed enterprises from the responsibility of paying pensions directly to their retirees. Under the existing practice prior to 1998, each month an SOE had to remit its pension contributions to SIAs as a percentage of the wage bill; then, the SOE at the same time requested pension benefits for its retirees. Instead of two payments being sent in opposite directions (contributions to the SIA and then benefits to the SOE), an SOE "remitted the difference" (*cha'e jiaobo*) by deducting from its pension contributions the amount that the firm was going to distribute as benefits to its retirees. This practice allowed SOE managers to make up whatever figures they wished so that they could minimize their contributions to the SIA as well as their distribution of pension benefits to retirees (Interview #053101).

State Council regulations issued in 1999 prohibited enterprises from paying pensions and placed this responsibility on SIAs. This measure, known in Chinese by the cumbersome label socialization of pension distributions (*yanglaojin shehuihua fafang*) had sudden, far-reaching effects. The regulations effectively cut the ties between pensioners and enterprises. As two Xinhua commentators stated, "retirees may go to nearby banks or post offices every month to receive the full amount of pensions provided by social security organs. Thus, their basic livelihood will be guaranteed." The Xinhua commentators also noted that "socialized distribution of pensions is common practice in all countries in the world. None of the countries which have established a social insurance system has provided pensions through enterprises" (Xinhua 2000a).

SOEs, now freed from having to pay pensions, gladly complied with the regulations that relieved them of the burden of distributing pension benefits. As a result, local governments that before had only collected fees for their pension funds now came under intense pressure to have sufficient cash on hand to pay local pensioners (Interview #070202; Interview #062802A). SIAs had to come up with enough funds on a monthly basis to distribute pensions to retirees within their respective cities. Pension protests that before had been diffuse by virtue of the fact that the unpaid pensioners went to SOEs to demand payment now had the potential to be concentrated at "city hall" or wherever local SIAs were housed. As a result, local governments had strong incentives to make enterprises contribute the full amount of their pension contributions to the pension pools.

Thus, the placement of responsibility for pension payments on urban governments quickly changed their incentives. Before, city officials could let SOE managers worry about how they would cover pension benefits, and if the firm in question was large enough, officials could arrange for bank loans to be directed to the firm to head off pension protests. With pension benefits now their responsibility, SIAs had strong incentives to collect enough pension contributions from local firms to ensure that retirees and laid-off workers could be paid what they were entitled to under various regulations.

Municipal officials understood that their political careers were at risk if they failed to deliver this support to pensioners and laid-off workers (Interview #062802B; Interview #060501). Various high-level conferences in 1999 and 2000, including the Fourth Plenum of the Fifteenth Central Committee that produced a major decision on SOE reform, all stressed the "two guarantees": the distribution of unemployment and retirement benefits through social insurance agencies and the responsibilities of local officials to deliver payments to laid-off and retired workers (Xinhua 2000b, 2000c). Nationwide between 1998 and 2000 the proportion of pensioners who drew their pensions from local SIAs rose from 48.4 to 81.1 percent and, in absolute terms, from 13.8 to 23.6 million retirees (Xinhua 2002). By year-end 2001, 98 percent of pensioners were said to have been receiving pensions from SIAs.

A database complied from eight hundred state and nonstate firms surveyed in 2000 illustrates the variation in the process of SIAs taking over responsibilities for pension distribution. (Further information on this survey data is found in chapter 4.) Of the 416 SOEs in the survey, a total of 204 (49 percent) were already having their pensioners paid directly from local pension pools by year-end 1999. Another 211 SOEs (50.7 percent) were engaged in "remitting the difference" arrangements with local pension pools, and one firm reported still paying its retirees directly. On the other hand, only 11 out of 211 urban collectives paid their employees from local social pools, whereas 112 (53 percent) still paid their retirees directly through the enterprise. Of eighty-nine recently "corporatized" state firms (a separate ownership category distinct from SOEs), only six reported having their employees paid directly by social pools. These data suggest strongly that municipal governments were in effect using their local social pools to look after the firms with the largest retiree populations (SOEs in the survey had a mean retiree population of 571, whereas urban collectives and other non-SOE categories had means of between 100 and 140 retirees per firm).

Following the transfer of pensions to SIAs, enterprises and local social security agencies continued to bargain over how much firms should remit to local pension funds as a percentage of their payrolls and whether retirees would be paid from enterprise accounts or from local pension funds.

(The dynamics of this interaction between SIAs and various forms of enterprises is the focus of chapters 4 and 5.) Although SIAs assumed responsibilities for pension benefits, they also refused to permit the aggregation of pension funds at higher levels. This made the creation of provincial pension funds, not to mention a national pension fund, highly unlikely. Localized pension funds at the urban level arose from the political and administrative responsibilities that the central government placed on local officials.

With these new responsibilities, SIAs saw a rapid increase in their administrative capabilities. The enlargement of SIAs is striking considering that in the late 1990s many government agencies were undergoing substantial restructuring that led to reductions in personnel allocations. According to an internal publication of the MOLSS, in 1994 SIAs had 3,305 offices within various levels of local government, from counties or urban districts to provinces. Total staff at that time numbered 38,988 (Ministry of Labor 1997, 149). By 1999, there were 63,229 staff (including sizable numbers of accountants, statisticians, and computer technicians) placed among 3,567 SIA offices (Ministry of Labor 1997, 288). By year-end 2004, the SIA bureaucracy had swelled to nearly 120,000 staff (over 200,000, if urban grassroots offices are included) among 7,293 offices nationwide (MOLSS 2005). Although there are no figures on budgetary resources for SIAs, it is safe to assume that the same rule held throughout the Chinese bureaucracy and that the increases in SIA staff corresponded to increases in SIA budgets. These SIA offices were funded through local governments, but much of their resources came from the administrative fees they could charge on the rapidly growing pension funds that they administered. Pension revenues collected by SIAs rose from 74 billion yuan in 1994 to 578 billion yuan ($69.8 billion) in 2004 (SSB and MOLSS 2005, 573).

Local SIAs also amass a great deal of information on individual citizens. A provincial head of a social insurance agency observed that the information he collected and managed was more detailed than the records kept by the public security bureau (Interview #040405A). The public security bureaus, he reasoned, collect information about an individual's place of residence and, of course, any legal transgressions. His and other SIAs possessed detailed information on each worker, including registration numbers and residence, current and past employers and places of employment, current and past earnings, social insurance contributions, and accumulated funds in personal accounts for pensions, health care, and so on. Although it is obvious that SIAs lack the coercive power of the public security bureaus, they claim to possess far more information on individuals.

Provincial-level SIAs also hold the personal dossiers of workers from bankrupt enterprises (Interview #030805A).

SIA officials often modestly claim that they can only implement, not make, policy. But in terms of staffing and resources, local SIAs are at least twice as large as the LSS bureaus that supposedly oversee the work of SIAs. In three of six provincial capitals that I visited, the provincial SIA building had marble and glass designs and other traits of a newly built office tower, whereas the provincial LSS bureau was housed in a drab, dusty concrete-block building with dozens of other provincial government bureaus. The rapid growth of SIAs during the 1990s demonstrates a new capacity of the Chinese state as a consequence of pension reform. And like any Chinese agency that possesses information, SIAs keep their operations and statistics a tightly held secret, not simply from foreigners but from other local governments and even the central government.

Although urban officials collaborated with SOE managers to externalize the costs of pensions, they also developed several formal policies and informal practices that allowed SOEs to dismiss state-sector workers who were not close to retirement age. The most prominent of these policies was a measure to designate some workers as laid off (*xiagang*). Under this policy, laid-off workers were put in a halfway house between their original employers and the labor market. Laid-off workers maintained formal labor relations with their original employers for up to three years by registering at the reemployment center of their firm. Laid-off workers were to receive a basic stipend from their original enterprise while they looked for employment elsewhere. They also had their social insurance fees paid on behalf of their enterprises to local SIAs (Interview #022305). In most cases, the prospects of state enterprise workers' finding another job were rather bleak, given the competition from migrant labor and the structure of the urban labor markets. After three years, laid-off workers had to cut relations with their employers. At this point, they were technically unemployed. If they registered as such with local authorities, they were eligible for payments from local unemployment insurance funds. After using up their eligibility for unemployment insurance (usually after two years), ex-SOE workers were lumped in with the urban poor and could apply for minimum income payments.

These policies and practices varied across region, but generally speaking the SOE workers who were too far away from retirement age were designated as laid off and could then apply for retirement benefits once they reached retirement age. The large state enterprises under central government supervision often managed to designate their workers as being retired even before they reached retirement age. But for most SOEs it was not possible to make such arrangements, and they channeled their workers toward the laid-off designation and eventually on to the rolls of the urban poor. The total accumulated number of laid-off workers over the five-year period ending in 2002 was 27.1 million. Official statistics suggest that 1999 was a peak year for designating laid-off workers—6.2 million workers were newly classified as laid off (SSB and MOLSS 2003, 134). By contrast, between 1998 and 2002, the number of people designated as retirees from enterprises (most of which were from state enterprises and urban collectives) rose from 27.7 to 32.6 million, with 1998 and 2002 being peak years in which approximately 1.8–1.9 million workers were added to the pension rolls (MOLSS 2003, 530).

By the early 2000s, local governments in some regions developed practices that allowed firms to avoid paying social insurance fees. For example, Shanghai pioneered a practice known as "agreements to keep social insurance" (*baoliu shehui baoxian xieyi*) or *xiebao*. Under this arrangement, SOEs continued to make payments for their workers' pension and medical insurance, but workers agreed to have their salaries terminated and to look elsewhere for employment. *Xiebao* was clearly much less costly for state enterprises than the formal *xiagang* designation, which involved the administration of reemployment centers and stipend payments for three years. *Xiebao* was also significant because SOEs continued to pay the social insurance fees of their workers. The nonstate firms that hired such *xiebao* workers saved considerable sums by being able to hire workers without paying 20–30 percent of their wages as social insurance fees (Interview #022305). Another labor market innovation by local governments, also in Shanghai, was the creation of labor service companies (LSCs), which essentially acted as labor contractors. LSCs provided to employers a pool of workers, with the assurance that their social insurance fees were paid for by the LSCs. Here again, nonstate firms that had few incentives to provide benefits to low-skilled employees could essentially evade the payroll tax associated with social insurance fees (Interview #022305).

The historical institutionalist approach helps to resolve some of the puzzling behavior of urban governments, which persisted in taking on the costly function of providing pensions and other benefits related to unemployment that they might otherwise have gladly left to local SOEs or to the central government. Partial property rights claims over state assets—a legacy of the Chinese economic transition—provided strong incentives for urban officials to collaborate with local SOE managers to restructure state assets in such a way that the most profitable could be retained and the firms losing money could be sold at fire-sale prices to preferred clients. The fiscal relationships and institutional norms that permitted urban governments to retain locally raised revenue further provided local officials with incentives to set up social insurance agencies that would collect social insurance wage deductions from local employers. Revenues from these wage deductions could be used to pay the social costs of SOE layoffs.

Urban governments and local firms differed sharply over the relative responsibilities and costs of social insurance provision (see chapters 4–5). Where their interests aligned, however, was on the question of national laws and regulations—both urban officials and business owners sought to preserve the flexibility that came with local administration. In this sense, it is difficult to ascribe to urban governments the function of veto players because there was, in policy terms, nothing to veto. At largely their own initiative, urban governments dismantled much of the state sector in the 1990s and shed some 40 million state-sector jobs. Urban governments could sell state assets in SOEs and assume the risks posed by the mass layoffs by distributing pensions as compensation to those left jobless by the process. Urban governments and the local SOE managers with whom they collaborated to dismantle the state sector faced rising worker unrest if the various policies they crafted to compensate SOE workers—pensions, laid-off worker stipends, minimum living allowances, and so on—failed to receive adequate financing.

PENSION PROTESTS, CELLULAR ACTIVISM, AND CASHING OUT

The workers who bore the brunt of SOE restructuring in the 1990s had experienced work and life under the old micro–welfare state in which SOEs provided broad benefits, including housing, medical care, and pensions, along with lifetime employment. The dismantling of the SOE sector meant not only lost jobs but also lost benefits and widespread protests over state efforts to revoke its social contract, in which it provided full-time work and guaranteed benefits in exchange for workers' political loyalty. The targets of the labor protests that followed were local state officials and SOE managers. This pattern of labor contention, in which SOE workers used labor laws to frame their grievances yet eschewed cross-factory or horizontal strategies of mobilization, has been labeled "cellular activism" (Lee 2008). Workers in rust-belt areas who received little if any compensation from SOE bankruptcies and mergers demanded that local officials, who often enriched themselves in these state-asset sales, provide them with a living wage in their forced (and usually early) retirement. Protests by ex-SOE workers often invoked pensions because they were institutionalized promises of compensation from the state to workers.

A vivid example of such protests can be seen in Ching Kwan Lee's (2007) recounting of the struggles in the northeast rust-belt city of Liaoyang in 2002. In what some claim was the largest protest in China since 1989, tens of thousands of workers from up to twenty factories in the city of Liaoyang (in Liaoning province) marched on the city government demanding that the authorities do something about their months-old backlog of unpaid wages, pensions, and unemployment assistance. The Liaoyang protestors directed their wrath at the city officials who had collaborated with local enterprises to invoke bankruptcy proceedings on the Liaoyang Ferro-Alloy Factory in 2001 (Lee 2007, 15–17). According to one of Lee's informants, enterprise managers had, just prior to the bankruptcy declaration, made off with the factory machinery, raw materials, and even doors and windows (Lee 2007, 27). When city officials continued to thwart legal efforts by workers to hold the enterprise managers accountable for their plundering of state assets and for their refusal to issue back wages and pensions, word spread to workers and retirees from other factories. The march eventually drew tens of thousands of workers and retirees, but it was largely spearheaded by the claims of the Liaoyang Ferro-Alloy workers.[1]

In virtually every pension protest in the 1990s and since, the targets have been local officials and state enterprise managers. Their zealous efforts in the 1990s to dismantle state enterprises and dump unemployed workers on to pension payrolls brought about a situation in many cities in which the number of claimants for pensions and unemployment assistance overwhelmed the available public funds of the local governments. Pensioners in Liaoyang and elsewhere in the northeast seemed well aware that their protests made a difference in persuading local officials to somehow come up with the unpaid pension benefits. The pensioners whom Lee interviewed in Shenyang had discerned a direct relationship between the size of their protests, which involved the blocking of major roads, and the amount and speed that local officials were willing to disburse unpaid pensions (Lee 2007, 21). Laid-off workers also targeted state enterprise managers and local governments in their protests (Cai 2005, 7).

In many cases, local officials and SOE managers had made personal fortunes in the restructuring of state enterprises. This fact was not lost on

---

[1] In fact, Lee provides evidence that the Liaoyang protest, which offered some signs of class-wide mobilization, was on close inspection actually more typical of the highly localized or firm-based labor mobilization that occurred elsewhere in China.

the retirees and workers whose pensions and wages remained unpaid for months on end. Large-scale protests in Chongqing, Baotou, and Daqing in 2002 and at a mine in Yangjiazhanzi in 2000 arose because laid-off workers and retirees received only small severance packages, especially when they were made aware of what retired officials had received (Kynge 2000; Bradsher 2002; *China Labor Bulletin* 2002; Pomfret 2002). To make matters worse, retirees had to continue paying insurance premiums for health care from these small pension benefits. A related source of pension protests was the practice by many local governments, in collusion with enterprises, of distributing a lump-sum payment to workers, based on the number of years they had worked (usually calculated as one month of pay for every year of service). This buy-out practice led to many problems when the funds ran out and workers petitioned at their enterprises or at local government offices to demand more compensation.

According to the provisions of the Bankruptcy Law of 1988 and a subsequent State Council notice in 1994, an enterprise going through bankruptcy proceedings had to clear up its unpaid wages and accumulated pension fees. Workers displaced by the bankruptcy were supposed to receive pensions drawn from the sale of the enterprise assets. Because urban governments had a strong financial interest in—and the ability to reap personal economic gains from—the corporate restructurings of state firms, the most valuable assets were transferred to the new corporate entity while the creditors, including workers and local pension funds, wound up with piecemeal distributions from the bankruptcy proceedings (China Labor Security Report 2002a). Although courts exerted pressure on firms to remit social insurance fees, the local governments that controlled the staffing and budgets of the courts consistently ensured that judges did not interfere with sensitive bankruptcy proceedings.

The accumulated evidence of a decade of protests by ex-SOE workers shows that they have had greater success in taking their pension claims to the streets than to the courts. In an illustration of the failed tactics of taking the matter to court, an estimated group of 1,000 retirees filed a rare administrative lawsuit against the Suizhou (Hubei province) Municipal Social Insurance Bureau in 2004 after repeated court rulings that went in favor of their former employer, the Tieshu Textile Mill. The retirees charged the Suizhou SIA with failure to pressure the Tieshu management to pay pensions in full, leaving each retiree with an average underpayment of 200 yuan per month. The charge suggests strongly that the Suizhou SIA did not take responsibility for the payment of pensions and that the Tieshu retirees were still dependent on their firm for partial pension payments. The pension case against the Suizhou SIA was just one part of a larger dispute involving 200 million yuan in unpaid wages, pensions, and other payments arising from the bankruptcy of the enterprise in 2003. In the end, Tieshu workers lost their court case and then staged large-scale demonstrations involving 2,000 workers and retirees in early 2004 (*China Labor Bulletin* 2004).

With the help of central government subsidies to provinces with the greatest levels of pension protests, local authorities began to make pension payments in a more timely fashion by 2002 (Lee 2007, 21). Local governments in the northeast and elsewhere increased pension benefits at a rapid pace. By 2005, average nominal pensions had risen to 9,251 yuan (Salditt, Whiteford, and Adema 2007, 28). We should be cautious in linking pension benefit increases directly to the threat of or past episodes of pension protest, but a number of informants argued that local officials were raising pension benefits at a rapid pace to deter social instability arising from protests by unpaid pensioners. One informant explained that, given the short tenure of mayors, they had every incentive to ignore the financial sustainability of pensions in the long run and to instead increase pension benefits to thwart social unrest in the short run (Interview #021805). Average pension benefits reached 11,100 yuan in 2007 (Ministry of Human Resources and Social Security [MOHRSS] 2008b).

Although jobless SOE workers engaged in cellular activism by mobilizing with workplace colleagues to demand a more just compensation from urban governments and state enterprises, current workers have pursued legal strategies to demand rights to pension coverage. Such demands have come largely in construction and other sectors with large numbers of migrant workers. In 2004, disputes with employers over rights to social insurance coverage became the leading cause of labor disputes, exceeding disputes over wages and labor contracts. In 2000, national labor dispute statistics classified 31,350 labor disputes in 2000 as arising from social insurance and welfare issues. This made up just over 25 percent of the total number of cases for that year (SSB and MOLSS 2000, 429). By 2004, the number of labor disputes said to involve social insurance and welfare issues had risen to 88,119, amounting to 33.8 percent of total labor disputes (SSB and MOLSS 2005, 525–26).

Workers have taken some of these disputes through the process of labor arbitration and eventually to the courts. In Hunan, thirteen workers whose labor contracts had terminated at a Xinhua bookstore pursued labor arbitration against their ex-employer in 2002 after they discovered that store management had not remitted pension fees on their behalf during the course of their three-year employment contracts. Despite the fact that the store management had paid each worker well in excess of the 300

yuan per month agreed to in their contracts, the labor arbitration committee found in favor of the ex-employees, and the store was ordered to pay
three years of unpaid pension fees, amounting to over 25,000 yuan (China
Labor Security Report 2002b). In another case, a group of 180 construction workers in Hefei took their former employer, the Anhui Provincial
No. 2 Construction Company, to court over a disputed amount of pension
contributions. A local court eventually compelled the firm to contribute
183,200 yuan toward the workers' pension accounts (Fan 2001, 10). In
Shenzhen, a group of 189 employees from the Jianye Construction Company in Shenzhen sought to recover money that Jianye had deducted from
their wages over a ten-year period for pension contributions to individual
accounts. These deductions accorded with pension regulations on individual accounts, but the Jianye management had sent the funds to the labor-
contracting company in Sichuan that had supplied the employees to Jianye
instead of to the Shenzhen SIA. Jianye Construction won on appeal because the court accepted its argument that the workers were not technically Jianye employees. "The laws are good, but the legal system doesn't
work," one of the workers told a foreign reporter. "If we had to do it again,
we would just protest" (quoted in Pan 2002).

In 2007, reports emerged of migrant workers in southern Chinese boom-
towns such as Shenzhen and Dongguan standing in lines for hours, even
for days in some cases, at local SIAs to withdraw their accumulated savings
from personal retirement accounts. According to press reports, migrants
were cashing out their pensions (*tuibao*) because they had decided to return
home or to seek employment elsewhere in China. They knew that they
would have no chance of ever seeing the money that they and their employers had contributed to their personal retirement accounts over the
duration of their work contracts. The wage deductions sent to the local
SIAs were very unlikely to be transferred to their home counties in Sichuan
or to other interior regions from which the migrant workers hailed. One
report estimated that 600,000 workers in Dongguan alone had cashed out
their pensions in 2007.[2] By late 2008, migrants were losing their jobs
rather than switching jobs, but the rationale for cashing out their pensions
remained. The phenomenon of cashing out was expected to grow more serious when thousands of factories in regions such as the Pearl River Delta
closed down.

The scene of migrant workers lined up outside of SIAs to withdraw their
pension savings presents a fitting contrast to the image a decade earlier of

---

[2] *China Labor News* (2008) translated into English the original article, which appeared in a
January 2008 investigative story in *Nanfang dushibao* (*Southern Metropolitan Daily*).

retired state enterprise workers' massing in the city streets of rust-belt areas to petition local authorities for subsistence payments after their firms had gone bankrupt. The ex-SOE workers demanded pensions from a state that had broken its promises of lifetime employment and guaranteed welfare benefits. Pensions were framed in terms of subsistence rights. A decade later, migrants in the high-growth regions demanded pension money that they rightly viewed as their accumulated savings. For migrants, pensions were not an abstract promise by the state but, rather, personal funds temporarily held by the state. These two contrasting demands by different groups of Chinese workers over the span of a decade reflect a fundamental change in how citizens conceived of pension rights. Pensions were once viewed as a social contract between the state and urban SOE workers in a command economy. Now, migrants, as well as the growing ranks of workers operating in the uncertainties of a fluid labor market, conceive of pensions as something to which they and the state have jointly contributed.

The contrasts between how older and newer segments of the Chinese workforce view pension rights are in part a story of generational change. They also demonstrate how institutional change, in this case the introduction of social insurance, alters the nature of the demands that workers make on the state. As ever larger segments of the Chinese urban workforce receive social insurance coverage, the nature of state-labor relations will undergo profound shifts. Workers who a generation ago were expected to be loyal subjects who received welfare benefits from a benevolent state are becoming contributors or taxpayers, who demand social services and accountability for the operation of pension and other social insurance funds.

In this chapter, I have identified the institutional sources that might account for the preferences and behavior of urban governments and of the workers who lost jobs in SOE restructuring. For urban governments, property rights claims over SOEs as well as the decentralized fiscal practices that gave them the control rights over locally generated revenues provided sufficient incentives to develop local welfare states based heavily on the financing of pensions. For jobless SOE workers, the nature of their subsistence rights claims stemmed from their experience and socialization into the norms of the work unit, with its guarantees of lifetime employment and welfare. The SOE workers were not haggling over benefits formulas but over the broad principle of pensions as pay for loyal service to the state and its production goals. More recent evidence of labor demands by non-SOE workers reveals a considerable contrast with those of SOE workers in the 1990s. After a decade of experience with labor law and social insurance regulations, these workers framed their demands in terms of legal rights and ownership claims to benefits such as pensions.

The next three chapters examine more precisely how institutions have defined the preferences and shaped the responses of local governments, firms, and the urban public toward pension policy. Given the considerable variation within each of these groups, a central task is to explain the contrasting views and actions taken toward pension policy and to discuss what such contrasts mean for the present and future shape of the Chinese welfare regime.

CHAPTER 4

Urban Governments, Social Insurance, and Rights to Revenue

The establishment of social insurance programs in the 1990s meant that large amounts of money began flowing into urban governments that, in most regions of China, faced serious revenue shortfalls. Although social insurance revenues and fiscal revenues were kept as separate accounts, it was not difficult for urban governments to use pension and other social insurance funds for expenditures on projects that would otherwise be funded by tax revenues. The opening of chapter 1 describes the ways in which the Shanghai government used funds collected by its SIA to invest in a number of local real estate and infrastructure projects. In this chapter, I look at the regional patterns in how urban governments raised and used social insurance revenue for pensions. My goal is to explain regional variation in the behavior of state agencies in charge of collecting and administering pension funds. The decentralized administration of pensions means that local SIAs collect and retain social insurance revenues without transferring the funds across regions for redistribution. Given that the primary redistributive element in pensions is intergenerational, local SIAs can legitimately retain pension funds by pointing to future obligations to local retirees, but such locally retained funds can be vulnerable to diversion, as seen in the Shanghai pension scandal and in other less publicized cases of the corrupt use of pension funds.

It is useful to begin with an overview of pension revenues and spending and to consider this in relation to actual tax revenues and public expenditures. Local governments at all levels in 2005 spent 404 billion yuan ($50.1 billion) on social insurance pensions (by far the largest portion of social insurance), and in the following year this figure rose to 490 billion yuan ($62.7 billion). Local governments in 2005 collected 509 billion yuan ($63.1 billion) in revenues for pensions from the employers and workers of the diverse array of enterprises, including foreign-invested firms. In 2006, local governments increased their pension revenues to 631 billion yuan ($80.8 billion). These pension expenditure and revenue figures exceeded all other individual categories of spending and tax collection by local governments. SIAs now collect approximately 45 yuan in revenues from local employers for every 100 yuan that local tax authorities collect in revenues.

Table 4.1 lists the top ten budgetary expenditure categories of local governments in 2005. The list includes items paid for via actual fiscal expenditures as well as social insurance expenditures. At the top of the list are social insurance pension benefits, at 404 billion yuan. This amount exceeds the leading category of budgetary expenditures, education (at 373 billion yuan), which was financed through the fiscal system. Local governments also paid over 106 billion yuan in civil service pensions to officials, as well as 2.1 billion yuan in rural pensions. Together this means that local governments spent 512 billion yuan on pensions. If we include the 158 billion yuan that local governments spent on social security subsidies—a large but unknown portion of which included transfers by provincial

TABLE 4.1
Ranking of 2005 fiscal expenditures and social insurance expenditures of local governments

Rank	Category	Amount (billions of yuan)	As a percentage of total fiscal expenditures (%)
a	Pension benefits	404.03	16.1
1	Education	373.00	14.8
2	Basic construction	267.58	10.6
3	Administration	241.92	9.6
4	Other expenditures	230.44	9.1
5	Public security and law	176.41	7.0
6	Social security subsidies (provinces to counties)	158.09	6.3
7	Urban planning	126.06	5.0
8	Other departments	116.62	4.6
a	Medical insurance benefits	107.87	4.3
9	Civil service pensions	106.60	4.2
10	Public health	101.56	4.0

Source: State Statistics Bureau and Ministry of Labor and Social Security (2006, tables 8–15, 23-38).
[a] Social insurance expenditure category.

TABLE 4.2
Ranking of 2005 fiscal revenues and social insurance revenues of local governments

Rank	Category	Amount (billions of yuan)	As a percentage of total fiscal revenues
a	Pension insurance revenues	509.3	34.2
1	Business tax	410.3	27.6
2	Value-added tax	264.4	17.8
3	Enterprise tax	174.6	11.7
4	Administrative fees	107.4	7.2
5	Personal income tax	83.8	5.6

Sources: State Statistics Bureau (SSB) (2006); SSB and Ministry of Labor and Social Security (2006).
a Social insurance revenue category.

governments to make up for pension deficits at lower levels—then the figure devoted to pensions is even larger. (A decade earlier, the absolute figure for pension expenditures was less than one-tenth of the 2005 levels, at 64 billion yuan, which still was the equivalent of approximately one-fifth of total budgetary expenditures.)

Table 4.2 lists the top five sources of revenues of local governments. The table includes both tax revenue sources and categories of social insurance revenues. Pensions are also at the top of this combined list, and they amount to 509 billion yuan in revenues. Pension revenues exceeded the leading source of tax revenue, the business tax, which was 410 billion yuan that year. Pension revenues collected as social insurance in 1995 were a fraction of 2005 levels in absolute terms but still were equivalent to 24.2 percent of the amount that local governments collected in actual revenues that year.

Table 4.3 shows how pension revenues compare against the fiscal revenues of local governments within ten provinces. At the top of the list is Sichuan province, whose local governments collected in pension revenues an amount equivalent to 90 percent of tax revenues. Also included among the top local governments are the rust-belt provinces and the poor, remote provinces of the interior (Qinghai and Xinjiang), all of which collected relatively low amounts of taxes but collected substantial amounts of pension revenues (very likely including unreported amounts of pension subsidies from the central government). Near the bottom of the list are the prosperous provinces that nonetheless collected pension revenues representing over one-quarter of the very large amounts they raised in tax revenues. When compared to aggregate local government revenues in 2005, pension revenues were equal to 34 percent of the amount that local governments col-

TABLE 4.3
Pension revenues as percentage of total local government revenues, 2005

Rank	Province	As a percentage of total revenues(%)
1	Sichuan	90.77
2	Qinghai	76.25
3	Jilin	71.46
4	Heilongjiang	65.78
5	Xinjiang	54.08
6	Liaoning	52.41
⋮	⋮	⋮
25	Zhejiang	27.15
26	Beijing	26.22
27	Shanghai	25.39
28	Guangdong	25.32

Sources: State Statistics Bureau (SSB) (2006); SSB and Ministry of Labor and Social Security (2006).

lected in tax revenues. In some counties in China, it is common for pension revenues to exceed the local tax revenues (Interview #060501).

Without knowing anything about the specific regions of China, we might reasonably expect that local governments would try to attract outside capital by creating the lowest possible social wages for investors. Higher payroll taxes in the form of social insurance could thwart the ability of some regions to attract and retain capital, as well as jobs. This is especially true in the Chinese fiscal system, in which local governments have such large responsibilities for public expenditures and also have pecuniary and political incentives to develop industries and to create jobs. Rather than imposing payroll taxes on investors, local authorities could seek to reduce welfare expenditures, or at least to finance local welfare expenses by raising money from some source other than enterprise owners and new investors.

But as the data presented in tables 4.1 to 4.3 show, there is considerable evidence that local governments in China are increasing their pension spending and increasing the revenues that they raise specifically for pensions. Local governments in some provinces are raising benefits faster than others, and some are raising revenues faster than others. Clearly, economic growth factors into this pattern because some of the fastest-growing areas (Shanghai, Guangdong, Zhejiang, and Jiangsu) rank highest in terms of pension benefits and pension revenues. Areas with higher per capita incomes should have also higher per capita pensions and higher revenues; the problem is not that pension revenues and benefits vary across regions. The local administration of pension revenues and benefits, however, acts as a major constraint on redistribution, even within provinces.

Redistribution is crucial to a viable welfare regime, and it is worth considering the possible outcomes in terms of pensions and their degree of redistribution in China. One possibility is that pension revenues are produced mainly by large state enterprises and that the savings are then redistributed (across generations) to retirees from the same group of large SOEs. A second likely outcome is that pension revenues are produced in the urban sector, by a relatively broad range of small to large enterprises and that urban retirees then receive pensions based on these revenues. A third potential outcome is that pension revenues are produced broadly, from all ownership sectors and possibly from universal coverage of all workers (rural and urban) and that benefits are then distributed both across generations and across ownership sectors to all retirees (rural and urban). Some regions of China resemble the first scenario and others follow the second; nowhere has the third outcome prevailed.

In the sections that follow, I examine the effects of two variables on the regional differences in pension redistribution. Regions that experience high inflows of capital and favorable demographic ratios, such as southern and eastern coastal China, are likely to differ in their capacities to collect social insurance revenue and in the uses to which they put such revenue. These regions stand in contrast with areas of China that have small inflows of capital and unfavorable demographic ratios. Variation in capital flows and demographics are likely to create differences in the scope and forms of pension revenue collection, in the extent to which local governments are willing to support regional redistribution of pensions, and in the likelihood of pension funds' being diverted for corrupt use.

Table 4.4 offers a preview of the discussion. Among local governments of the interior and northeast provinces, the revenue base is narrow and the redistributive element in pensions is low—state enterprises are providing funds for SOE retirees, and even then not without significant subsidies from the central government. In the southeast region and in Shanghai, pensions are redistributive in the sense of transferring pension revenues from a broad base of private and foreign-invested firms to SOE retirees (although Shanghai is more highly redistributive than the southeast region). Because Shanghai and the southeast region enjoy pension surpluses drawn from a broad base of employers and workers, the potential for the corrupt use of pension funds is also the highest.

We begin with a simple regression analysis of the variation in provincial revenue and expenditure patterns, and then turn to qualitative evidence from specific regions.

TABLE 4.4
Summary of regional pension administration

Region	Scope and primary source of social insurance revenues	Degree of redistribution	Potential for corrupt use of pension funds
Interior	Narrow; large SOEs	Low; possibly negative with labor outmigration	Medium
Northeast	Narrow; SOE sell-offs and surviving SOEs	Low; with some subsidies from center	Low
Southeast	Broad; foreign-invested and private enterprises	Medium	High
Shanghai	Broad; all sectors including civil servants, farmers, migrants	High	High

Note: SOE, state-owned enterprise.

VARIATION IN PENSION REVENUES AND EXPENDITURES

As noted in preceding chapters, pension benefits in China have risen dramatically under pension reforms (a term that usually denotes retrenchment or cutbacks in pension benefits for future or current pensioners). Figure 4.1 shows the rapid expansion in social insurance pension expenditures on a per capita basis across the thirty-one Chinese provincial-level governments since 2000. The increase in nominal pensions is substantial even in a period of low inflation. Some of the poorest provinces, such as Tibet, Qinghai, and Ningxia, are among the top ten provincial governments in per capita pensions, along with the richest provincial governments, such as Shanghai, Beijing, Guangdong, and Zhejiang.

Figure 4.2 shows the absolute amount of social insurance pension revenues and their rapid expansion since 1995. Here the rank order of provincial governments, arranged by the amounts their local SIAs collected for 2005, is a closer approximation of richest to poorest, with Guangdong, Jiangsu, and Shanghai at the top of the list. Officially reported provincial pension revenue statistics, however, include an unknown amount of subsidies that the central government transfers to particular provinces each year to make up for deficits between pension revenues and benefits. (The absolute amount of central government pension subsidies is reported but not the specific amount distributed to each province.) An internal (i.e., classified) statistical report of local finances for 2002 shows that the central government spent 50.5 billion yuan on such pension subsidies, and that three northeastern provinces (Liaoning, Heilongjiang, and Jilin) received about

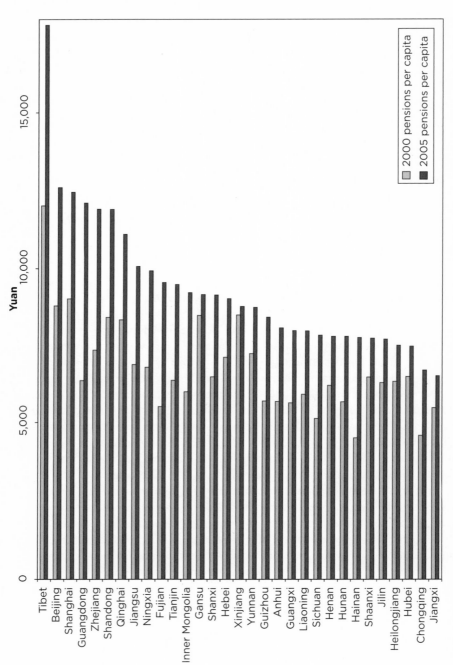

Figure 4.1 Increase in per capita pension benefits by province, 2000–2005. *Sources:* State Statistics Bureau and Ministry of Labor and Social Security (2001, 2006).

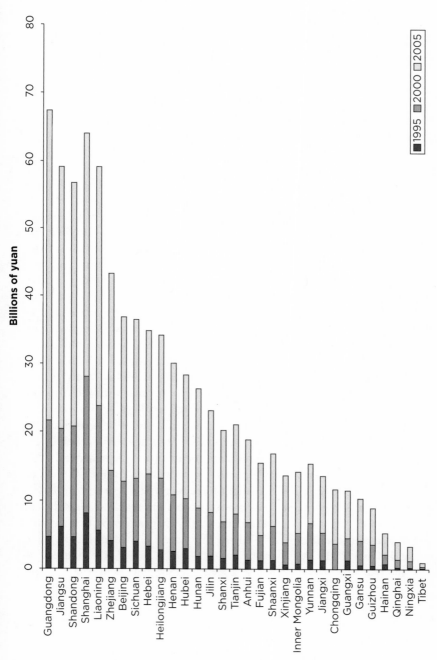

Figure 4.2 Pension revenues by province, 1995–2005. *Sources:* Ministry of Labor (1997); State Statistics Bureau and Ministry of Labor and Social Security (2001, 2006).

13.5 billion yuan of these subsidies, or 26.7 percent (Ministry of Finance 2003, 267). By contrast, the richer provincial governments of Guangdong, Zhejiang, Jiangsu, and Shanghai received a combined total of only 1.1 billion yuan in pension subsidies that year. We do not know from open sources how much each province received in subsidies in 2005; still, it is certain that the northeast provinces would be placed much farther down the list than they appear in figure 4.2 to reflect the actual pension revenues collected exclusive of central government subsidies.

A few caveats are in order about the use of the data from provincial-level governments. The ideal data set would be one that lists revenues and their sources for each municipal-level government in China. The only publicly reported data, however, come from provincial reporting to the national statistics authorities. We can use the sum of what cities in a province say they have collected, and we can analyze variation in pension revenues across provinces. In addition, local SIAs are said to calculate pension coverage by taking the total number of registered employees at a firm and then reporting all of its workers as having pension coverage. In fact, it is common for a share of enterprise employees to not have pension or other social insurance coverage, especially if they are migrant labor or somehow contracted as temporary labor. The discussion that follows this section confirms this point. It is also true that local authorities have to be careful not to exaggerate the number of workers reported as being covered by social insurance because this would lead to the expectation by higher levels of government that pension and other social insurance revenues should also rise along with the number of contributing or covered workers. With these caveats in mind, we can use the provincial data to reach tentative confirmations for the hypothesis that levels of capital inflows and age demographics explain the variation in pension revenues and benefits across provinces.

Because the pension revenues reported by provincial authorities include the amount that a given province might have received in pension subsidies from the central government, it is important to subtract these subsidies to determine how much local governments within a given province actually raised in pension revenues. The Ministry of Finance provided this information for the year 2002 (Ministry of Finance 2003, 267). We can, then, estimate the pension revenues for 2002 by regressing variables that control for economic levels, inflows of new urban workers, and pensioner population.

An ordinary least squares (OLS) regression helps us answer the question of whether provinces that attracted more FDI and increased their nonfarm workforces were able to collect more in pension revenues. The two models in table 4.5 show that, after controlling for economic development levels and pensioner population, provinces that had high levels of FDI were able to collect higher levels of pension revenues two years later. (The time lag was introduced using the assumption that it would take at least two years for FDI effects to be felt in terms of new jobs and payrolls for which social insurance agencies could collect revenues.) Model 1 attempts to control for the fact that the pension revenues of a given province in 2002 depended on its pension revenues in a base year—in this case, the year 2000. Model 1 shows that, after controlling for this factor, an additional US$1 billion that a province attracted in FDI was associated with approximately 560 million yuan ($67.6 million) in additional pension revenues. Yet the pension revenues for the baseline year of 2000 might be inaccurate if it includes the subsidies that a province received from the central government. In Model 2, this baseline year is taken out, and the FDI variable remains significant and increases in magnitude. In Model 2, increases in the number of nonfarm workers are now also associated with increases in pension revenues. Moreover, in Model 2, the number of pensioners in 2000 is now positively associated with greater pension revenues,

TABLE 4.5
Explaining pension revenues, 2002

	Model 1	Model 2
	β	β
(Constant)	−0.551 (0.673)	−1.593 (0.959)
Change in nonagricultural workforce, 1995–2002 (millions)	0.227 (0.143)	0.370* (0.210)
Per capita GDP 2000 (yuan)	0.000 (0.000)	0.000** (0.000)
2000 pension revenue (billions of yuan)	1.433*** (0.262)	—
2000 pensioners (millions)	−2.244 (1.759)	6.827*** (0.885)
FDI 2000 (billions of US$)	0.563*** (0.175)	1.093*** (0.216)
	$F=115.2$ Significance$=0.000$ $r^2=0.96$	$F=61.7$ Significance$=0.000$ $r^2=0.911$

Notes: Ordinary least squares (OLS) regression. Dependent variable is Actual 2002 pension revenue (billions of yuan). Values in parentheses are standard errors. * indicates $p<0.10$; ** indicates $p<0.05$; *** indicates $p<0.01$. FDI, foreign direct investment.

suggesting that provinces with more pensioners to support were under pressure to increase pension revenues. Both models explain a great deal of the variation in the dependent variable (over 90 percent), but the problem of not knowing the actual revenues (i.e., ex-subsidies) makes it difficult to employ an accurate baseline-year measure. Nonetheless, the fact that FDI is significant in both models suggests that the provinces that are receiving FDI are also able to collect greater pension revenues, all else being equal.

By next comparing the same variables with the distribution of pension benefits, we can see to what extent per capita pension benefits are greater in provinces with higher levels of FDI. In this case, we can use more recent data because we do not need to rely on the data for the only year in which actual (ex-subsidies) pension revenues are available. Table 4.6 shows the results of an OLS regression in which the dependent variable is per capita pension benefits for 2005, with the same explanatory variables as we used in the models to predict pension revenues. Here, again, FDI is substantively and statistically significant. After we control for per capita GDP, the provinces with higher levels of FDI also had higher pension benefits. The results also show that provinces with higher numbers of pensioners had lower pension benefits, after we control for per capita GDP.

TABLE 4.6
Explaining pension benefits, 2005

	Model 1	Model 2
	β	β
(Constant)	9,653.235*** (869.518)	2,762.73** (1160.23)
Change in nonagricultural workforce, 1995–2005 (millions)	−67.084 (138.215)	16.868 (85.388)
Per capita GDP 2003 (yuan)	0.100* (0.049)	0.043 (0.031)
2005 pensioners, (millions)	−1,556.608*** (531.626)	−907.365 (339.082)
FDI 2003 (billions of US$)	515.610** (238.634)	343.338** (148.083)
Benefits per retiree, 2000	—	1.002*** (0.150)
	$F=4.31$ Significance$=0.008$ $r^2=0.399$	$F=18.16$ Significance$=0.000$ $r^2=0.784$

Notes: Ordinary least squares (OLS) regression. Dependent variable is per capita pension benefits, 2005 (yuan). Values in parentheses are standard errors. * indicates $p<0.10$; ** indicates $p<0.05$; *** indicates $p<0.01$. FDI, foreign direct investment.

The regression models in tables 4.5 and 4.6 suggest that FDI—which others have shown serves as a substitute for private capital in China (Huang 2003; Gallagher 2005)—brings about higher levels of pension revenues and that higher levels of pension revenues create higher levels of pension benefits. Because we know that the vast majority of the 51 million Chinese retirees were once in the state sector, the findings suggest that in one sense pension reforms have achieved a limited degree of redistribution. With the important proviso that all pensions are localized, the regression models suggest that the dynamic foreign-funded and private sectors are financing the needs of retirees from the state sector. But for regions with very little FDI, low pension revenues also mean low pension benefits, even after we control for per capita GDP. In addition, the fact that all pensions are locally financed also tells us that intraregional redistribution is severely limited. Pension revenues are redistributed locally within an urban pension pool, not even within an entire province and certainly not nationally (except, of course, for the 50 billion yuan that central governments deliver in subsidies to poor provinces; compared to the 500 billion yuan spent on pensions, this is not a significant amount). The fact that the regression models used provincial-level data should not conceal the fact that all but a few pension pools in China are administered at county and city levels. The genuinely provincial-level pools are actually cities with provincial-government rank: Shanghai, Beijing, Tianjin, and Chongqing.

The results thus highlight a larger problem in the Chinese welfare regime. The inequalities in economic development are leading to inequalities in welfare provision. The most dynamic areas of China, which draw foreign investment and create jobs, are those regions where the most pension revenues are being collected and where they are being distributed to local retirees. But pensioners, except for Shanghai, are not concentrated in the areas with high levels of FDI and other capital inflows. Instead, retirees are predominantly found in rust-belt regions in which both capital and labor have undergone substantial declines since the 1990s. As the sections that follow reveal, variations in capital flows and economic development generally have created different patterns in the scope and forms of social insurance revenue collection, in the redistribution of these revenues, and in the diversion of these funds for other uses.

THE SOUTHEAST

The pattern of pension revenue collection found in southern and eastern China has been strongly influenced by the liberalization of labor markets and booming investment. Local governments operate in dynamic environments with rapidly expanding firms and wage bills for their employees. Local governments have developed an array of tactics to monitor private-sector firms and their employees. This is not to say that local governments have succeeded in bringing about full or even substantial compliance with social insurance regulations by local firms. But local governments and SIAs have devised a number of innovations to gain a share of the lucrative and expanding wage bills that have grown with the expansion of capital flows to their areas. These localities also face generally positive demographics. For Guangdong, the migration of labor swelled the ranks of nonfarm workers to 31.5 million in 2005, up from 22.9 million in 1995. Yet the local SIAs had to support a relatively low number of retirees, totaling 2.3 million in 2005. This abundance of workers and a relative scarcity of retirees resulted in a potential support ratio of 13.7 to 1. We treat the support ratio as *potential* because not all of the nonfarm labor force had pension coverage. In fact, in 2005, official statistics showed 18.0 million Guangdong workers covered by pensions. Still, this estimated coverage rate of 57 percent appears to be well above the reported rates in 1995, when the ratio of covered workers to nonfarm workers was 19 percent (Ministry of Labor 1997; State Statistics Bureau [SSB] and Ministry of Labor and Social Security [MOLSS] 2006). Ching Kwan Lee (2002, 199) reports that in the late 1990s only 5.4 percent of foreign-owned enterprises, 3.2 percent of township and village enterprises, and 0.3 percent of private and individually owned firms were paying into the local pension funds in Guangdong. For Zhejiang (1.6 million pensioners) and Jiangsu (3.0 million pensioners), a similarly favorable potential support ratio prevailed by 2005, with Zhejiang at 15 to 1 and Jiangsu at 9 to 1 (SSB and MOLSS 2006). Given the challenges posed by monitoring so many firms of varying size and scale, local governments in southern and eastern China have failed to achieve high rates of pension coverage in percentage terms, but they have increased the number of covered workers in absolute terms, and with expanded coverage has come an increase in pension revenues. The abundance of revenues and the creation of sizable pension funds increased the likelihood that local governments would use pension and other social insurance funds for spending on unrelated projects, if not for corrupt uses by local officials (National Audit Office 2006).

A municipal SIA official in a city from this region responded to a question about the most difficult challenge in expanding pension coverage by pointing to the dynamism of the private and foreign-invested sector. The "creative destruction" of capitalism that has fueled the boom of cities and towns in southeast China also made it extremely difficult to establish a social safety net in terms of pensions or other forms of contributory social insurance. Although, this official explained, labor authorities can be assured that most foreign-owned firms will pay contributions in full and on time, it is difficult to gain compliance from small private firms and Hong Kong– or Taiwan-invested firms (Interview #022105).[1]

He and other local officials uniformly denied that new investors bargained with local governments over social insurance payments. Nevertheless, virtually every other informant who was not a government official said that such bargaining was commonplace (Interview #021905; Interview #022405). The existence of these bargains often turned up when potential buyers of private or foreign-invested enterprises conducted due diligence prior to securing a deal to purchase the assets of a firm. One important consideration, informants explained, was the extent to which the firm had made prior arrangements with local officials to reduce social insurance contributions. Usually a large employer could work out an arrangement to pay a flat fee rather than the 30–40 percent payroll tax called for in the regulations. Legal and financial advisors to private equity firms and other purchasers of Chinese assets were especially wary of getting stuck later with having to pay past pension contributions and, thus, sought to address this with local governments by either making up for the arrears or continuing to enjoy the favorable policy of the previous owners of the firm. At the very least, an enterprise manager could readily underreport the base wage for pension contributions or simply leave large portions of the workforce off the official payroll. Migrant workers often preferred higher wages to pension contributions, given their long time horizon until retirement and the uncertainty that the local government collecting the contribution today would pay the pension benefit in the far-off future (Interview #030805A; Interview #110604; Ye 2004, 100–104).

Beginning in 2000, several southern and eastern provinces, most notably Guangdong and Jiangsu, empowered local tax agencies to collect social insurance contributions. Prior to this time, social insurance agencies, formally under the local department of LSS, had collected social insurance fees from firms, generally with great difficulty. Under the new arrangement, tax authorities deposited social insurance contributions (approximately three-fourths of which were pensions) in special accounts with the local departments of finance. This measure also took place elsewhere, outside the southern and eastern provinces, including in several interior provinces. The effect of this transfer in agencies was felt most directly in southern and eastern provinces, however. In Shenzhen, for example, the reported

---

[1] This observation is consistent with Ye Xiangqun's (2004, 93–113) conclusions from his study of a central Chinese city in which he conducted field work in 2000.

number of pension contributors rose from 750,000 at year-end 1998 to 1.3 million in late 2000 (MOLSS 2000, 318; 2001, 410).

Giving the local tax authorities the power to collect social insurance revenues had both advantages and drawbacks. As a municipal official noted, the tax authorities had far more data on firms than did the SIAs, but the type of information that tax authorities possessed—generally the number of employees at an enterprise and their levels of pay—was not precise enough for social insurance purposes.

> When the tax bureau notifies us that a new firm has registered, it might have 1,000 employees, but a few months or a year later, it might have half that many, or it might have twice that many. But all we have is the information that a firm is registered with 1,000 employees. The tax authorities are most interested in getting information about the profits and losses of a firm so they can calculate the relevant taxes. They aren't going to put that much pressure on a firm to accurately report employees and wages. (Interview #022105)

Despite these drawbacks and the challenges posed by the rapid growth of private firms, southern and eastern cities also developed new mechanisms to inspect enterprise payments. In Jiangsu province, for example, a number of cities hired private auditors (usually former officials in the audit bureau) to carry out inspections of enterprise accounts for wage bills, payrolls, and pension contributions to ensure that private firms were paying on behalf of their workers. Moreover, firms remitted reports to both the tax bureau and audit offices, which the SIAs inspected for consistency with the employment and wage data that they had received from firms (Interview #030705).

Local governments used a number of incentive mechanisms to encourage officials, whose budgets and pay they controlled, to expand both pension coverage and revenues. One city gave its urban officials seven performance quotas related to social insurance, chief among them the number of covered workers and increases in them, the amount of social insurance revenues collected, and the number of investigations of local firms. Salaries for SIA officials were roughly split between a fixed and a flexible income. If insufficient funds were collected for social insurance, the official was not eligible for the bonus covering the social insurance collection quota. When asked if these quotas were credible as incentives, a group of SIA officials asserted that indeed they were because they could make a large difference in one's pay. Moreover, it was quite common for officials not to meet their quotas. Promotions were also based on the ability of officials to meet social insurance quotas (Interview #030705).

Local governments that failed to collect enough in pension revenues to pay local pensioners could receive subsidies from the provincial government, but not without close scrutiny. In 2004, two out of three urban districts in one city raised more than they spent on pensions, and four out of six rural counties in the same city failed to collect enough to cover pensions for their approximately 150,000 retirees. According to officials, the provincial government was very strict when it dispensed subsidies because the province received very few subsidies from the central government. The burden of proof was on local officials to show that they had failed to collect sufficient pension revenues. "It's not like you can just say [to the provincial government], 'we have a deficit' and then they hand you the money. They're very strict" (Interview #030705).

It remains rare for provincial governments or municipalities to report publicly their pension revenues, but the Guangdong provincial statistical authorities did so in the online edition of their 2005 provincial yearbook. According to this data, in 2004 local governments in the province collected 35.4 billion yuan in social insurance pension revenues (Guangdong Statistics Bureau [GSB] 2005). Of that amount, 6.4 billion yuan (18.1 percent) came from the large state enterprises whose pensions were under provincial management after 1998. Despite the billions of dollars in FDI in Guangdong cities such as Shenzhen, Dongguan, and Foshan, only Shenzhen remitted more than the large SOEs in Guangdong. Dongguan accounted for 7.3 percent of total pension revenues, Shenzhen for 21.2 percent, and Foshan for 7.6 percent. These figures help us better understand the statistical relationships previously discussed. FDI does not necessarily mean greater compliance with social insurance payments, but simply provides a large payroll base from which SIAs can collect revenues. Guangdong province had both the largest amount of FDI and the largest amount of social insurance pension revenues in the mid-2000s, but its local governments still relied on SOEs for 18 percent of their pension revenues. Local SIAs could have collected much more from foreign-invested and private-sector enterprises.

There is abundant evidence that local governments and their SIAs came up with innovations to monitor and collect social insurance revenues from their local firms, but the fact that they enjoyed favorable demographics (i.e., large numbers of workers and relatively fewer retirees to support) meant that the surpluses were vulnerable to misappropriation. After 2000, pension revenues were put into special accounts whose disbursement required the signatures of both the local LSS department and the local finance department. These special accounts had been set up in response to the widespread misuse of pension funds. An MOLSS study conducted by the Auditing Department of the Ministry of Finance determined that, between 1986 and 1998, city, county, and prefectural governments spent an estimated 10 billion yuan in pension funds on investments and other projects that had nothing to do with pensions (Shi 1999, 159–60). Guangdong province accounted for 1.86 billion yuan out of a national estimate of 7.7 billion yuan in misappropriated social insurance funds as of mid-2000 (MOLSS 2002, 707).

When asked about this problem, an urban SIA official from a city in Guangdong explained that before 1998 such "experiments" were permitted by the highly ambiguous regulations on the allocation of surplus pension funds: "We were collecting funds, and we had to have some way to maintain and increase the value of the funds; we entrusted the funds to a management company that put the money in the bank. The banks are at fault if they were not regulating the funds properly. This was a prominent problem, and we were no different from the rest of the country" (Interview #022105). A 2004 report by *Caijing* magazine, based in part on an inquiry by the Guangzhou Municipal People's Congress, estimated that prior to 1996 a total of 890 million yuan in social insurance funds had been put to illegal uses and that 85 percent of the total was invested in real estate projects (*Caijing* 2004). Although local governments have since set up social insurance fund supervision offices and made some progress in recovering the lost funds from the 1990s, the favorable demographic trends and pension surpluses enjoyed by many southern and eastern cities will continue to make these funds vulnerable to being used for general (and personal official) expenditures.

THE NORTHEAST

In the urban areas of northeast China, SIAs faced the opposite problem from those in the booming southern and eastern coastal provinces. Rather than trying to extract revenues from a fast-growth dynamic economy, these SIAs had to coax out revenues largely from a state sector that had undergone rapid transformation. Bankruptcies and mass layoffs gave SIAs a shrinking base of firms from which to draw social insurance revenues. Rising numbers of pensioners and their public protests for adequate pension and unemployment compensation created an urgent revenue imperative. Much of the revenue reported by these local firms came, in fact, in the form of pension and other social insurance subsidies from higher levels of government.

The restructuring of the state sector had a dramatic impact on pensions and other social insurance programs in the northeast. The rapid decline in the number of state-sector workers turned millions of workers from social insurance contributors into pensioners. In Liaoning province, for example, the number of pensioners rose from 646,241 in 1989 to 3.15 million in 2003 (Ministry of Labor 1997, 30; SSB and MOLSS 2004, 568). Pension expenditures rose from 5.1 billion yuan in 1995 to 15.5 billion yuan in 1999 and to 25.6 billion yuan in 2003 (Ministry of Labor 1997, 75; SSB and MOLSS 2000, 77; 2004, 555). Jilin and Heilongjiang registered similar magnitudes of increased expenditures on pensions. This was at the same time that the collapse of state-owned and collective enterprises in the northeast put millions of workers out of jobs, and thus no longer contributed to the pension revenue base.

Given the lack of pension surpluses, local governments in the northeast could not engage in the same pension fund diversions that occurred in the high-growth regions of China. Still, the evidence suggests that the revenue collection methods resembled the classic patterns found in what Xiaobo Lü (2000) describes as organizational corruption—the use of state social-ist practices of fixing quotas; the belief in the efficacy of propaganda; and, most seriously, the practice of local protectionism, which shrouds public finance and administration in secrecy. When asked to discuss obstacles to the expansion of pension coverage, provincial- and municipal-level offi-cials commonly responded that no such obstacles existed and that every-one who should be covered was covered. They stressed the effectiveness of their "propaganda work" in effecting a change in public attitudes and awareness about pension contributions (Interview #030805A; Interview #030905A; Interview #040405A). When it was pointed out to them that the statistics suggested that roughly half of the local urban workforce re-mained uncovered, officials either challenged the numbers or said that anyone who did not now have pension coverage was not eligible for it, for example, party and government officials whose pensions were paid from budgets, or migrant workers, or the self-employed.

During interviews, officials said their primary task was to ensure that pen-sions were paid to current beneficiaries in full and on time. Pensions were a "social stability tool," said one informant (Interview #030905C). Pensions had failed in this function in the 1990s, or resources were lacking to finance them. Most informants, including several pensioners, agreed that since 1998 pension arrears were now less of a problem. One informant noted, however, that if the central government pension subsidies were suddenly cut off, so-cial unrest would quickly revive. He speculated, "I worry about major insta-bility in the future; who knows, we might end up like the Soviet Union" (Interview #030905C). Many northeast informants made the argument that the area deserved subsidies because, during its heyday as a manufacturing center, all the profits went to the central government. It was only fair that the center now return those profits in the form of subsidies.

With such a potentially explosive situation, northeast officials had strong incentives to both curb pension expenditures and squeeze pension revenues from the base of existing firms. Local governments turned down retirement applications from the workers of firms that had fallen behind on pension payments (Interview #053101; Interview #060501). In contrast to the practices that evolved in the south and east, where local governments devised new ways to monitor private firms, northeastern officials relied on more coercive compliance mechanisms. A number of provincial-level officials noted that they had certain incentive mechanisms in place, but generally they expressed a lack of faith in the use of material incentives to reward local officials for collecting fees or expanding coverage (Interview #030805A).

In the northeast, the general rule since 2000 had been for SIAs, rather than tax authorities, to collect social insurance contributions. The exception was Liaoning, where tax bureaus collected the pension contributions. In the relatively prosperous Liaoning port city Dalian, however, the SIA collected all social insurance contributions; in other Liaoning cities, the tax bureaus collected such levies on behalf of SIAs (Interview #040405A).

Provincial SIAs in the northeast had also developed performance quotas for the expansion of coverage and collection of funds. The provincial government of Jilin made contracts with city governments to fulfill the revenue targets for pensions. If the target was fulfilled, officials got a nominal bonus, which might represent an increase of a few percentage points in their salary, an official explained. Yet this official, like others in the northeast, was highly ambivalent about these material incentives. He said that the honor and recognition of fulfilling the goal were more important than the bonus. Moreover, he pointed out, it was common for local governments to make agreements to meet quotas of all sorts, so the responsibility system in place for pension fees and the expansion of pension coverage was nothing special (Interview #030805A). There was no punishment for not fulfilling the pension revenue and related quotas. In Liaoning, the provincial government also made contracts with lower levels of government to fulfill the pension revenue targets and permitted any excess collections to be retained for use in the collection targets of the following year. In April 2005, a major push was underway to expand coverage, involving the provincial governor and department chiefs of six to eight provincial agencies. The target was private firms, small firms of fewer than eight employees, and the self-employed. The goal was to use quotas with local governments to increase the total number of pension contributors from 7.5 million to 10 million by late 2006 (Interview #040405A).

With the exception of dynamic cities such as Dalian, with its large inflows of new capital, the scarcity of new firms or potential contributors meant that a new investor had a great deal of leverage to negotiate favorable social insurance policies with the local government. According to an informant at a benefits-consulting firm, any investor who started a firm with good prospects for job creation in the northeast could essentially bargain for the social insurance fees that would be paid to local governments on a flat-rate or other basis (Interview #021905). This generalization was consistent with an account given by a northeast informant about a privatized state firm. This enterprise was able to negotiate with local SIAs to provide pension coverage through a commercial life insurance company. In so doing, the firm essentially withdrew from the public pension scheme (see chapter 5; Interview #030905C).

The Liaoning experiment and its diffusion in 2005 to other provinces in the northeast shows the ability of the central government to successfully impose discipline on local pension administration. As noted in chapter 2, the central government compelled Liaoning officials to "wall off" individual accounts and to refrain from using the money intended for these accounts to pay current retirees. By April 2005, the provincial SIA had accumulated 13.8 billion yuan ($1.7 billion) in individual accounts. The difficulty at that point, according to one official, was where to invest such money. Liaoning officials, under advice from the World Bank, were encouraged to place these funds in what was regarded as the safest investment— the state banks. But, as one official noted, "banks have risks too" (Interview #040405A). With the amount invested expected to reach over 15 billion yuan in 2006 and eventually 50 billion yuan, this official expressed the wish to invest the funds in assets that would yield higher returns. "We want to be able to invest 20 percent in equities, like the National Social Security Fund, but we're not allowed to," he said. Such pressures to increase the value of funded individual accounts, yet with few safe alternatives for such investments, highlight the dilemma that many SIAs with surplus funds faced in the mid-2000s. They could get very low or even negative real returns through bank deposits, or they could plunge into the shady world of loaning such surpluses to entities that promised higher rates of return (as happened in Shanghai).

The central government spread the Liaoning experiment to two other northeastern provinces in 2005 and then to nine other provinces thereafter, including many provinces in the interior. As was the case in Liaoning, these provincial governments required substantial subsidies from the Ministry of Finance to fund the empty individual accounts.

INTERIOR PROVINCES

Local governments in many interior provinces lack the availability of social insurance revenues that those in the southeast enjoy, but unlike the governments in northeastern cities, they also do not face large concentrations of pensioners and others jobless from state-sector restructuring. With some important exceptions, many interior counties have mostly rural townships and therefore few urban workers who can claim pension rights.

Of foremost concern to interior provinces is the fact that the outmigration of labor to the coastal cities and factories has created a very serious regressive or negative redistribution problem. Feng Xiugan, a private business owner from a Chongqing county and a vice chair of a county National People's Political Consultative Conference, noted in a 2005 interview in *Nanfang Zhoumo* (*Southern Weekend*) the consequences of labor migration on pensions. Based on a 2003 survey that Feng and two colleagues carried out of more than 14,700 migrant workers from the county who worked in twenty cities, approximately 90 percent of migrant workers reported receiving no pension coverage (and approximately 83 percent said that they did not want to buy pension insurance coverage in the first place). Feng noted that all the migrant workers (not just those in the survey) working in eastern provinces who were not covered by pensions, and even those who were, would eventually reach retirement age and that it would be up to local governments in western provinces to provide for them. In other words, even if coverage were extended to all migrant workers, the money they had contributed to pension funds in eastern cities would very likely remain there. Feng's report noted that his county alone had sent more than 100,000 workers eastward, and he estimated that with pension coverage they could have contributed between 300 and 400 million yuan to the pension funds of local governments in eastern provinces. Localized pensions thus contributed to an already serious imbalance between the west and east. Feng offered a few back-of-the-envelope calculations. He noted that if 250 million migrant workers nationwide were covered under pension insurance and jointly with their employers paid approximately 180 yuan per month into a national pension fund, this would create 500 billion yuan in pension revenues in one year. After ten years of accumulations, this would amount to 5 trillion yuan ($620 billion) in principal alone. With the interest earned on such a large amount, the problem of pensions for migrant workers would be easily resolved (*Nanfang Zhoumo* 2005).

The pension rights of women migrant workers appear to be especially undermined and not simply because their pension contributions are going to local governments. In fact, their employers appear to be dodging making pension contributions altogether. According to a *China Youth Daily* report, the Women's Federation found in a 2006 survey of nearly 6,600 women migrant workers in the cities of Beijing, Guangzhou, Wuhan, and Chengdu that fewer than one in four had some form of social insurance. Only 23.8 percent were covered under medical insurance, 19.1 percent had workplace injury insurance, and 15.8 percent had pension insurance. Only 40 percent of those surveyed had signed labor contracts (*China Labor Bulletin* 2006).

Labor migration from the interior provinces cost the local governments of these provinces a great deal in forgone pension revenue that they might have received if there were some form of national pooling. Even as it was, local governments in the interior and their SIAs faced serious obstacles in gaining compliance from many large state enterprises. In part, this problem arose from the fact that many cities were (and continue to be) dominated by very large SOEs that originated during the "third front" strategy of the 1960s, when the Maoist government established large-scale heavy industrial plants away from the coast in the event of an invasion. These factories, their suppliers, and local governments have had to cope with the pension and unemployment costs in a fashion similar to the local SIAs in the northeast. As figure 4.1 shows, average benefits in many interior provinces have risen substantially and exceeded the pension benefits found in the northeastern provinces. Tibet, Qinghai, Ningxia, and Inner Mongolia have per capita social insurance pensions that compare with those of Beijing, Shanghai, and the wealthier coastal provinces.

Because of the construction of large SOEs during the "third front" era, it is common to find firms whose leaders equal or outrank in protocol the officials from the SIAs charged with enforcing social insurance collections. Predictably, the local SIAs face great difficulty in collecting social insurance levies and in bringing large SOEs into compliance with social insurance regulations. These large SOEs, which in some cases have branch factories in several provinces, proved especially troublesome for even provincial governments to bring into compliance with social insurance regulations.

The case of a dispute in the late 1990s between a large SOE in Sichuan province and local governments illustrates the pressures that the latter had to apply to the most important sources of social insurance revenues in their jurisdictions. Panzhihua Steel (Pangang) has been based since the early 1970s in the town of Panzhihua, a company town. (Given its remote location, it is said that "if there were no Pangang, there would be no Panzhihua.") Many of the party secretaries and mayors of the city are former directors or senior party officials at Pangang, which itself enjoys a vice-ministerial ranking (*fubuji danwei*). This means that the director of Pangang holds the rank of a central government vice minister. The significance of this in terms of policy implementation is that, short of direct orders from a supervising ministry or bureau in Beijing, the only office that could issue a binding order to the director of Pangang was the governor of Sichuan province.[2]

With a workforce numbering 100,000 and very few retirees, owing to its relatively short history, Pangang and its directors felt no strong obligation to comply with orders from the Sichuan SIA to remit pension and other social insurance funds for its workforce. By 1998–1999, Pangang had accumulated over 300 million yuan ($36.2 million) in unpaid social insurance contributions, earning it the distinction of being the firm with the largest such delinquencies in China. When the Sichuan Labor and Social Security Bureau pressed the issue, Pangang management reported that to make up what it owed in social insurance contributions it would have to cut its wage bill by 100 million yuan over the coming year, which it promptly did. But the Pangang management allegedly failed to follow up the wage cut with further payments to social insurance. When the director of the Sichuan Labor and Social Security Bureau went to investigate along with four office directors, the head of the Pangang personnel department refused to meet with them. The position of Pangang was that, because the enterprise had few retirees, it was not reasonable for it to have to pay so much in social insurance. In subsequent discussions with Panzhihua municipal LSS officials, with whom the enterprise officials were apparently more willing to engage in negotiations, Panzhihua agreed that Pangang could reduce its payments to the city pension and other social insurance pools. This was an understandable outcome given that the Pangang officials had far more bargaining power compared to the city labor officials, whose direct supervisors, the mayor, and party secretary were both former Pangang managers.

It is revealing that Panzhihua city officials, and not Sichuan provincial officials, took the initiative to resolve this impasse. Panzhihua LSS officials ultimately appealed to their administrative superiors in Beijing at MOLSS, which obviously took an active interest in the case, given the amount of money involved. Nonetheless, when MOLSS dispatched a vice director of its Social Security Bureau to Pangang, the enterprise director is said to have countered that, considering the credits of the firm to so many other state enterprises in China, "the State Council owed *him* money." It was not until the following year, when the Pangang Communist Party Committee received an order from the CCP Central Committee that Pangang managers

---

[2] The following account is from Interview #060501.

were finally persuaded to comply with social insurance provisions. Pangang agreed to resolve its unpaid social insurance debt of 300 million yuan by making payments of 100 million yuan over three years.

A similar sort of conflict between provincial and municipal governments, on the one hand, and the managers of national corporations and the heads of agencies regulating these corporations, on the other, occurred over pensions. Firms under the control of the national oil corporations PetroChina and Sinopec frequently resisted their incorporation into local social insurance pools. Because these corporations had scattered oilfields and refineries located near many small and relatively poor urban areas, the employees of these facilities faced substantial losses in pension benefits when their firms were brought under provincial or municipal pension administration. Kun-Chin Lin cites the example of the Luoyang Refinery in Henan province, whose employees protested against the incorporation of the firm into the local social insurance fund because they were well aware that the 800–1000 yuan per month that pensioners received in 2002 would be drastically reduced when the retirees of the firm came under local government administration (Lin 2009).

Enterprises in the interior were frequently found on the "shame lists" of enterprises that the MOLSS publicly revealed as the leading evaders of pension and other social insurance fee payments. In January 2002, MOLSS listed thirty-three enterprises that owed more than 10 million yuan ($1.2 million) in overdue pension contributions, along with the amounts they were in arrears. Seven of these enterprises were in Chongqing (with the Chongqing Steel Corporation owing a nation-leading 71.2 million yuan in unpaid pension contributions). Other firms on the list were based in cities such as Lanzhou, Xian, and Wuhan (MOLSS 2002). Such firms were also prominently featured in investigations published by the local media. The MOLSS journal *China Social Security* followed up one of these local media reports with a 2000 article that investigated several large enterprises in Ningxia (Jiang 2000, 4).

Like local governments in the southeast, those of interior provinces that had pension surpluses also found it easy to divert their pension funds to alternative uses. According to a Sichuan informant, pension collection in many counties was higher than the actual fiscal revenues, and local governments with budgets stretched thin would use pension funds for other purposes (Interview #060501). In fact, according to this informant, it was common before State Council regulations were issued in 1998 for local governments to use pension funds to inject cash into financially troubled banks or even to build new office towers for local government offices, including that of the SIA. Following 1998 State Council regulations, Sichuan authorities also issued rules that made it necessary for both financial departments and SIAs to sign off on the disbursement of pension funds—a measure that allowed one agency to thwart attempts by the other to misuse the pension funds but that also presumably opened avenues for their mutual cooperation in the misuse of pension surpluses.

Local governments of the interior provinces, like those of the northeast, drew on a narrow base of large-scale SOEs that had survived restructuring. Pensions were thus redistributive to a limited extent, with money transferred from large SOEs to local pensioners whose enterprises had been downsized or eliminated. This made the degree of redistribution much like that in the northeast. Unlike the northeast, urban and provincial governments in the interior provinces encountered the issue of labor outflows in which migrants from their counties paid into the pension pools of the coastal cities in which they worked. In this case, pensions were arguably regressive in their redistribution because the migrants of poor regions were paying into pension funds that would support the retirement benefits of retirees in the wealthier coastal cities.

SHANGHAI

The Shanghai pension scandal shows the local cadre and crony capitalist coalition at its finest. Before 2006, Shanghai had been the paragon of welfare and social policy reforms in China. Shanghai officials had successfully transferred the welfare functions of its state enterprises to local government agencies. The 2.9 million retirees of the city in 2005 drew their pensions from local banks, and 5.4 million workers contributed to pension and other social insurance accounts. In addition to these employees formally covered under social insurance, civil servants and public-sector workers (e.g., teachers, police, and sanitation workers) had been required since 1993 to contribute to the city pension fund. They contributed at the same levels as the employees of urban enterprises (8 percent for employees, 22.5 percent for employers). Outside Shanghai, civil servants and employees of public-sector units (*shiye danwei*) are exempt from having to make pension contributions; their pension benefits come directly from the government budget. The city even stood out for providing special social insurance coverage to residents of its surrounding rural townships and for its policies providing social insurance to migrant workers. But with such a broad safety net came a large amount of funds to manage. The same agency that took the money in made the decisions about how to manage the funds.

It is perhaps not a coincidence that the Shanghai pension scandal occurred in the city that is both the wealthiest and most rapidly aging in China. Shanghai is well known for its prosperity and rapid expansion under the economic reforms, yet it is also facing the most serious demographic pressures of any city in China. In 2005, its ratio of nonfarm workers (including migrants) to retirees was only 2.7 to 1. The retiree population of 2.9 million will continue to grow over the next decade. Shanghai officials also have a massive source of payrolls from which to draw a combined contribution (from workers and employers) of 30.5 percent of wages. Still, the city each year spends all its pension revenues, except for those designated for enterprise annuities, on benefits for current workers. Even the 8 percent of wages that is supposed to be earmarked for workers' personal retirement accounts is used on current benefits (Interview #040605). In this respect, Shanghai is no different than nearly all other locally managed pension funds in China—personal retirement accounts are "notional" or, in blunter terms, empty.

Shanghai officials responded to the pressures of a demographic challenge and the availability of large payrolls from local enterprises in two ways. First, the local government and SIA expanded the basis of coverage for social insurance to include categories of workers that elsewhere in China are not required to pay into social insurance funds. Civil servants and public-sector employees have contributed to the city pension fund since 1993. The Shanghai government has also drawn in migrant workers and residents of rural counties by offering them low-priced, low-benefit pensions. In 2002, the Shanghai authorities introduced comprehensive insurance for migrant workers, which allowed them to remit nominal amounts for pension and medical coverage. The same year, the local government enacted township insurance for the residents of newly urbanized townships in the counties surrounding Shanghai (Interview #022305; Interview #021805). The intent was to provide pensions to peasants whose land had been requisitioned. The policy has also given enterprises the opportunity to relocate to these towns and put their urban employees on a substandard township social insurance scheme. The comprehensive insurance program for migrants has, in effect, been privatized by being placed under the operations and management of the Shanghai branch of China Life (which is a state-owned firm, to be sure, but also a commercial entity that handles pension and health insurance for an estimated 2 million Shanghai participants; Interview #040605).

The second response of the Shanghai authorities to the aging population and large payroll base has been to collect revenues far above and beyond what was permitted under central government regulations. This allowed the Shanghai SIA to turn over large sums of pension funds to private agents for assorted and often questionable investments. According to national pension regulations in 1997, enterprises were required to turn over to SIAs an amount equal to a certain percentage of the base wage (ranging from 20 to 30 percent, depending on the province). The national regulations put a ceiling on these contributions; if an employee earned more than three times the local average wage, then the employee and firm were to use as the basis of the pension contributions the three-times average wage figure. For example, in Shanghai the local average wage in 2004 was 1,847 yuan per month, which resulted in a ceiling of 5,511 yuan. If an employee earned more than that—as surely a large number of Shanghai professionals did—then the employer would only remit in pension fees 30.5 percent of 5,511 yuan. But the Shanghai SIA ignored this cap. It collected 30.5 percent of the actual basic wage or basic salary, which could run well above 10,000 yuan for many executives and professionals in the city. The Shanghai SIA treated the difference between the capped contribution and the actual contribution as "supplemental pension insurance." Through this scheme, the Shanghai SIA had amassed by 2004 a pension fund estimated at between 8 and 10 billion yuan.[3] Shanghai businesses, especially those with high-salaried employees, were willing to accept this arrangement because the higher pension contribution resulted in a substantial tax deduction and, thus, lower taxes.

The surplus pension funds were effectively privatized when the Shanghai SIA contracted with commercial fund managers in Shanghai to manage these funds in exchange for a guaranteed return. No one, save for officials and the managers themselves, knew who these managers were or the specific arrangements that had been made with them for managing this special pension fund (Interview #012505; Interview #021905). "It's all very lacking in transparency," one close observer of Shanghai pensions remarked in 2005 (Interview #012505). Informants that I interviewed during field research in 2004–2005 said that Shanghai authorities had farmed out an estimated 10 billion yuan (US$1.25 billion) to commercial fund managers to invest in essentially any assets they chose, provided they guaranteed a particular rate of return (Interview #012505). An official from the Shanghai Labor and Social Security Bureau said in an interview, "We can call this pension privatization," although he refused to

---

[3] Details in this passage were provided by informants in Interviews #022405, #021905, and #110904.

confirm the amount of money involved (Interview #040605).[4] The Shanghai SIA was also a large shareholder in several companies listed on the Shanghai and Shenzhen stock exchanges (Xinhuanet 2002). National pension regulations explicitly prohibited local SIAs from investing pension funds in anything other than government bonds and bank deposits. In the months following the Shanghai pension scandal, local officials declared that they had recovered all the funds that had been diverted, but this is difficult to believe given how far the network of loans extended (*China Daily* 2007).

The practice of essentially ignoring the maximum that enterprises would owe in social insurance fees gave Shanghai its 10 billion yuan pension fund, which the Shanghai SIA designated as a supplemental pension fund so as to appear that it was following the central government regulations on this special but rarely used source of pension revenues. The fact that the Shanghai SIA contracted with local businesses and investors to guarantee a much better rate of return on these funds than they could receive from legal channels for pension investments is revealing. Just as SIAs in Liaoning and other northeastern provinces now have management responsibilities over several billion yuan in funded individual accounts, the pressure of future claims on these funds means that SIAs must seek ways to enhance their value. Yet because of the immature state of capital markets in China, there are few vehicles other than the highly turbulent stock markets in Shanghai and Shenzhen. Even though many of the investments of the Shanghai supplemental pension fund were clearly based on political connections between businesses and Shanghai political kingpins, diversifying the pension fund across asset classes to provide a modestly higher return at a calibrated amount of risk was in many ways a rational move for Shanghai SIA director Zhu Junyi.

The evidence from Shanghai confirms a general pattern suggested in our regression analysis. Essentially, the Shanghai SIA has redistributed the social insurance revenues generated by its thriving foreign-invested and pri-

---

[4] Personal retirement accounts were spent on current benefits; thus commercial fund management companies were not involved in managing the investments of personal retirement accounts, as is the case in Chile and other countries that have privatized pensions. Nonetheless, it is accurate to say that the only surplus pension funds that Shanghai possessed were being handled by commercial fund managers—and based on the revelations of the Shanghai pension scandal, funds were also loaned out to investors and projects of considerable risk. The ownership forms of the fund management companies were complex, and in some cases partly state-owned, but they were usually commercially driven entities that received licenses to invest the city public pension funds.

vate sectors to the state-sector employees who lost jobs through early retirements and SOE restructuring in the 1990s. Although this pattern of
redistribution suggests something resembling a rich-to-poor redistribution
of wealth, it has come at the cost of the intergenerational transfers of
wealth for which pensions were originally designed. The 36.2 billion yuan
in pension expenditures that Shanghai distributed in 2005 to its 2.9 million
retirees included all the money from the individual retirement accounts of
current workers, whom the Shanghai government will one day need to
compensate for spending their money on today's pensioners.

Even the success of Shanghai in expanding coverage may come at the cost
of adequate financing for its future retirees. One analyst, who also provides
informal advice to the Shanghai Labor and Social Security Bureau, expressed concern about the proliferation of different pension schemes for
different segments of the workforce, noting that the pension pool of the
city was going to come under increasing pressure because of the shrinking
base of state enterprises and the latitude given to small and medium private firms to contribute at rates far below what is called for in the national
pension regulations (Interview #021805).

As a provincial-level government, Shanghai has both the highest levels of
redistribution and the greatest levels of corrupt management of pension
funds. The contrast with Beijing and its provincial-level government is instructive. Beijing has a relatively more favorable support ratio of 5.7 to 1. It
has also enjoyed large inflows of FDI and other investment spending. In
terms of demographics and capital flows, it is therefore more like the governments of southern and eastern China. Beijing has also followed a pattern of pension redistribution similar to that in the cities of the southeast-
ern region. Large inflows of migrant labor and capital have allowed SIA
officials to gain a substantial increase in social insurance revenues. Between
1995 and 2003, Beijing absorbed approximately 1.9 million new workers,
up from 6.0 million in 1995. The Beijing pension coverage rate by 2003
stood at 38.8 percent of the nonagricultural workforce. Beijing officials attributed the increase in pension revenues and participants to an incentive
system that they introduced in 2000, in which district governments were
allowed to retain whatever pension revenues they collected over a certain
quota. The policy yielded an increase in pension revenues (Beijing receives
no subsidies from the central government) from 9.6 billion yuan in 2000
to 16.6 billion yuan ($2.0 billion) in 2003, or an increase of 73 percent
(Interview #110604). When a given locality receives a large influx of labor
and capital, as Beijing did in the late 1990s, the contribution base expands
and becomes a resource from which governments can collect revenues. To
date, the Beijing SIA has not fallen into the practices that the Shanghai SIA

engaged prior to the scandal. The Beijing municipal government has not lacked for corrupt officials in the past. It would not be out of the question to discover one day the corrupt use of SIA funds, especially among the district governments in Beijing, which were allowed a rather long leash to collect and retain pension revenues if they fulfilled their quotas for the Beijing SIA.

The behavior of SIAs in different regions in China shows that local pension administration, and welfare provision in general, is highly compromised not so much by the inability of local agencies to extract revenues but by the tendency of local governments to retain control rights over pension funds. This inability to pool pension funds at higher levels means that revenues from the vastly wealthier cities in coastal China do not reach the much poorer cities and their pensioners in the interior. Although central government subsidies suggest some degree of redistribution, the fact that the Ministry of Finance has pressured provincial governments to fund individual accounts offsets the potential for redistribution and creates far greater pressures on provincial governments than on the center to prepare for financing the future cohorts of retirees as population aging grows acute, beginning in 2015. Moreover, as noted in the discussion of the interior provinces, there is a substantially regressive element to pensions when we consider that several tens of millions of migrant workers from these provinces pay money into the accounts of local governments on the coast, where they are employed, and not into the accounts of their home cities in the interior, whose governments will be asked to provide them with pension benefits when these workers eventually reach retirement age. Patterns of redistribution vary across regions of China, but it remains to be seen how and why business owners—and which types of firms—would cooperate with local governments to establish a welfare regime heavily centered on pensions and heavily financed through payroll taxes.

CHAPTER 5

How Employers Shaped China's New Welfare Regime

China's economic reforms enhanced the power of business owners, who in turn have strongly supported the political status quo of CCP rule. Business associations have succeeded in their efforts to gain beneficial regulations from government authorities (Kennedy 2005). In their political orientations, business owners are ambivalent about, if not suspicious of, democratic political competition that might weaken or overturn CCP rule (Dickson 2003; Tsai 2007). In this chapter, I examine the power of business and its relations with the state from a different and largely unexplored angle—the rapid expansion of welfare spending in China, which has largely been financed through very high payroll taxes amounting to 40 percent, and even higher in some locations. The rapid expansion in social insurance revenues and expenditures (see chapter 4) was financed almost exclusively through levies on businesses. The rise of social insurance in China therefore constitutes an important test for the cooperative relations between government and business. Like employers anywhere, business owners in China can be expected to resist demands from the state to finance social protections if it means higher production costs, greater regulatory scrutiny, and so on. Business opposition to welfare policies in China, or preferences for certain policies over others, has exerted a powerful influence on the design and shape of China's new welfare state.

The CCP under Hu Jintao has staked its political legitimacy on the expansion of welfare provision to achieve more balanced growth and remedy the social problems that have come with rapid economic expansion. Although CCP elites may have a stake in creating a "harmonious society" to enhance popular support, business owners have reasons to avoid or evade payroll taxes necessary to finance such welfare measures. But there are several conditions under which certain welfare programs can become attractive to businesses. Businesses may view such programs as necessary to stabilize or lower labor turnover. Some businesses may view welfare measures as a way to undermine the cost advantages enjoyed by their lower-cost competitors. Welfare programs can also allow businesses to dump slack labor if governments can pick up the tab for the costs associated with unemployment and retraining.

The preferences of business owners were instrumental in the design of most contemporary developed welfare states. Recent work by scholars exploring welfare state development in twentieth-century Europe has shown that employers were not uniformly opposed to the expansion of social policies that provided workers with different forms of social insurance. In early-twentieth-century Europe, the political conflict was in many respects over the questions of who would be covered and who would control the social insurance funds and their administration. Isabela Mares notes that assigning responsibility for the administration of social insurance—to state agencies, unions, or employers—was "one of the most divisive political questions throughout the history of welfare state development" (2003, 234). As she shows in the cases of France and Germany, employers divided sharply over proposals such as workplace injury insurance and unemployment insurance, with some demanding a great deal of firm-level discretion over the administration of social insurance and others favoring universal coverage in which administration was entirely in the hands of state agents or unions. Others have also found strong evidence that business owners and employers had a decisive influence on the formation of welfare legislation during the New Deal in the United States. As Colin Gordon notes, "U.S. welfare policy has been, in large part, a business measure in progressive clothing" (1991, 67).

Employer preferences for social policy most often divide over a crucial aspect of social policy design. Under contributory social insurance (for pensions, unemployment insurance, health insurance, etc.), revenues are raised largely through payroll taxes and, thus, through the employer. By contrast, with universal coverage, funds for the same types of insurance are raised through income taxes and through individual premiums paid by individuals. Universal coverage programs funded in this way thus do not involve direct levies on employers. Contributory social insurance can be costly for firms. Still, some firms prefer it to universal coverage because they can retain control over the administration of the social insurance funds. As Mares points out (2003, 239) larger firms and those in favorable market positions can shift the costs of social insurance on to consumers in the form of higher prices. For small firms, the cost of contributory social insurance is simply too much of a burden, and they are likely to oppose social policies altogether, or at least be more willing to accept designs based on universal coverage rather than on contributory social insurance in which they have to remit high payroll taxes. Moreover, firms that compete for skilled workers want to retain discretion over social insurance by being able to reward skilled workers with favorable social insurance benefits and to exclude low-skilled workers. In the early stages of welfare state formation in France and Germany, employers aligned themselves for and against proposed social insurance policies depending on the size and skill levels of their workforce (Mares 2003).

The discussion in the sections that follow shows that important differences based on the form of ownership divided employers during the introduction of new social policies in China. The opaque political process in China makes it difficult to discern the extent to which businesses and their associations actually lobbied for particular welfare policy designs. But, as is often the case in Chinese public policy, conflict over policy begins *after*, not prior to, the introduction of a particular law or regulation. In other words, conflict over compliance and implementation allows us to discern preferences and stances on policy questions. Following the introduction of social insurance measures in the 1990s, the interests and preferences of three segments of Chinese businesses became apparent, and these groups varied substantially in their compliance with the social insurance provisions and in their willingness to remit social insurance revenues to authorities: (1) large SOEs, including those under central government administration; (2) smaller locally administered SOEs and urban collectives (generally smaller firms run by district governments of cities); and (3) private-sector enterprises, including foreign enterprises.

Large SOEs wanted to retain their own pension administration, if possible within their supervising ministry. Such firms and their managers wanted favorable pension arrangements that came with the higher status of their firms in the administrative hierarchy. These SOEs came into sharp conflict with local governments, which tried and eventually gained the ability to regulate the social insurance collections from these very large, lucrative sources of social insurance revenue. Local SOEs faced an entirely different welfare policy calculus. Local SOEs and their bureaucratic handlers had to consider the market pressures from nonstate firms and the looming debt burdens of local SOEs. Local governments had a direct interest in the resolution of these debt burdens and overstaffing. Local SOEs and local governments collaborated to change the corporate identity and structure of local firms, including bankruptcies and mergers (including those with foreign firms), and used pension reforms to turn over to local governments those workers made jobless by the restructuring. The third category, private firms, including wholly foreign-owned firms, sought to avoid social insurance levies altogether and essentially bargained with local officials to reduce social insurance payments and workforce coverage. Many large-scale export-oriented private and foreign-invested firms avoided social insurance fees by exempting "temporary workers" from coverage.

CENTRAL STATE ENTERPRISES

The battles between enterprise managers who evaded the payment of social insurance fees and the local SIAs that collected them were featured prominently in the Chinese media beginning in the late 1990s. The most intense conflicts over the evasion of social insurance payments in the 1990s occurred between SIAs and large SOEs under the regulation of central government ministries. The following quotation from a county-level SIA official in Sichuan is representative of how officials viewed the behavior of many large SOEs:

> In order not to remit pension insurance fees, some enterprises rack their brains, giving every thought to how they might play tricks on the collecting agencies and wage a see-saw battle with them. Some enterprises even talk about taking aggressive action by bringing the social insurance agencies to court, suing them for chaotically collecting fees [*luan shoufei*]. (Liao 2002, 161)

As noted in chapter 4, executives of these firms often outranked in terms of protocol the mayors and even provincial officials who ordered them to remit their social insurance fees to local social insurance agencies. National social insurance regulations in 1998 ordered all enterprises within a given jurisdiction of a municipal government social insurance agency to remit fees to that government rather than to the central government ministries, as had been the practice before 1998. Large SOEs remained under central government regulation, but they were to pay their social insurance levies to the local governments in which their firm, or a branch factory of their firm, was located (Interview #062802B; Interview #060601A; Interview #070302). These central SOEs became the "cash cows" supporting local SIAs.

The case of a local government that had a major dispute with a large, centrally administered SOE over social insurance payments shows the extent to which local governments went to draw social insurance revenues from these large SOEs. A municipal government in Sichuan province got into a dispute with a large SOE that I call here National Engine.[1] National Engine had always been supervised by an industrial ministry of the central government and became part of an enterprise group owned by a central government agency. As of summer 2001, the enterprise had 14,000 workers, of which 4,000 were "not at workposts," and another 900 employees were considered formally "laid off" (*xiagang*) and placed in the firm's reemployment service center. Some 3,000 employees were nearing retirement age. Finally, some 200 employees were actually past retirement age but could not yet formally go through the retirement procedures because the city SIA refused to approve the application by National Engine to retire them. By mid-2001, National Engine had paid out 1 million yuan in pensions from its own funds to these would-be retirees. The reason the city SIA officials had suspended its approval of the National Engine retirement applications was that the company owed the local SIA an estimated 100 million yuan, most of which was in unpaid pension contributions.

As it turned out, National Engine was in arrears by such a staggering amount through some deft maneuvering on the part of the municipal government. As the National Engine managers noted, it had earlier been awarded a "progressive unit" certificate for its social insurance work. National Engine had accumulated the 100 million yuan ($12.1 million) social insurance debt because of a transaction that the municipal government had arranged with another SOE (called here "City Steel") that was under the ownership of the city government. City Steel was a supplier firm to National Engine, and after several years of supplying goods to National Engine on a credit basis, City Steel had uncollected payments of 100 million yuan. But, at the same time, City Steel had amassed a debt of its own in unpaid social insurance fees to the municipal SIA. When the city government decided to convert City Steel into a shareholding corporation in 2000, city officials wanted to make the City Steel shares more attractive to investors by first cleaning up its social insurance debt. They did this by going to National Engine and offering to cancel its 100 million yuan debt to City Steel in exchange for National Engine's taking on the 100 million yuan in unpaid social insurance fees to the city SIA. This transaction shifted the unpaid social insurance fees from City Steel to National Engine. As a

[1] The following account was conveyed in Interview #060401.

National Engine manager put it, "Their delinquent payments to the social insurance office became *our* delinquent payments to the social insurance office." In accepting this debt reshuffle, however, National Engine had unwittingly obtained a demanding new creditor in the form of the city SIA. Authorities there now viewed National Engine as they would any other firm that had unpaid social insurance fees. SIA officials told National Engine managers that until National Engine made an up-front payment of 4.2 million yuan to cover three years worth of future pension obligations for its 200 would-be retirees, SIA officials would not permit the 200 workers to retire. With a backlog of 200 retirees, plus another 3,000 workers within three years of retirement, National Engine found itself in an especially difficult position.[2]

Such disputes were not limited to Sichuan province. In Shanghai, the municipal government in 1999 and 2000 clashed with and ultimately triumphed over the managers at Baoshan Steel (Baogang), which was among the largest SOEs in the city. Managers at Baogang were reluctant to turn over their 2 million yuan in annual pension contributions to local authorities. The leaders of the Shanghai Municipal Party Committee finally ordered the leaders of the Baogang enterprise party committee to comply (Interview #070302). The municipal government of Taiyuan (Shanxi province) also pursued a very large firm (with approximately 60,000 employees and 20,000 retirees) within the city to remit an estimated 200 million yuan in unpaid pension contributions, although evidently with less success (Liao 2002, 162).

After the 1990s, large SOEs under central government supervision could no longer rely on administrative rank to evade local government measures to collect social insurance fees. As a National Engine manager reflected of the relationship between his firm and the city government, "We're now under local government rule. It's hard for us to even go to the provincial government [for dispute resolution]. The reason is that local governments have to think about social stability and the political problem of disturbances by workers and retirees. The local government transfers this political function to us. So we have to undertake obligations like monitoring Falungong." He also noted that "the city government treats the local enterprises with special policies but is much tougher on central government enterprises" (Interview #060401).

---

[2] When asked why they did not go to their bureaucratic superiors in Beijing for support in the matter, the National Engine managers countered, "Oh, we did. And they not only refused to give us any financial support, but they scolded us for agreeing to the transaction in the first place" (Interview #060401).

SIA authorities often reported that they relied on the regulatory powers of other local government agencies to compel enterprise managers, especially those from large SOEs, to remit social insurance fees. One critical component of this effort was the licensing regime under which firms apply for certifications. These include annually renewable documents related to business licenses, tax compliance, public health, family planning (for the one-child policy), and others. Authority for approving these documents comes under different local agencies, and SIA officials reported colluding with their counterparts in these agencies to revoke or deny approval if a firm was delinquent on its payments to social insurance funds (Interview #052801; Interview #053001; Interview #053101). Another common, although controversial, measure was for local SIAs to deny approving retirement procedures for enterprises that had not paid their social insurance fees (Interview #060401; Interview #060501).

Municipal governments also sought compliance with pension and social insurance policy by pursuing newly formed enterprise groups in the state sector. During the 1990s, in accordance with the Company Law of 1994, SOEs reorganized as joint stock and limited-liability corporations. Frequently with the encouragement of local authorities, state enterprises reorganized into enterprise groups that include both healthy, profitable firms and a good many that were near bankruptcy. SIA authorities used the structure of the enterprise groups to punish the entire group if one of its group member firms fell behind on social insurance payments. In an enterprise group based in Jilin province, for example, one of the branch factories had accumulated unpaid social insurance fees. The municipal SIA responded by punishing the entire group of thirteen enterprises by threatening to withhold approval of the wage inspection certificate of the group. Moreover, LSS authorities put pressure on enterprise group managers by refusing to pay pensions to the seven hundred current retirees of the group (who had begun drawing their pension payments from local LSS agencies following socialization in September 2000) (Interview #060101B).

Finally, local authorities used public information channels to expose firms that had not paid pension contributions. Many LSS offices and their SIAs have whistle-blower sections that receive reports from employees or others about firms that have made false reports or otherwise sought to avoid pension contributions. Urban governments frequently broadcast reports on the Central Television network of local enterprises that refuse to pay their pension contributions. This draws public attention to alleged violators and to the managers of firms that have fallen into arrears (Interview #053001; Interview #060101A; Interview #053101; Liao 2002, 162). At the national level, the MOLSS in fall 2001 issued a public list of twenty enterprises that were more than 10 million yuan ($1.2 million) behind on their payments to pension pools (Xinhua 2001); all these were large SOEs. In early 2002, MOLSS followed up this publicity campaign by releasing a list of thirty-three enterprises that had by then achieved the dubious distinction of amassing more than 10 million yuan in back payments to pension funds (see also chapter 4). This time, however, the amount that each firm owed was specified, and in its announcement MOLSS averred that the firms listed "had the ability to pay their fees but still fell into arrears on basic pension insurance fees" (Ministry of Labor and Social Security [MOLSS] 2002).

This conflict between local governments bent on collecting social insurance fees and large SOEs took on serious dimensions in 1998. That year, the central government attempted to take the administration of pension funds away from large state corporations and hand them over to the SIAs of the provincial governments. Before this time, many of the largest state enterprises with nationwide operations, such as those in banking, insurance, petroleum, mining, and railroads, were permitted under State Council regulations from the early 1990s to form their own social insurance funds for pensions, unemployment, and other purposes. By 1998, eleven such pension funds were under the control of individual ministries that regulated the national corporations. As of December 1997, firms in these sectors employed 13.9 million workers and managed pensions for 4.2 million retirees (MOLSS Social Insurance Management Center [SIMC] 2000, 169), representing approximately one-eighth of the 33.5 million retirees nationwide in late 1997 and just under one-sixth of all retirees from state enterprises (State Statistics Bureau [SSB] and MOLSS 1998, 479). The pension funds of the national corporations collected 35.6 billion yuan ($4.3 billion) in contributions in 1997 and distributed 30.6 billion yuan to their retirees. Thus, the central government agencies that regulated the eleven national corporations controlled more than 26 percent of the 134 billion yuan in pension fees collected nationwide in 1997.

The central government managers of the pension funds of the eleven national corporations tended to arrange relatively generous pension benefits for their employees, and at substantially lower contribution rates. In Sichuan province, for example, the average officially reported pension for a retiree in 1997 was 400 yuan per month, whereas retirees from the Sichuan enterprises and offices of one of these eleven national corporations received about twice that, or 800 yuan ($97) per month (Interview #060501). In Shanghai, pensioners who had worked in the local firms of one of the eleven national corporations were entitled to pension benefits that ranged from 30 to 100 percent higher than the average Shanghai pension (Jiang and Li 1999, 13). The enterprises that belonged to the eleven national corporations had to remit only 4–5 percent of their payroll as pension fees, whereas all other enterprises had to follow the local government remittance rates of 20 percent and higher.

In 1998, the central government sought to reduce these disparities in retiree benefits and to standardize pension policy more generally by transferring the sector-based pension funds to provincial government administration. These funds were effectively consolidated on September 1 of that year, but the officials of the eleven national corporations nearly bankrupted the Chinese pension system in the process. Knowing that they were soon going to transfer several billion yuan in accumulated pension funds to provincial SIAs, the managers at the eleven national corporations took advantage of the opportunity to invoke massive retirements from these firms and to provide these retirees with much higher than average benefits. In the first eight months of 1998 leading up to the September 1 transfer of the pension funds of the eleven national corporations, nearly 800,000 retirees of dubious qualifications (in terms of age) were added to pension registries (Zhao and Xu 1999, 7). An estimated 55 percent of these were early retirees in their forties and even thirties. The bottom line in terms of finances was alarming; only 4 billion of the estimated 14.7 billion yuan ($1.8 billion) in surplus pension funds ended up moving from the national corporations to the provincial SIAs (Jiang and Li 1999, 11).

Central government officials in charge of implementing pension reforms thus learned a costly lesson from their hasty attempt to consolidate control over the fragmented pension funds. Among them was then-premier Zhu Rongji, who by many accounts intervened forcefully to insist that the eleven national corporations turn over their pension funds to provincial government control. The lesson was that any attempt to consolidate pension funds from one level of government to another could easily result in the evaporation of vast amounts of pension fund money. This is why provincial governments have encountered such difficulty in combining pension funds from the municipal and county governments—the latter will quickly use the funds on early retirements before they turn over the funds to the provincial government.

Although the eleven national corporations and their managers lost the battle over control of social insurance pension funds, they won a significant policy victory in 2004 that allowed them to retain control over new sources of pension funds. As noted in chapter 2, the central government introduced supplemental pensions under the management of individual firms in 2004. These enterprise annuities can be introduced by any employer, but according to most experts, the firms most likely to pursue them are large SOEs and various branch enterprises of national corporations in sectors such as telecommunications, energy, airlines, and banking. With their monopoly profits, these firms can reduce their tax bill by making tax-deductible contributions on behalf of their employees. This tax deduction policy was highly controversial and opposed by the Ministry of Finance, according to informants (Interview #012505). Even more controversial was the provision that allowed these supplemental pension funds to be managed by commercial entities such as banks and insurance companies rather than by the local SIAs. Originally, SIAs had the right to collect and administer supplemental pensions. Indeed, it was these supplemental pensions that provided the revenue source for the Shanghai SIA to collect extraordinary payroll levies and eventually to distribute its pension funds to various corporate cronies of party secretary Chen Liangyu (see chapter 1).

LOCAL GOVERNMENTS AND LOCAL STATE-OWNED ENTERPRISES

Local governments vigorously pursued large, centrally managed SOEs for their pension and other social insurance fees, but they took an entirely different approach with the local SOEs that they directly administered. Facing strong pressures to dismantle the financially troubled local SOEs, local governments had to consider the risks posed by surging unemployment and mass layoffs that would ensue with the restructuring of local SOEs. The wave of SOE bankruptcies and mergers that took place in the late 1990s did create mass unemployment and led to periodic episodes of resistance among those who lost their jobs at state enterprises (Cai 2002). Yet local governments and the SOEs they administered found in pension reforms an appealing program that allowed them to cope with the problem of indebted and overstaffed SOEs. If local social insurance agencies had amassed enough revenues by the late 1990s, the workers in the troubled SOEs could be retired, even if they were not yet near retirement age. If the local social insurance revenues were not sufficient, as was usually the case in rust-belt regions such as the northeast, then local governments and SOE managers collaborated to provide workers with severance payments from SOE bankruptcies, sales, or mergers. Those who could not be placed within the pension system were considered laid off, and nominally at least, retained their social insurance coverage from their enterprises. As noted in chapter 3, cities with sizable pension revenues invoked SOE layoffs and put workers on pensions, whereas cities that lacked such revenues came up with short-term or one-off payments to workers. The more prosperous a given city, the more it would use pensions as part of SOE restructuring.

This means that in regions in which pension resources were most needed, such as the northeast, local governments that restructured SOEs did so without providing workers with adequate pensions or severance pay.

This general pattern (identified in chapter 3) can be confirmed using firm-level data from a survey conducted in 2000 by a team of researchers under the guidance of scholars at the Economics Institute of the Chinese Academy of Social Sciences (CASS). The CASS survey sampled eight hundred state and nonstate enterprises in four Chinese provinces and twenty cities. The sample was drawn from an initial set of 680 state enterprises that were first surveyed in 1990 and then resurveyed in 1995. When survey administrators attempted to locate the original 680 firms, it turned out that 236 of them had not survived the restructuring of the late 1990s. The 444 surviving firms were surveyed in 2000, and 11 of these had changed ownership form between 1995 and 2000.[3] A look at the traits of firms from both groups, including the 236 exiting firms and the 433 remaining SOEs, allows us to see to what extent the firms that disappeared also had significantly higher social costs in the form of workers at or near retirement.

The survey data showing the manner in which firms shed workers is revealing. Table 5.1 shows the stark differences in how SOEs released workers compared with non-SOEs. Between 1994 and 1999, a total of 159,810 workers in the sample left SOE employment. Of these, nearly 145,000 (90.4 percent) of the workers were released through retirement, as opposed to dismissal, resignation, or transfer. By contrast, out of the 72,145 who left collective-sector employment, nearly 40,000 (55.3 percent) did so through dismissal. Roughly the same proportion of those separated from corporatized firms did so through dismissal. It appears that SOEs, unlike non-SOEs, shed workers by retiring them and then relied on transfers or negotiated arrangements with local governments to offer financial support for those left jobless.

This clear contrast in the manner in which state and nonstate firms released workers strongly suggests important constraints on the ability of state enterprises to use flexible labor policies to compete domestically and internationally. Instead of adjusting the labor force in response to market conditions, SOEs channeled their excess workers through retirement and pension procedures. In the survey, enterprise directors were asked to offer their assessment of specific management problems believed to be common among Chinese firms. One such possible management problem was that

---

[3] The survey-takers in 2000 also collected data on 232 urban collectives, 92 corporatized firms, 33 private and joint-venture firms, and 10 firms that fit into none of these ownership categories.

TABLE 5.1
Personnel reductions by ownership form, 1994–1999

	SOE	Collectives	Joint stock	Limited liability	Private	Joint venture
Number of firms	431	218	17	74	12	21
Dismissals	4,929	39,924	885	14,548	1,842	2,523
Retirements	144,498	10,698	316	5,130	456	2,334
Resignations	6,032	15,088	251	6,987	640	1,811
Transfers	4,020	3,324	67	1,081	123	424
Total reduction in personnel, 1994–1999	159,810	72,145	1,517	28,453	3,048	7,128

Source: Chinese Academy of Social Sciences Economics Institute data set on SOEs, 1995–1999.
Note: SOE, state-owned enterprise.

managers "lacked the authority to hire and fire workers," in other words, that they had to seek approval from some external authority, such as a local industrial bureau, the board of directors of the firm (which might well contain local officials), or the local Communist Party Committee. Table 5.2 shows a cross-tabulation of how directors of SOEs, collectives, and limited-liability firms viewed constraints on making labor force adjustments. (Other ownership forms were left out for simplicity and because of their relatively small numbers.) Slightly over one-half the respondents reported that a lack of autonomy to hire and fire workers posed a management problem for them. But the clear contrast lies in the ownership of the firm because 83 percent (316 out of 380) of those claiming some or many difficulties in hiring and firing workers were from SOEs. Large and significant majorities of collective and limited-liability firms (81 and 72 percent, respectively) reported no difficulties in their ability to hire and fire workers.

The CASS survey data also show the significant differences between state enterprises that ceased operations between 1994 and 1999 and those that remained in business over the same period. Table 5.3 shows a striking contrast as of year-end 1994 in the employment levels, average wages, value of industrial output, productivity, and profitability of the 444 surviving firms and the 236 firms that exited after 1995. The surviving SOEs in the sample were larger employers, with higher average wages, productivity levels, and profits. The industrial output value of the surviving firms was on average approximately eight times greater than that of the exiting firms, and surviving firms reported over three times the productivity of exiting firms.

Table 5.4 presents the results of a multivariate regression to explain the patterns of firm exit. This model estimates 92.4 percent of the cases of firm

TABLE 5.2
Ownership form and managerial autonomy

Does lack of autonomy to recruit and dismiss labor pose a managerial problem?

| | Ownership form | | | | | | | |
| | SOE | | Collectives | | Limited liability | | Totals | |
	n	%	n	%	n	%	n	%
No difficulties	117	27.0	189	81.5	54	72.0	360	48.6
Some difficulties	217	50.1	43	18.5	16	21.3	276	37.3
Many difficulties	99	22.9	0	0	5	6.7	104	14.1
Total	433	100.0	232	100.0	75	100.0	740	100.0

Source: Chinese Academy of Social Sciences Economics Institute data set on SOEs, 1995–1999.
Notes: Pearson $\chi^2 = 206.9$; $p < 0.001$. SOE, state-owned enterprise.

TABLE 5.3
Traits of SOEs at year-end 1994: SOEs that would survive 1990s restructuring and those that would not

Status of enterprise	Average annual wage, production workers (yuan)	Total workers and staff	Industrial output value (millions of yuan, 1990 prices)	Gross profits (millions of yuan)	Annual output per employee (yuan/ worker)
Present in 2000 (n=444)	4,406	2,563	115.64	1.18	49,333
Not present in 2000 (n=236)	3,604	901	14.43	−0.775	15,077

Source: Chinese Academy of Social Sciences Economics Institute data set on SOEs, 1995–1999.
Notes: Values are the means, as of year-end 1994, for each category of enterprise. SOE, state-owned enterprise.

exit among the 681 firms with available data, compared to 62 percent without these variables in the model. After controlling for size of the firm based on employees, firms with both higher output value and higher taxes in 1994 were less likely to exit in the late 1990s. The taxation variable shows that SOEs that contributed more taxes were less likely to have exited production; SOEs that paid none or few taxes (because they were unprofitable) in 1994 were more likely to have ceased production in the late 1990s. Consistent with central government policy, the larger firms were retained while smaller firms were "released," but the model suggests that local governments also thought in terms of tax revenues and not simply of dismantling small firms while retaining large ones.

TABLE 5.4
Likelihood of firm exit for SOEs between 1994 and 1999

	β	Standard error	$\exp(\beta)$
Constant	60.069***	7.979	n/a
log(1994 employment)	0.593	0.875	1.810
log(1994 output value)	−8.314***	0.982	0.000
Production workers, 1994 (%)	0.032*	0.018	1.033
log(1994 average wage)	−0.557	1.413	0.573
Hiring autonomy	−0.070	0.159	0.932
Level of regulatory agency	0.093	0.255	1.098
Retirees (%)	0.138***	0.051	1.148
log(1994 taxes)	−0.325	0.302	0.723
Mining dummy	−0.193	0.808	0.824
Machinery dummy	−0.214	0.545	0.808
Utilities dummy	−19.481	12,987	0.000
Food dummy	−0.623	0.741	0.537
Chemical dummy	−0.838	0.606	0.433
Metals dummy	−0.567	0.649	0.567
Furniture-paper dummy	−1.169	0.750	0.311
Sichuan dummy	−0.045	0.587	0.956
Shanxi dummy	−1.061*	0.604	0.346
Jilin dummy	−0.251	0.560	0.778

Source: Chinese Academy of Social Sciences Economics Institute data set on SOEs, 1995–1999.

Notes: Binary logistic regression. $n=681$. * indicates $p<0.10$; ** indicates $p<0.05$; *** indicates $p<0.01$. Percentage correctly predicted, 92.4%; −2 Log likelihood=269.824; Nagelkerke $R^2=0.769$; n/a, not available; SOE, state-owned enterprise.

The results in Table 5.4 also show significant patterns in terms of industrial sector. When compared with textiles, the generally more capital-intensive sectors had a lower likelihood of firm exit (although the furniture and paper firms were considerably less likely to exit than were textiles). The textile-sector SOEs, facing heightened competition, were producing goods that sold at lower prices and were no longer capable of remitting taxes. As a consequence, they faced a relatively greater likelihood of liquidation in the late 1990s.

The results also show that regional variation can explain firm exit. All else being equal, a firm's being located outside of Jiangsu province considerably lowered the likelihood of firm exit. For example, in the case of Shanxi province, the coefficient is significant and suggests that SOEs in Shanxi faced a 66 percent lower probability of firm exit than those in Jiangsu province. This result could be explained by a more competitive environment in Jiangsu that provided increased opportunities for employment outside the state sector. Of greatest significance for our purposes, the proportion of retirees of a given firm was a significant explanatory variable for firm exit. Firms that had a larger share of retirees to manage (compared with workers) in 1994 had a 14.8 percent increase in their probability of exit. Local governments and local firms appeared more willing to liquidate firms that had larger shares of retirees, even after we control for other traits such as enterprise size and tax remissions.

The CASS survey also sheds light on the efforts of local governments to collect pension revenues from local enterprises. Enterprise managers in the 2000 survey were asked to state the percentage of their wage bill that they contributed to the local pension pool in 1999. According to State Council regulations, this rate should be the same for all firms within the same city, depending on the pool to which a firm contributed. Thus, when enterprises from the same city responded to this question in the survey, the rate should be the same. But in fact, the 778 firms that responded to this question varied considerably even within the same city. Pension contribution rates from the seventy firms located in the city of Chengdu ranged from well above to far below the municipal government official rate of 25 percent of the basic wage bill. Only thirteen enterprises reported paying at the official 25 percent level. The rates that other firms paid ranged from 16 percent (in two cases) to 32 percent (in one case). This raises the obvious question: which types of firms were the local SIAs levying with higher and lower pension contribution rates?

A broader analysis of the entire data set provides a clear answer. Table 5.5 reports the results of an OLS regression to explain the variation in the pension contribution rates reported by enterprises in the year 2000. If firms were strictly abiding by pension regulations, the only significant coefficients in the table should be for region because different provinces and cities can levy contribution rates within certain limits laid down in the 1997 central government regulations. But, as we see in table 5.5, after we control for region, scale, and productivity, SOEs paid approximately 2 percentage points higher in payroll levies for pensions than did non-SOEs (collectives, corporatized SOEs, and private firms). The coefficient for the regional dummy variables shows that, compared to Jiangsu province, firms in the other three provinces (Jilin, Shanxi, and Sichuan) paid lower payroll taxes, all else being equal. This finding is expected because cities in a given province have the ability to set their pension contribution rates at a level based on what their expected pension burdens will be in the future; provincial governments usually set a ceiling. Of greater significance in table 5.5 is the scale variable, which shows that, all else being equal, pension contribution rates fall as we move from larger to smaller enterprises. This should not occur because, as we have noted, all firms in a given city were supposed to remit the same proportion of the wage bill in pensions.

TABLE 5.5
Pension contribution rates, 2000

	Model 1		Model 2	
	β	Standard error	β	Standard error
Constant	25.576***	0.442	24.628***	0.592
Gross profit	0.000	0.000	0.000	0.000
Scale	−0.739***	0.161	—	—
Sichuan dummy	−0.494*	0.289	−0.523*	0.295
Shanxi dummy	−0.617**	0.300	−0.577*	0.306
Jilin dummy	−0.862***	0.284	−0.863***	0.288
SOE dummy	1.932***	0.227	1.904***	0.318
Administrative agency rank	—	—	−0.140	0.104
	$n=800$		$n=800$	
	$F=27.06$		$F=23.27$	
	Significance = 0.000		Significance = 0.000	
	$r^2=0.178$		$r^2=0.157$	

Source: Chinese Academy of Social Sciences Economics Institute data set on SOEs, 1995–1999.

Notes: Ordinary least squares (OLS) regression. Dependent variable is pension contribution rates as % of wage bill. * indicates $p<0.10$; ** indicates $p<0.05$; *** indicates $p<0.01$. Scale variable: 1=large; 2=medium; 3=small. Rank variable: 1=central; 2=provincial; 3=city; 4=county; 5=none; 6=other. SOE, state-owned enterprise.

The coefficients in table 5.5 suggest that even within individual ownership categories, smaller firms were paying lower contribution rates than large firms. The most significant finding is that SOEs were paying larger payroll taxes than non-SOEs, all else being equal. In some regions, this practice was actual policy—for example, in Jilin province the manager of a large SOE complained that his firm, and its various factories, had to pay 25 percent of its wage bill in pension contributions, whereas the local SIA allowed his competitors in joint-venture and private firms to pay 20 percent of their wages as social insurance pension contributions (Interview #030805B).

A second model presented in table 5.5 tests whether local governments in charge of collecting pensions also set different contribution rates on firms depending on whether they were regulated by central government ministries, provincial government departments, city governments, or others. The tensions between local SIAs and central government SOEs noted in the previous section might also be reflected in the different contribution rates that central government SOEs had to pay compared to locally regulated SOEs. Yet as Model 2 in table 5.5 shows, this was not the case. The variable for "administrative agency rank" does suggest that contribution rates fell slightly as we descend the administrative hierarchy from central government to county (and even to "none" for private-sector firms), but the coefficient is not statistically significant. Scale was omitted from Model 2 because of the close association between scale and administrative rank.[4]

THE PRIVATE SECTOR AND LOCAL GOVERNMENTS

Local governments appear to offer local SOEs that survive restructuring favorable treatment in terms of their payments for pensions and other social insurance fees. Nonstate enterprises, including collective, private, and some foreign-invested firms, pose a different challenge. On the one hand, large private and foreign-invested firms offer a potentially rich source of revenue for social insurance. On the other hand, all private firms are more difficult to monitor compared with state-owned firms. This is especially true for small and medium enterprises, whose workforces can include large numbers of mobile and informal labor. Even in Shanghai, with its enviable pension collection rate, only 4.3 million out of a working-age population of 8 million (including migrant labor) participated in pension and other social insurance pools during the mid-2000s. This gap in Shanghai and in many other cities in China is largely the result of small nonstate firms remaining outside the grasp of local SIAs. According to several reports, private and foreign-funded enterprises most commonly evade social insurance payments by falsely reporting the wage bill or by falsely reporting the number of registered workers, or both (Interview #021905; Interview #022305). According to statistics reported in a 2005 study in the Chinese journal *Economic and Social Development*, coverage rates in a survey of 508 firms in ten large cities found that only 12.1 percent of private-sector workers received coverage (Wei 2005, 82).

Some also argue that workers at these firms either fear being fired if they report to local SIAs or because of the wage deductions involved, such workers do not want employers to transfer social insurance payments to local pools (Chen T. 2002, 182; Interview #070302). Thus, both managers and employees have at least some reason to avoid making pension and other social insurance contributions to local SIAs. Moreover, given the small scale of many collective and private firms and their relative mobility, they are both difficult and costly for local SIA offices to monitor. With

---

[4] Even when non-SOEs were excluded from the analysis, contribution rates still did not vary in any statistically significant way based on the administrative rank of SOEs.

much larger enterprises in the state and urban collective sectors, it makes little sense for SIAs to go after noncontributors from small firms because the ultimate take in social insurance fees from a successful investigation of a firm with few employees would likely be less than the staff and resources involved in enforcement. Finally, local officials are reluctant to undertake a vigorous collection of pension and social insurance fees when doing so might erode the profits of nonstate firms that are important sources of revenues and employment. Areas with large numbers of Taiwan- and Hong Kong–invested firms in Guangdong and Fujian provinces are notorious for dodging social insurance fees (Interview #052801; Chen T. 2002, 181).

Collection problems are complicated by the fact that workers in smaller private-sector firms, especially in service-sector enterprises, are very reluctant to have their wages deducted for contributions to a local social insurance fund because they are likely to be working on a seasonal or short-term basis before switching jobs or returning home. This reluctance holds especially true for pensions, which are the largest deductions from a workers' wages and take the longest to accrue rights—fifteen years under current regulations. A survey of sixty-three private enterprises in Zhengzhou (Henan) discovered that only eighteen firms provided pension insurance coverage for their entire workforce (Xiao 2004). These forty-five firms were not willing to provide pension coverage to reemployed laid-off workers or to migrant workers. The enterprises surveyed argued that local officials would misuse the pension funds. Because their own employees have strong reason to suspect that they will never see the pension benefits, small and medium firms that use migrant labor can easily evade social insurance payments altogether.

Manufacturing-sector workers interviewed in focus group discussions (see chapter 6) in six Chinese cities explained that, especially in private-sector enterprises, employers simply gave them the choice of purchasing social insurance or not. Four out of eight private-enterprise workers in Nanjing said that they had to make their own arrangements with their local SIA to purchase social insurance because their employer would not provide them with coverage (Nanjing private enterprises, #1–8).[5] Other focus group participants explained that private-sector firms were notorious for lowering the amount of social insurance fees paid to SIAs by, in effect, understating the earnings of their workers. A common ruse was to pay a given worker 400 yuan as a base wage, for example, and 400 yuan in various forms of extra pay. Social insurance fees (20–30 percent, depending on

---

[5] See table 6A.9. Information on the focus groups can be found in chapter 6.

the city) would be calculated based on the 400 yuan base wage rather than the 800 yuan in actual earnings (Foshan private enterprises, #3).[6]

A Foshan private enterprise manager at a textile firm employing approximately two hundred employees said in an interview that only older employees had pension coverage and that new employees did not. Given the amount of turnover in the workforce of the firm, this manager explained, she did not blame the workers for not wanting pension insurance when they had little chance of being able to keep their coverage when they switched firms (Interview #031605). Turnover was also linked with low coverage rates in a study from the early 2000s in Shenzhen. Firms that did not provide social insurance coverage had a turnover rate of 40–60 percent, whereas firms that did provide social insurance coverage had a turnover rate of 10 percent (Zhao 2002). The Foshan textile firm manager also noted that workers from outside Foshan were especially reluctant to pay into the local pension fund because they stood little chance of ever seeing the money when they retired. Instead, she explained, her employees wanted and got coverage under major medical and workplace injury insurance plans sold by China Life (Interview #031605). Migrants in Beijing also were essentially exempted pension coverage, and SIA officials there focused primarily on major medical and workplace injury insurance for migrants (Interview #110604).

Urban residents interviewed also reported a general tendency among employers to gladly collude with their employees to evade social insurance levies. A taxi driver from a rural Shanghai county explained that it was commonplace for taxi companies to avoid social insurance payments. "If you ask for social insurance, the company will provide it for you, but if you don't want it, they're glad not to have to pay it" (Interview #031205). Another common pattern among many self-employed was to retire early, draw a pension, and continue to find employment. One such informant had "enough to get by on" in pension income, but did not have any social insurance coverage because he did not want to pay the fees on his own (Interview #030705).

Even if local SIAs cracked down on the self-employed and on the small private- and service-sector firms, their payoffs in terms of social insurance revenues would be small. In several cities, SIAs offered lower pension contribution rates for the self-employed than for enterprises (Interview #030705; Interview #030805A). In one province, for example, owners of small firms with fewer than eight employees could pay at 18 percent of the wage bill rather than the 28 percent levy that applied to larger firms in the province

---

[6] See table 6A.9.

(Interview #040405A). The inclusion of the self-employed and very small firms was basically voluntary (Interview #110604; Interview #030705; Interview #030805A). One city SIA simply allowed the self-employed to sign up for pensions by self-reporting their income levels at anywhere from 60 to 300 percent of the local average city wage and to then pay 20 percent of that income level (Interview #030705). Personnel and enterprise managers were also generally skeptical that SIAs would ever be able to prevent evasion by small firms, by firms that employed largely migrant labor, and by the self-employed (Interview #031605; Interview #031905).

In marked contrast, large private and foreign-owned firms are much more attractive to SIAs because they offer a potentially lucrative revenue base for social insurance. One astute analyst of pension regulatory problems discerned from intensive interviews with SIA officials in a central Chinese city that foreign-owned firms of large multinational corporations were largely compliant with social insurance regulations but that the smaller Chinese firms that simply had a share of foreign-invested capital generally evaded social insurance regulations (Ye 2004, 153–58). As noted in chapter 4, foreign-invested and private firms can bargain with local social insurance agencies for lower rates than those levied on state enterprises. SIAs find this acceptable because (as discussed in chapter 4) regions with foreign-invested firms also have the highest payrolls and are thus a potentially rich source of pension revenue, even if they are not made to pay the full amount required by local regulations.

In a northeastern province, an informant related a well-known account of a former urban collective, now a private firm, and its efforts to opt out of the local social insurance pool. Management at this firm calculated that if the firm registered its workers with the local SIA, it would have to pay approximately 100 yuan per month per employee. But if they bought commercial insurance instead from a local insurance company, they would pay approximately 54 yuan per month and receive about the same benefits. Management opted for the latter, and now has its several thousand employees covered under a well-known insurance company instead of the city SIA. Even though this was patently in violation of the social insurance regulations, the city SIA accepted this arrangement. The SIA was now off the hook in terms of having to be responsible for paying pension benefits to the retirees of this firm. As the informant who related this story concluded, "I really think that the power of SIAs is on the decline; they cannot manage so many private enterprises, small firms, and the self-employed. In addition, the base of their revenues, SOEs and their payrolls, is shrinking" (Interview #030905C). Another pension expert concurred on this point: "Pension finances are in an extremely shaky situation" because of the reduction in SOEs, the main source of pension revenues (Interview #021805).

Several reports on labor conditions in foreign-owned factories in Guangdong province found, among other violations of Chinese labor law, a pattern of limiting the provision of social insurance to formal employees only. China Labor Watch (CLW) reported in 2004 that the factories of Kingmaker Footwear Holdings, a Taiwanese-owned supplier to Timberland, provided social insurance only to its staff but not to production workers at its Zhongshan factory employing 4,700 (China Labor Watch 2004). In Guangzhou, a factory owned by Proctor and Gamble had a labor-contracting arrangement with a LSC known as Bestfriend, in which the workers supplied by Bestfriend were classified as "temporary" labor and received no social insurance (China Labor Watch 2005). The Dongguan Elegant Top Shoes company provided no social insurance to its 5,500–6,000 employees, according to a 2001 CLW report (China Labor Watch 2001).

The evidence on social insurance payment enforcement by enterprises in Zhejiang province, which is dominated by private capital and has both large and small private firms, is instructive. More private capital simply provided a greater source of revenue, even though compliance rates were still comparatively low. According to MOLSS statistics, Zhejiang province has seen the most rapid rise in both revenues and coverage, in absolute terms. The Zhejiang coverage rate (workers covered as a share of total nonfarm workforce) rose from 18.2 percent in 1995 to 33.0 percent in 2005. The total number of covered workers rose from 2.8 million to 8.0 million. Zhejiang local governments collected 4.1 billion yuan in pension revenues in 1995, and 29.0 billion yuan in 2005 (Ministry of Labor 1997; SSB and MOLSS 2006). In 2001, the Zhejiang People's Congress issued a regulation that established a "labor and social security unified annual inspection" system. This measure essentially ordered firms and individual entrepreneurs who did not comply with social insurance payments to be subject to audits and the withholding of business licenses by the local tax and commercial regulatory agencies (Wenzhou Municipal Government 2002). Although such measures apparently had some effect on expanding coverage rates and increasing social insurance revenues, the fact remains that smaller firms fell essentially outside the ambit of the SIA regulations.

The reasons for low coverage rates among private enterprises can thus be divided into structural, political, and cultural. In structural terms, it is simply not worthwhile for SIAs or tax authorities to pursue delinquent firms with so few employees when the returns from doing so are minimal. In political terms, collaboration between local cadres and capitalists to maintain growth and employment means that social insurance coverage is subject to bargaining; a firm with sufficient leverage can threaten to move elsewhere unless it receives favorable treatment on tax and social insurance payments. In cultural terms, the attitudes and beliefs that workers and employers hold toward the ability of local government agencies presents a serious constraint on the ability of SIAs to collect social insurance revenues. Anecdotal evidence suggests that private firms and their employees do not trust local government agencies to fairly administer social insurance funds and, at worst, expect them to divert the funds, as seen in the numerous local pension scandals. This point is explored further in chapter 6.

Welfare regimes in China, as elsewhere, are politically divisive because they introduce a new source of revenue for the state and a new expense for business owners. When welfare programs are based on social insurance—the idea of pooling large amounts of money to finance the costs of health care, pensions, unemployment, and so on—the conflict between business and government can intensify. Yet the fault lines in this conflict do not simply divide employers and government agencies into antagonistic camps.

In China, firms varied significantly in their willingness to comply with the payment of social insurance and in their assertion of control rights over pension administration. Large SOEs wanted to retain their own pension administration, if possible, within their supervising ministry. Such firms and their managers wanted favorable pension arrangements that came with the higher status of their firms in the administrative hierarchy. These SOEs came into sharp conflict with local governments that tried and eventually gained the ability to regulate social insurance collections from these very large, lucrative sources of social insurance revenue. Local SOEs faced an entirely different welfare policy calculus. Local SOEs and their bureaucratic handlers had to consider the market pressures from nonstate firms and the looming debt burdens of local SOEs. Local governments had a direct interest in the resolution of these debt burdens and overstaffing. Local SOEs and local governments collaborated to change the corporate identity and structure of the local firms, including bankruptcies and mergers (some with foreign firms), and used pension reforms to turn over to local governments those workers made jobless by the restructuring. The third category, private firms, including wholly foreign-owned firms, sought to avoid social insurance levies altogether and essentially bargained with local officials over reduced social insurance payments and reduced workforce coverage. Many large-scale export-oriented private and foreign-invested firms avoided social insurance fees by exempting so-called "temporary workers" from coverage.

The conjunction of state enterprise restructuring and the rapid increase in the number of pensioners and pension benefits was no accident. Local SIAs in China fought with large state enterprises over the control of pension funds. At the same time, local SIAs assisted smaller SOEs and their managers by restructuring and using pension funds to compensate workers laid off in the process. In the case of private-sector enterprises, SIAs showed much less interest in enforcing social insurance provisions, except when they were large private enterprises with substantial employment and thus lucrative sources of social insurance revenue. Social insurance in China was and remains primarily an issue of collecting funds from large-scale corporations, including SOEs and private or foreign-invested firms, and redistributing them to local retirees.

The pattern in which China's large state enterprises restructured and abandoned their functions of welfare provision resembles in many respects the transformation of welfare capitalist firms in the United States during the 1920s. The largest U.S. corporations, which had once provided paternalistic programs for housing, health care, and pensions for employees, turned over these functions to state governments by the late 1920s. These same corporations eventually supported New Deal welfare legislation. As Gordon notes of the U.S. corporations that had once engaged in welfare capitalism, "rather than simply dumping their pension and unemployment programs (which some did anyway), most preferred to force competitors, consumers, and taxpayers to pick up the tab" (1991, 176).

As Hu Jintao pushes a domestic policy agenda based largely on the expansion of welfare programs and coverage, the success of this undertaking will depend largely on how and whether CCP policymakers consult business owners in the process. Private-sector employers and small enterprises are likely to support moves toward universal coverage of their workers if they can be persuaded that the wage deductions will provide adequate social insurance. Yet, given the power of large SOEs, whose managers are closely allied with the Beijing officials and policymakers, it is far more likely that the future path of the development of the Chinese welfare state will continue in the direction of expanded provision for the state sector and its employees and retirees.

CHAPTER 6

Public Opinion and Pensions

Social insurance consciousness is very high among the people. They have trust in the social insurance pension system because it's a government program. Maybe they're not clear when they hear the word "social insurance" but once you explain to them that the government and the Communist Party and operate the social insurance pension system, they have trust, because they have high levels of trust in the government and the Party.
URBAN OFFICIAL (INTERVIEW #030705)

I would rather starve to death than participate in social insurance! Officials always steal social insurance funds.
MIGRANT WORKER (INTERVIEW #022105A)

In the previous two chapters, I have dealt with issues of local state accumulation or the extraction of funds used to build the fragmented Chinese pension system; in this chapter, I turn to the question of how the public views pensions. How do the victims of the 1990s mass layoffs in China, who now make up a large share of its pensioners, assess government programs such as pensions? As the quotations demonstrate, official assessments of strong public support for pensions in China and for the government officials who administer pensions can be easily contradicted by comments from Chinese citizens who voice a passionate mistrust of government. Can public mistrust of officials lead to the rejection of public pensions?

Recent studies of labor in China have examined how Chinese workers interpreted and responded to the massive transformation of the world of state socialism and its replacement with the instability and risks of the labor market. Workers frequently protested the injustices and inequities associated with the end of state socialism. In some protests, workers invoked the powerful symbol of Mao Zedong to resist the closure of state enterprises and to point out the loss of their once-high status in the Maoist era (Cai 2005; Lee 2008; Hurst 2009). These studies also stressed that worker responses to the end of state socialism, with its promises of lifetime employment and welfare benefits, invoked cellular, or workplace-specific, contention rather than strategies of horizontal coordination across work units or of classwide mobilization. The cellular mobilization strategies of jobless SOE workers reflected the institutional legacies of workplace solidarity over alternative forms of identity and mobilization. Yet even migrant workers in cities such as Shenzhen also mobilized on the basis of the workplace, albeit with different strategies and goals (Lee 2008).

This response to the end of socialism by urban workers allows us to revisit the concept of historical institutionalism noted in earlier chapters. Historical institutionalists contend that preferences and behavior are not guided by an autonomous logic of rational calculation of costs and benefits but are, instead, heavily influenced by existing, usually long-standing, institutions. Under this view, the attitudes and responses of workers toward pensions and welfare more broadly derive not from income or education levels but from the extent to which a worker experienced employment under work-unit socialism. As would be expected, the defense of work-unit socialism figured prominently in the pension protests of the 1990s. On the other hand, Marc Blecher (2002) has used survey research to show that SOE workers seemed to accept the principles of the market allocation of labor and other goods or to acquiesce in what Blecher labels "market hegemony." Even if market hegemony reigns supreme among Chinese workers, it is not clear how workers would view the provision of government programs to protect them from the risks of labor markets. Based on Karl Polanyi's (1957/2001) central thesis, the commodification of labor in China should be accompanied by demands for state protection from the market. But demands for state protection can take many forms. Some workers might invoke past state promises to resist the dismantling of their welfare benefits, whereas others might use welfare rights to demand inclusion in new or existing welfare programs. Historical institutionalism offers some predictions about how the public, and different groups within society, would be expected to respond. SOE workers should defend the institution of workplace welfare provision and potentially resist the transformation to a social insurance based model with welfare programs handled by local government agencies. Non-SOE workers, or those young enough to have missed the experience of work-unit socialism altogether, should have their preferences about and views on welfare shaped by their experience in new labor market institutions, such as labor laws and social insurance.

Public opinion surveys in China during the 1990s suggest that urban residents supported the status quo of the work unit as the central institution in the provision of welfare. Respondents were firmly opposed to the policy of replacing the provision of welfare by the work-unit by externalizing the costs of public pensions on to society. A 1996 survey of urban views toward welfare in Guangzhou and Shanghai found that 78 percent of the respondents in Shanghai and 82 percent of the respondents in Guangzhou disagreed or strongly disagreed with the statement that "One should not rely upon the work unit for the provision of retirement benefits since the work unit is nothing but a work place" (Lee and Wong 2001, 85). An even higher proportion of respondents (ranging from 90 to 96 percent in both cities) agreed with the statements that "To ensure social stability, the state has an obligation to provide retirement pensions for staff and workers in Guangzhou/Shanghai." Only 45 percent of respondents in Guangzhou and 32 percent of respondents in Shanghai agreed with the statement that "Since retirement pension is a personal matter, everyone should make their own arrangements" (Lee and Wong 2001, 85). Peter Lee and Chack-Kie Wong conclude that urban residents exhibited a "high welfare dependency orientation" (2001, 90).

We could argue, however, that by the 2000s (and perhaps even earlier) Chinese urban workers made demands for welfare protections and pension support not because they possessed a lingering orientation of dependency on the state but because they were in the throes of a highly uncertain labor market. A considerable proportion of the Chinese urban workforce who are now working outside the state sector have undergone either a switch in jobs or a switch in the ownership of the enterprise at which they were employed. These workers are likely to have developed their views of welfare provision less from being informed by work-unit socialism than from their actual experience of having lost jobs or having seen their employment status drastically changed as their firms underwent ownership changes. This cohort of urban workers might have strongly mistrustful views of local officials—whom they have seen benefit from reforms at workers' expense—yet might also view the Chinese state as responsible for providing them with greater compensation in the form of welfare and greater protection from the new labor market forces to which they are now exposed. Their attitudes may be more accurately characterized as reflecting demands for social protections in a market economy, not some nostalgia for or defense of work-unit socialism.

As we have seen in preceding chapters, urban governments and their allies in local state firms collaborated to shed unprofitable SOEs during the 1990s, and in the process they created large pension debts to those laid off in SOE restructuring and to future generations of retirees. The viability of this strategy depended on the use of pensions to satisfy the demands of two crucial sectors of the urban workforce: pensioners (including legal retirees and those given pensions as unemployment compensation from SOE restructuring) and urban workers. In the analysis in the sections that follow, I show that retirees were more likely than current workers to state that they had benefited from pension reforms. Retirees were also more likely than workers to have greater confidence in the future of the ability of the Chinese government to provide pensions. On other issues, such as proposals to increase the retirement age or to pass a social insurance law, the views of retirees and workers coalesced, in strong opposition to retirement age changes and in strong support of a social insurance law.

The data used in this chapter are drawn from the results of the 2004 Beijing Area Study (BAS; conducted in March 2005) and from the content of six focus groups held in March 2005 in four cities. The sampling methods and other background on the survey and focus groups can be found in the appendix of this chapter. In the sections that follow, the 593 respondents in the BAS were categorized as retirees (216), unemployed (99), and working (278). Table 6.1 displays some basic demographic information for these groups. The average age of the retirees in the sample was only 56.3—well below the legal retirement age for men and just above the retirement ages of fifty-five and fifty for white-collar and blue-collar women. Of these retirees, 65.3 percent were women. Retirees also had an average of 10.5 years of education and had significantly lower average household incomes than those who were working. The ninety-nine respondents in the sample who were either unemployed or between jobs had on average 10.1 years of education and lower monthly household incomes than the retirees. Men

TABLE 6.1
Demographic data from Beijing Area Study 2004

	Working (*n*=278)	Retired (*n*=216)	Unemployed (*n*=99)	Total (*n*=593)
Age (years)	43.05 (7.93)	56.33 (5.81)	45.33 (7.12)	48.27 (9.38)
Education (years)	12.51 (2.97)	10.52 (2.92)	10.12 (2.61)	11.39 (3.08)
Household income (yuan/month)	5,244 (8,310)	3,099 (6,249)	2,281 (6,226)	3,968 (7,377)

Notes: Study conducted in March 2005. The mean is reported for each group; values in parentheses are standard deviations. Among the 617 respondents in Beijing Area Study (BAS) 2004, 24 reported their occupational status as "student" or "housework" and were not classified as working, retired, or unemployed.

made up the majority of the working and the unemployed groups in the sample. The test of significance for these data is shown in table 6A.1.[1]

The participants in the focus group study, drawn from manufacturing-sector workers in state and private enterprises, are listed in the table 6A.9.

MAIN PROVIDER OF PENSIONS: STATE, EMPLOYER, AND INDIVIDUAL

One of the crucial questions in the political conflict over pensions is who bears the primary responsibility for the old-age needs of citizens. The mix of occupational, private, and state-financed pensions varies widely across countries, and public opinion surveys also show considerable differences in the level of support for the state as the primary provider of pensions. Yet, even after control variables are introduced for age, income, and other demographics, public opinion varies considerably across countries when it comes to assigning the obligations of the state, the employer, and the individual worker for financing pensions, health care, and other forms of social insurance (Gelissen 2001). Some have noted that each of the three welfare regime types noted by Gosta Esping-Andersen (1990) corresponds to a coherent set of public preferences about welfare policy. For example, F. John Mehrtens (2004) shows that in liberal economic regimes such as those found in the United Kingdom and United States, public opinion toward pensions reflected more emphasis on individual saving, market solutions, and a minimal role for the state. By contrast, in social democratic regimes, such as Sweden, the public expressed preferences for a welfare policy in which the state takes a central role, especially in the financing of pension benefits.

In the BAS, respondents were asked to identify what they felt should be the primary funding source for an individual's pension: state finances, contributions from employers and employees, private contracts between individuals and companies (such as insurance firms), or other. As shown in table 6.2, nearly 62 percent of the BAS respondents said that the state should be the main source of pension benefits, and approximately one-third of respondents stated that contributions from employers and employees should serve as the primary source of pensions. Only 1.4 percent favored commercial insurance as the primary source of old-age income. This roughly two-to-one preference for state-provided over employer-provided pensions among BAS respondents puts them in a group comparable with French and British respondents to the same question in a 2001 Eurobarometer survey, in which

---

[1] All tables numbered 6A can be found in the appendix to this chapter.

TABLE 6.2
Views on responsibility for pensions (%)

Who do you think should be the main provider of pensions?

Mainly provided by the state	Mainly provided by pension contributions from employers and employees	Mainly provided by individuals purchasing commercial insurance	Other	Total (*n*=589)
61.8	33.8	1.4	3.1	100.0

citizens from twenty-one EU member states were surveyed (Janky and Gal 2007, 15).

Table 6A.2 uses a multinomial logistic regression model to analyze variation in the response categories in Table 6.2 based on the variables of age, income, education, gender, and employment category (retired, unemployed, or working). The coefficients presented in table 6A.2 (in which "mainly by the state" is the reference category) highlight a number of significant points. Of greatest interest is the distinction between those who preferred the state and those who preferred employers' and employee contributions to serve as the main source of pensions. The coefficients show that older respondents were much more likely than younger ones to place responsibility on the state for providing pensions, compared with any other categories of responses. Moreover, the unemployed were much more likely than retirees or the employed to place responsibility on the state for providing pensions, compared to employers or individuals. In a separate regression model (not shown in table 6A.2), there was no significant difference in responses between SOE workers and those employed outside of SOEs.[2]

The focus group discussions showed that worker preferences for having the state as the primary source of pensions arose from the belief that the state, as well as employers, had abandoned its obligation to provide pensions and other forms of welfare. In all six focus groups, workers argued that the costs of financing their health care and retirement needs had fallen entirely upon their shoulders. "The trend now is for individuals to pay [for social welfare needs]. The state and the enterprise don't care about you

---

[2] This finding may reflect the coding of workers and their ownership sectors; those who were employed in state enterprises that had undergone ownership transformation into joint stock or other ownership forms were coded as "non-SOE" workers. These "non-SOE" workers and SOE workers are likely to have similar attitudes toward welfare provision based on their having both experienced work in SOEs prior to the SOE reforms.

anymore" (Beijing private enterprises, #3). "These days the best thing is just to rely on oneself" (Foshan private enterprises, #4). "Relying on others isn't realistic" (Foshan private enterprises, #2). Moreover, participants expressed anxieties about how to cover hospital expenses should they or family members be struck by an illness or suffer an accident. Contrary to the stereotype that Chinese citizens retain traditional beliefs regarding children supporting their parents in old age, none of the focus group participants expected to rely on his or her children for financial support. Many participants (among them some who had already retired) pointed out that they could not possibly ask their children, who were struggling with young families of their own, to provide financially for them (Beijing private enterprises, #3). Respondents also uniformly stated that they were concerned about the low-quality housing in which they lived. In a further contrast to a widely held piece of conventional wisdom, focus group participants were not saving their money to finance their future pension needs. Whatever savings they did have were to be directed toward education and medical expenses. In this sense, preferences for making the state the central provider of pensions, as reflected in the BAS results, should be interpreted not as support for the status quo but, rather, as a demand for the state to serve as the main source of welfare provision.

CONFIDENCE IN THE CHINESE PENSION SYSTEM

Table 6.3 shows that respondents possessed a high degree of confidence in the future of the Chinese pension system. A total of 81.4 percent of BAS respondents stated that they were very confident or somewhat confident in the future of the pension system, whereas 18.6 percent of the respondents reported that they were not very or not at all confident. This is an important finding because we might expect Beijing respondents to possess a greater degree of skepticism regarding pensions—after all, public protests that garnered such attention in the early 2000s arose over the inability of the local state agencies and SOEs to distribute pension benefits. With the dismantling of many SOEs, millions of pensioners were vulnerable to having their pension benefits suspended. Yet, in the BAS at least, respondents appeared to have maintained a high level of confidence in the future of the Chinese state to distribute pensions.

The ordered probit regression model in table 6A.3 shows that, after we control for age, education, income, and gender, retirees were more likely than those still active in the labor market (i.e., the unemployed or workers) to express confidence in the future of the Chinese pension system. This

TABLE 6.3
Confidence in the future of pensions

How confident are you in the future of the social insurance pensions system?

Very confident	Somewhat confident	Not too confident	Not at all confident	Total (n=570)
12.50 (%)	68.90 (%)	16.80 (%)	1.80 (%)	100.0 (%)

pattern of retirees having greater levels of confidence in the pension system than current workers could be reinforced by the generally positive conditions reported in terms of pension coverage and access to pension benefits. For example, of the 278 respondents who said they were currently employed, only 28 (approximately 10 percent) said they did not have pension coverage. Among the unemployed, the coverage rate was much lower, with 39 out of 99 (or approximately 40 percent) lacking pension coverage. Among the 217 retirees, 143 reported that they received social insurance pensions. For the seventy-three retirees who reported lacking social insurance pension coverage, a very large share would have had access to pensions by virtue of having worked as public officials. At least sixty-seven of the retirees had been employed in government, party, and other public-sector workplaces that would have made them eligible for civil service pensions rather than social insurance pensions. Of the 143 retirees who reported receiving social insurance pensions, only 4 said that they had experienced a delay in receiving pensions. Only twenty-seven retirees reported that they frequently or sometimes worried about delays in receiving their pensions. The relatively high levels of confidence among the survey respondents who were retired probably reflects their generally positive experiences with social insurance pensions or their employment status as civil servants who received their pensions directly from government budgets.

The focus group discussions showed that this confidence in the future of Chinese pensions appeared to be based on assessments that pensions were too important for the government to neglect. A Beijing worker reasoned that, "If you can't get a pension, the state will be in chaos. This affects a large number of people, and if they don't get pensions, how will the state not be in chaos?" (Beijing private enterprises, #1). A forty-five-year-old Nanjing private enterprise worker also argued that pensions were much too important for social stability for the government not to take measures to see that pensioners received their benefits, whatever costs this entailed (Nanjing private enterprises, #4). Some focus group participants did express a degree of doubt as to how much of their current contributions they would see when they reached retirement age. "I pay the money [into social insurance pensions], but I don't know whether it will have any value [in the future]" (Foshan private enterprises, #4). Pension policy was always changing, some noted, and this led to uncertainty (Foshan private enterprises, #5 and #2).

TRUST IN THE ADMINISTRATIVE ABILITIES OF THE GOVERNMENT

One of the crucial links between public opinion and the ability of local government agencies to collect social insurance fees from employers and workers is the extent to which citizens trust these agencies. As seen in chapter 5, enterprise managers often evaded pension contributions out of concern that the agencies administering them were going to spend them for other purposes. One of the BAS questions attempted to measure the degree of trust that respondents held toward local government agencies, the central government, and commercial insurance companies. After explaining to respondents that central and local government agencies were in charge of collecting, managing, and distributing social insurance pension funds and that commercial insurance companies handled commercial pension funds, survey-takers then asked respondents to rate their degree of trust in central government agencies, local government agencies, and commercial insurance companies.

Table 6.4 shows that Beijing respondents placed substantial levels of trust in central and local governments, but they felt just the opposite regarding commercial insurance companies. A strong majority of respondents (84.5 percent) said that they somewhat trusted or very much trusted the central government to administer pensions, whereas a lower proportion (75.2 percent) placed some or a high level of trust in local governments to administer pensions. Given the conventional wisdom that the public regards local governments as the source of governance problems but has a greater degree of trust in the central government, we might have expected a greater gap in levels of trust between the two. In Beijing, which has seen its share of corruption scandals among local officialdom, over three-fourths of BAS respondents nonetheless appeared willing to trust the local government to handle pensions. One plausible explanation for the relatively high levels of trust expressed in the central and local governments is the fact that the wording of this question very likely cued respondents to draw a distinction between government agencies at both levels (central and local) and commercial insurance firms. As reported in table 6.4, respondents expressed very low levels of trust in commercial insurance firms, with

TABLE 6.4
Trust in government versus trust in commercial insurers

Central government offices and local government offices are the agencies responsible for handling the social insurance pension of the state's social security system; commercial insurance companies are the entities that manage commercial pension insurance. We would like to know your level of trust in the following entities: Do you very much mistrust, trust not very much, somewhat trust, or trust very much?

Agency	Very much mistrust (%)	Trust not very much (%)	Neutral (%)	Trust somewhat (%)	Trust very much (%)
Local government (n=593)	1.3	12.8	10.6	62.4	12.8
Central government (n=593)	1.7	6.6	7.3	59.7	24.8
Commercial insurance firms (n=590)	7.1	36.9	31.9	22.5	1.5

Note: After the text of the question was stated, each respondent was read the name of the entity and then was read the list of responses (including "neutral") for each entity.

only 24 percent stating that they very much trusted or somewhat trusted the commercial insurance companies to administer pensions. A total of 44 percent of respondents expressed mistrust or very little trust in commercial insurance companies.

The regression results from table 6A.4 show that there was no significant difference in levels of trust among retirees and workers regarding commercial insurance firms or the central government. Commercial insurance companies were viewed as untrustworthy by both groups, and the central government was regarded as trustworthy by both groups.[3] Table 6A.4 also shows that BAS respondents who were retirees were more likely than workers to express lower levels of trust in local governments. The relatively lower levels of trust in local government among retirees compared to workers and the unemployed could reflect their relatively more positive assessment of the central government or their consideration of past cases of corruption among Beijing municipal officials (if that were the case, workers should have also expressed this concern, however).

---

[3] The only significant variable in the model for trust in the commercial insurance companies was gender—men were more likely to express higher levels of trust in commercial insurance for retirement needs than were women.

The prediction posed at the outset of this chapter—that workers who experienced employment under the institution of work-unit socialism would have significantly different views of welfare than those who did not—finds partial confirmation in these results. Older workers were more likely than younger workers to say that the state should be the main provider of pensions, and retirees expressed greater levels of confidence in the future of China's pension system. On the question of trust in administering pensions, both older and younger BAS respondents far preferred government agencies to commercial entities. In this instance, public attitudes reflect the status quo—public pension funds will remain by far the dominant vehicle for pension savings in China, despite the growth of supplemental pensions offered by insurance companies and banks. Given the fairly deep support for the state as the main provider of pensions in China, the discussion now turns to the issue of pension rights. Do urban residents link pensions to citizenship, or do they continue to view them as a benefit tied to their place of employment? How does the urban public view the expansion of pension rights to migrant workers and peasants?

RIGHTS TO PENSIONS

Tables 6.5 and 6.6 show several responses regarding legal rights to pensions. The BAS found strong support for universal pension coverage. Respondents were nearly unanimously in agreement (98.2 percent) with the statement that Chinese citizens should receive pensions as a basic right.

TABLE 6.5
Views on pension rights

	Strongly agree (%)	Agree (%)	Disagree (%)	Strongly disagree (%)
Receiving pensions is a basic right of all citizens. (*n*=586)	59.0	39.2	1.5	0.0
China is not at the level of prosperity for all citizens to receive pensions. (*n*=586)	27.3	52.2	18.4	2.0
If the government passes a social insurance law or pension law, my pension would be guaranteed. (*n*=586)	47.2	48.5	1.8	0.2

Note: "Don't know" responses not included.

TABLE 6.6
Views on pensions for farmers and migrant workers

In terms of receiving pension benefits, do you think the following groups should receive, relative to urban residents, the same benefits, greater benefits, or less benefits?

Group	More (%)	Same (%)	Less (%)
Farmers (n = 563)	11.2	60.6	28.2
Migrant workers (n = 561)	8.4	66.3	25.3

Note: Respondents could also choose the categories "should not receive [pensions]" and "do not know."

Moreover, in response to a statement that the passage of a social insurance or pension law would guarantee pension benefits, a near-unanimous 95.7 percent of respondents agreed. Respondents were also asked to consider their stance on the claim that China was not prosperous enough to provide pensions to all citizens. (In fact, this survey item appeared immediately before the item in which respondents were asked to consider if pensions were a basic right.) As reported in table 6.5, 79.5 percent of respondents agreed or strongly agreed that China was not yet prosperous enough to provide pensions to all of its citizens.

While the BAS respondents, when cued by survey items, appeared to support the idea of pensions as a basic right that should be enshrined in law, it is significant that focus group participants never raised the issue of rights to pensions or the need for a pension law in any substantive way. Focus group participants mentioned law (as an abstract concept) three times in the context of regulating the labor and welfare practices of private enterprises, but never explicitly connected pension rights as being better ensured by legal protections. This omission of any direct reference to legal protections for pensions and other forms of welfare is curious, given that in interviews with urban residents conducted for this study informants stressed how important it was to have laws to protect rights. A Beijing informant, for example, explained as follows:

Social insurance is a complicated matter. Without a law, then officials can do this and that, pay this and that, delay paying this and that, and generally cause a lot of trouble. It really won't do to not have a law. Without a law, you can't take anyone to court if you have trouble getting your pension. We should be able to go to court and sue—that's the best way to run a social insurance system. (Interview #120904)

Another urban informant stated, "China is now the way America was in the 1920s and 1930s, just starting a social security system. But the big difference is that the American government passed a law; here in China we need a social insurance law too, but I really doubt we will get one, because of the Chinese Communist Party. They like to steal people's money too much" (Interview #120604).

Regardless of whether BAS respondents thought in terms of rights, they and focus group participants elicited broad support for the practical question of providing pensions to rural residents. BAS respondents were asked whether farmers and migrant laborers should receive pension benefits at the same levels as urban residents, pension benefits at higher or lower levels than urban residents, or no pensions at all. Table 6.6 shows that BAS respondents were unanimous in support of at least some pensions for farmers (*nongmin*) and migrant workers (*wailai mingong*). Three-fifths of BAS respondents (60.6 percent) said that farmers should receive the same level of pension benefits as urban residents. A slightly larger proportion (66.3 percent) also said that migrant workers should receive the same level of pension benefits as urban residents.

The results of the ordered probit regression in table 6A.5 show that age and education were significant variables in increasing the probability that a respondent stated that migrants and farmers should receive less in pension benefits. Retirees, when compared to workers and unemployed, were more likely to support higher levels of pensions for farmers and migrants.

Focus group discussions also revealed a broad level of support for the rights to the same level of pension benefits for peasants and migrant workers. Focus group participants generally felt that, if pensions were based on an individual's contributions to the nation and society, then migrant workers and peasants deserved equal treatment with urban workers (Changchun state enterprises, #2, #7, and #8). The general sentiment was that, having literally built so much of urban China, migrant workers were deserving of some form of government pension and medical benefits. Participants in the Nanjing focus groups noted with sadness that peasants had no medical insurance and that, if they suffered a serious illness, they could only "wait to die" (Nanjing state enterprises, #2 and #7; Nanjing private enterprises, #3). This point of consensus among focus groups was consistent with the Beijing survey results that reflected strong support for universal pension coverage.

Focus group discussions generally also expressed a high degree of sympathy for migrant workers and a feeling that the government owed migrants something in retirement for all their bitterly hard work. The consensus view among focus group participants was that migrant workers should have social insurance coverage, including for pensions (Foshan private enterprises, #7 and #2; Nanjing state enterprises, #3 and #5). Some participants argued that migrant workers were willing to receive a few hundred extra yuan in pay from their employers in lieu of having their pay deducted for social insurance (Foshan private enterprises, #3). In this respect, migrant workers had low levels of consciousness (*yishi*) regarding social insurance (Foshan private enterprises, #5).

Perhaps the strongest opinions elicited during the focus group discussions related to the issue of inequality in pension coverage and benefits. In all six focus groups, at least one participant brought up the fact that Chinese officials receive far higher benefits than do ordinary urban workers. Most often a focus group participant would raise the issue of official corruption as a sort of reference point when discussing their current livelihood and thoughts concerning retirement. Some participants stridently objected to the fact that officials enjoyed high salaries, low expenses (because their health care and housing were virtually free), and generous retirement benefits courtesy of the state budget. "What qualifications do they have to get so much money?" asked one participant (Beijing state enterprises, #1). A forty-two-year-old Nanjing factor worker complained that "officials can still be working at age 80 and not necessarily be thinking about retiring—it's really unfair. We workers at the bottom levels don't have any sense of security" (Nanjing state enterprises, #4).[4] Focus group participants also noted that family members of retired cadres received free medical care and other perks. A production worker at a private enterprise in Nanjing drew a contrast between how reforms had affected officials and workers: "If I were in a government agency, I would definitely say that the reforms were good. Why? Because I'm fat and rich, right? But [as a worker] I have no benefits, and no way of making gains. I'm a worker, we're all front-line workers, the most bitter, most tired, most busy, and most poor" (Nanjing private enterprises, #6).

Moreover, focus group participants felt that workers now faced all the risks of the labor market and had to pay to insure against such risks, whereas officials who faced no risks were eligible for pension benefits that would be two to three times greater and also enjoyed free medical care for whatever illnesses they or their families encountered. Last but not least, officials stood little chance of losing their jobs.

The BAS results as well as the content of the focus group discussions revealed a strong sense of pension rights based less on the idea that they were

---

[4] In fact, the Chinese government and the CCP have explicit rules about the retirement age for officials, generally at ages sixty to sixty-eight. Thus, this focus group participant was not technically accurate in claiming that cadres could work to age eighty.

an employment benefit to be provided by an employer and more on the notion of citizenship and contribution to the nation. By introducing legislation such as the draft SIL, which received widespread public comment in January 2009 prior to its likely passage later that year, the PRC government took a popular step to align policy with preferences elicited by the Chinese public. Yet, in expanding its pension and health-care insurance system, the Chinese government will also face, as have numerous other governments, the prospect of having to increase the retirement age to cope with the costs of financing retirement benefits for a growing share of the population that will look to the state as the main source of its old-age income. Such a proposal is likely to encounter fierce opposition in China, as it has elsewhere when retirement age increases have been proposed. As the discussion that follows suggests, even proposed changes to the gender-specific retirement ages, in which women retire earlier than men, have little support among women.

RAISING THE RETIREMENT AGES

BAS respondents voiced strong opposition to the proposal to raise current retirement ages. The relatively early retirement ages in China (fifty for women on production lines, fifty-five for women in staff positions, and sixty for men) were, as noted in previous chapters, established in 1951. Table 6.7 shows that a substantial majority of respondents, or 72.8 percent, disagreed or disagreed strongly with the statement that the government should gradually increase the retirement age.

The regression results reported in table 6A.6 show that age was the only variable that was significant in increasing the likelihood of disagreeing with the statement. (Even then, the coefficient was above the threshold of $p = .05$.) This finding is not surprising because older respondents at or near retirement age should be more steadfast in their disagreement (i.e., more likely to strongly disagree) with the idea of raising the retirement age.

TABLE 6.7
Views on raising the current retirement age

The government should gradually raise the currently stipulated retirement age.

Strongly agree	Agree	Disagree	Strongly disagree	Total ($n = 581$)
8.3%	18.9%	50.8%	22.0%	100.0%

There was no significant difference in how retirees versus workers and the unemployed responded to the statement. With across the board opposition to raising retirement ages, it is not surprising that none of these demographic or other variables can explain variation in responses to this question. But the model whose results are shown in table 6A.6 lacks statistical significance, and we should treat the coefficients with caution, if not reject the results altogether.

Equalizing the retirement age, we might suppose, would receive support from women who could then stay in the job market longer. Instead, as shown in table 6.8, a majority of respondents (approximately two-thirds) disagreed or strongly disagreed with the claim that the retirement ages between men and women should be equalized. The regression model in table 6A.7, which is statistically significant, shows that gender was not a factor in changing the odds of choosing a response category. In other words, women were no more likely than men to agree with the statement proposing to make retirement ages equal. In addition, there was no significant difference in responses between retirees and workers and the unemployed. The only variable that seemed to be associated with a respondent's being more likely to disagree with the statement was years of education, a finding that is difficult to explain since more years of education might be expected to be associated with support for equal treatment in retirement ages for women and men.

Given the highly uncertain employment opportunities for women in their fifties, longer participation in the labor market was apparently not as important as receiving access to pension benefits five years before men are eligible (and, for women production workers, ten years before men are eligible). Interviews and focus group discussions revealed that women at or near retirement age were strongly opposed to even a gradual extension of their retirement age designed to equalize their years of workforce participation with men. They argued that receiving a pension starting at age fifty or fifty-five—or even earlier, in the case of jobs with hazardous working conditions—was preferable to participation in a labor market in which

TABLE 6.8
Views on equalizing retirement ages for men and women

The legal retirement age for men and women should be the same.

Strongly agree	Agree	Disagree	Strongly disagree	Total (*n* = 602)
11.0%	22.6%	56.5%	10.0%	100.0%

they encountered consistent age and sex discrimination (Beijing private enterprises, #6, #8, and #4).

AWARENESS OF PENSION REFORMS

As many politicians in Europe and North America have discovered, pension retrenchments are highly controversial because, regardless of their complexity, they threaten to alter a very popular social program. Pension reforms also break an implicit promise by the state to society to guarantee specific cash benefits funded by the state. Paul Pierson and others have noted that pension reform advocates can circumvent public opposition to unpopular measures by hiding the costs of reform in complicated provisions in reform legislation (Pierson 1994; Madrid 2003). Although this strategy means that reformers cannot arbitrarily cut benefits to current beneficiaries or simply raise retirement ages, it does mean that strategies such as calculating benefits differently or phasing in gradual retirement age increases can hide the costs. Would-be opponents might fail to mobilize against such reforms because the provisions are simply too difficult for the public to grasp.

In China, pension reforms were reported in the media throughout the 1990s and 2000s, and enterprise labor unions and personnel departments issued numerous briefings to employees on the specifics of the new pension system. One BAS question asked respondents whether they knew that pension reforms had taken place in China—a substantial portion of the respondents were not aware of these reforms. As presented in table 6.9, survey respondents were split nearly evenly between those who said that they knew of pension reforms and those who said that they did not. The unemployed had the lowest levels of awareness of the pension reforms, with only one-third saying that they knew about them. Among workers and retirees, only just over half said that they knew about the pension reforms.

This lack of awareness that the Chinese government was undertaking pension reforms is an important finding.[5] Changes to pensions are a hotly contested issue across the globe, and public reaction acts as a major political constraint on government efforts to retrench or reform pensions. If a substantial portion of the urban public in China were unaware of the very

---

[5] Stockmann (2009) uses the same BAS data set to show that education and self-reported attentiveness to the issue of pensions were the best predictors of respondents' reporting that they were aware of pension reforms.

TABLE 6.9
Awareness of pension reforms by groups of respondents

Did you know that China has carried out social insurance pension reforms?

	Group			
	Working	Retired	Unemployed	Total (*n* = 593)
Know (%)	54.7	52.3	33.3	50.3
Don't know (%)	45.0	47.7	66.7	49.6

existence of pension reforms, then pension reform advocates in the government, in addition to being unaccountable to the public, faced much weaker political constraints on pension reforms. But, as noted in previous chapters, the urban governments that initiated pension reforms did so largely in conjunction with SOE reforms. If the BAS had included a question asking whether respondents knew about the SOE reforms, a large majority would probably have stated that that they did know. Still, the fact that a considerable portion of the BAS respondents said that they did not know about the pension reforms, combined with the high levels of confidence and trust that BAS respondents put toward the Chinese government to administer pensions, suggests failings in one of the fundamental objectives of the reforms—the promotion of a greater role for individuals' taking responsibility for saving for retirement.

Table 6.10 shows how BAS respondents said that they fared under the pension reforms for the 297 respondents who claimed to know about the reforms (and who were willing to answer this question). A majority of those who were aware of the pension reforms either put their gains and losses as being equal (49.0 percent) or could not say how they had fared (16.9 percent).

Table 6.11 shows in cross-tabulation form the results for how retirees, workers, and the unemployed thought they fared under the reforms. Two important findings are apparent from this table. First, those who said they lost more than gained from pension reforms (n=48) were about equally distributed across the unemployed, retired, and workers. In other words, opponents of reform were not concentrated in any of the occupational groups.[6]

---

[6] When the full sample was analyzed (although it was a questionable step to include respondents who said that they did not know about pension reforms), those who said that their losses exceeded their gains were also roughly equally distributed in the three occupational categories.

TABLE 6.10
Perceived gains and losses from pension reforms

With pension reforms, do you think your gains exceed losses, gains and losses are the same, or losses exceed gains?

Gains exceed losses	Gains and losses are the same	Losses exceed gains	Don't know	Total (n = 297)
17.9%	49.0%	16.2%	16.9%	100.0%

The second important finding is that, among the retirees, a majority (51.8 percent) said their gains and losses were about equal, whereas 28.1 percent said that they had gained more than they lost. Only 13.2 percent of retirees said that they had lost more than they gained from pension reforms.

Table 6A.8 shows the results of a multinomial regression designed to test whether being retired made any difference in how respondents answered this question. The model introduces controls for variables such as income, education, gender, and age. As the analysis shows, after these control variables are held equal, being in the labor market (as either a current worker or as unemployed) significantly raised the probability of respondents' stating that they had lost from the pension reforms compared to stating either that they had gained or felt neutral. In other words, retirees were far more likely than workers and unemployed to have stated that they gained from the pension reforms rather than stating they had lost.

The focus group discussions revealed several patterns that help explain the level of information and perception of how the reforms affected individuals. Focus group participants on occasion voiced concerns that they had suffered under the pension reforms. But most, consistent with the survey results, found it difficult to pinpoint specific gains or losses from the reforms. Participants in virtually all focus groups, when asked about how familiar they were with the specifics of the pension regulations, admitted that they were not clear about the complicated provisions by which pension benefits were calculated. Nor did they understand clearly that deductions were taken from their wages to pay for pension and other forms of social insurance.

The focus group discussions suggest that we should distinguish between the inability of urbanites to assess their gains and losses from the pension reforms and the assessment of how adequate they thought pension benefits would be when they retired. On this count, focus group participants uniformly and strongly agreed that retirement would bring a substantial

TABLE 6.11
Cross-tabulation of perceived gains and losses from pension reforms by group of respondents

With pension reforms, do you think your gains exceed losses, gains and losses are the same, or losses exceed gains?

| | | Group | | | Total |
		Working	Retired	Unemployed	
Gains exceed losses	*n*	21	32	0	53
	%	13.9	28.1	0.0	17.8
Gains and losses	*n*	75	59	12	146
are the same	%	49.7	51.8	37.5	49.2
Losses exceed gains	*n*	19	15	14	48
	%	12.6	13.2	43.8	16.2
Don't know	*n*	36	8	6	50
	%	23.8	7.0	18.8	16.8
Total	*n*	151	114	32	297

Notes: $\chi^2 = 42.6$; significance < 0.000. $\Phi = 0.379$; significance < 0.000

decline in their livelihood. One participant in the Nanjing focus group of state enterprise workers stated that "once you retire, your living standards definitely decline" (Nanjing state enterprises, #8). Others also felt that they would at best receive a pension providing them with barely enough to live on and that they would lack any prospects of obtaining a postretirement job capable of supplementing their income (Nanjing state enterprises, #5 and #7; Changchun state enterprises, #2 and #1). Some of the focus group participants were recently retired workers in their early fifties, who had their own as well as family members' medical costs to support. One fifty-two-year-old plastics factory worker (Changchun state enterprises, #2) estimated her monthly expenses at 500–600 yuan could barely be met with her pension and that, if she needed medicine or medical care, the money would have to come from elsewhere.

Urban workers in China expect a great deal more from the state than they are now being given in terms of social protections. These attitudes are in part a legacy of state socialism, but the findings from the BAS and from the focus groups show that demands on the Chinese state to provide pensions and other social welfare measures stem much more from their experience of life in a highly competitive and highly uncertain labor market. Costs once borne by work units are now the responsibility of the individual worker. Not surprisingly, urban workers want the state to provide a greater assurance that the risks they face can be cushioned in some way by payments from the government and from their employers. Those nearing retirement, who suffered the most under the pension reforms, have serious misgivings and feel a sense of inequity at the privileges enjoyed by retired government officials. Workers who are near retirement also anticipate suffering lower living standards.

Somewhat paradoxically, the expectation among urban workers that the state can and should provide a broader safety net undermines the policy goals of the government. The point of pension reforms in China was to create alternative, market-based sources of welfare supply, especially for pensions. Public resistance to the state policy to diversify the sources of pension financing is reflected in the exasperated tones in which a highly placed MOLSS official whom I interviewed in 2002 spoke. "We Chinese must start thinking about pensions in a different way," he observed, "If you don't have enough income after you retire, then you should first scold yourself, then scold your boss, and lastly scold Jiang Zemin" (Interview #062802B). Instead, he noted, Chinese citizens were still and would probably continue to blame the government—to "scold Jiang Zemin"—for having inadequate savings for retirement.

It is important to stress that these high expectations that the state should provide pensions are not unique to China and that, in fact, this sentiment may be stronger in less-developed welfare states than in mature ones. As John Gelissen (2001) finds in a study of attitudes toward pensions among EU countries, the highest levels of support for public pensions and the weakest levels of support for nonstate sources of pensions were found in countries with the least-developed welfare systems. In Spain, Portugal, and Greece, where old-age income support came largely from familial and community sources and public expenditures on pensions were relatively low, respondents placed far greater weight on the role of the state in providing pensions than did respondents in the advanced welfare states of Sweden, Germany, and France (Gelissen 2001, 500–501). A question posed in a 2001 Eurobarometer survey asked respondents to identify what they felt should be the main source of pensions: the state or public pensions, occupational pension funds (i.e., employer and employee contributions), or private channels such as insurance companies. This survey found that 57 percent of respondents favored public pensions as the main source of pensions, with 7 percent choosing private channels (Janky and Gal 2007, 5). As we have seen, the BAS included the same question, and the results were not dramatically at variance with the respondents in the Eurobarometer survey. As noted in table 6.2, nearly 62 percent of the BAS respondents said the state should be the primary provider of pensions, whereas 33.8 percent indicated that employers and employee contributions should form the main source of pension provision. Further research on public opinion about pensions, involving migrant laborers and rural residents, would help reveal the extent to which the views among urban residents are held more broadly by Chinese citizens.[7] Moreover, survey questions that ask respondents to compare specific welfare policies, such as pensions, health care, unemployment insurance, and others, could help identify which groups tend to attach greater priority to certain policies over others. Findings from postsocialist transition countries suggest that pensions have broad support—and are thus more difficult for governments to change—compared with unemployment and social assistance programs (Lipsmeyer 2002).

Chinese policymakers are relatively well-insulated from organized social forces that could apply the sorts of interest group pressures that exist in pluralist political systems, but they appear to be well aware of public reaction as a potential constraint on policy choice. The strongly held views about retirement ages and pension rights discussed in this chapter suggest that the Chinese government had to tread cautiously in what might seem reasonable reforms to public pensions. Chapter 2 shows in part how Chinese policymakers eventually reined in what was considered sound policy— modest increases in the retirement age, the inclusion of civil servants in pension reforms, and so on. (By stark contrast, the Cuban government in January 2009 raised the Cuban retirement ages for men and women by five years. It did so after reportedly holding town hall meetings at which 99.1 percent of the three million citizens in attendance supported the increase in retirement ages [Weissert 2009].) But the main constraint on the ability of the center to make policy comes less from the public and more from the urban governments that proved so decisive in the making of the highly fragmented Chinese pension system. This fragmentation has created a widely disparate pension system in terms of benefits and eligibility. More broadly, pension fragmentation has locked-in the already uneven gains and losses from economic growth in China. We now turn to this relationship between pensions and uneven growth.

---

[7] The China Urban Labor Survey, conducted in late 2001, sampled over 8,109 adults in five cities on their labor market status and social insurance coverage. Here, again, the sample was limited to those with urban residence permits. Regarding social insurance, the survey found that only 56 percent of respondents had health insurance coverage. This figure ranged widely from a 87.4 percent coverage in Shanghai to 39.1 percent coverage in Shenyang, as of late 2001 (Giles, Park, and Cai 2006).

APPENDIX TO CHAPTER 6

Surveys and Supplementary Tables

THE SURVEYS

The BAS has been conducted on an annual basis by the Research Center for Contemporary China since 1995; the 2004 BAS was conducted in spring 2005. The BAS includes a standard list of questions related to Beijing residents' assessment of Chinese reform policies, as well as demographic data such as individual and family income and expenditures. The BAS includes a special section each year of several questions related to a current issue. The 2004 BAS included special sections on media consumption, perceptions of foreign countries and their citizens, and pension reforms. The BAS target group is the registered urban population of residents eighteen to sixty-five years old, randomly drawn from fifty communities (*shequ, juweihui*) in eight urban districts. The BAS uses the probabilities proportional to size (PPS) sampling method. For the 2004 BAS, 1,099 individuals were contacted and 618 surveys were completed—a response rate of 56.1 percent.

The second survey was done by Horizon Research, a public opinion and marketing research firm based in Beijing, which was commissioned to carry out a series of focus groups in different cities in spring 2005. The purpose of the focus groups was to collect public opinion and attitudes in a more open-ended fashion than is possible within the constraints of a social survey questionnaire. The six focus groups were carried out in March 2005 with six groups of manufacturing-sector employees—state enterprise workers in Beijing, Nanjing, and Changchun and workers employed in firms other than state enterprises in Beijing, Nanjing, and Foshan. Focus groups consisted of eight individuals recruited from different firms through-out each city (see table 6A.9). The focus group composition was designed to detect differences in how workers from state- and privately owned manufacturing firms viewed pensions and social security. The geographic selections were made on the assumption that the attitudes of workers in cities such as Changchun, which has served as a base for state industry, and Foshan, home of many foreign joint venture and private firms, would pro-vide evidence to explore the hypothesis that workplace experience exerts a heavy influence on attitudes toward pensions and the role of the govern-ment in financing them. The Beijing and Nanjing focus groups included separately convened sessions of both state and nonstate enterprise workers. Chinese moderators employed by Horizon led the focus group discussions, which lasted from 90 to 120 minutes. The sessions were recorded on audio and video (participants were unaware of this), and a transcriber later pro-duced a full text of the remarks made in the focus groups. The moderators of the focus groups had copies of the Beijing pension survey and were in-structed to lead participants in a discussion of some of the questions in the survey (though without structuring the discussion to proceed as a survey response).

SUPPLEMENTARY TABLES

The remaining tables in this appendix correspond to the survey results re-ported and discussed in the chapter. Tables 6A.2–6A.8 contain the results of multivariate regression models that seek to control for factors such as age, gender, income, and education, to test to what extent being in the retired group is associated with a particular response category in the survey ques-tions. Table 6A.1 confirms, using multinomial regression, that the retirees were older, less educated, and more likely to be women than men than were the workers. It also demonstrates that (after we control for income, educa-tion, and age) the unemployed, compared to workers, were more likely to be women than men.

The variables used in the appendix tables are defined as follows:

Income: monthly household income (yuan)
Age: years
Education: years
"Men": dummy variable, where 1=man, 0=woman
"Retirees": dummy variable, where 1=retired, 0=unemployed/laid-off or
    working
"Unemployed": dummy variable, where 1=unemployed/laid-off, 0=retired
    or working

TABLE 6A.1
Demographic difference among workers, retirees, and unemployed: Test of significance

Variables	Retired			Unemployed		
	β	Significance	exp(β)	β	Significance	exp(β)
Intercept	−13.967 (1.567)	0.000		2.128 (1.108)	0.055	
Age	0.338 (.030)	0.000	1.401	0.013 (0.018)	0.473	1.013
Education	−0.160 (0.052)	0.002	0.852	−0.271 (0.052)	0	0.763
Income	0.000 (0.000)	0.233	1	0.000 (0.000)	0.043	1
Men	−2.55 (0.322)	0.000	0.078	−0.501 (0.274)	0.067	0.606

−2 log likelihood = 711.4
χ^2 = 490.8; significance < 0.000
Nagelkerke R^2 = .647

Notes: See table 6.1. Multinomial logistic regression results, in which the reference category is "workers." Values in parentheses are standard errors. Values in boldface are significant coefficients ($p < 0.05$).

TABLE 6A.2
Views on responsibility for pensions

Who do you think should be the main provider of pensions?

Variables	Mainly by contributions from employers and employees			Mainly by individuals purchasing commercial insurance		
	β	Significance	exp(β)	β	Significance	exp(β)
Intercept	−0.239 (0.896)	0.790		1.997 (3.151)	0.526	
Age	−0.025 (0.013)	0.061	0.976	−0.132 (0.044)	0.003	0.876
Income	0.000 (0.000)	0.829	1	0.000 (0.000)	0.145	1
Education	0.010 (0.032)	0.761	1.01	0.042 (0.141)	0.765	1.043
Retirees	0.036 (0.280)	0.898	1.037	2.274 (1.262)	0.072	9.718
Unemployed	−0.759 (0.286)	0.008	0.468	0.591 (0.972)	0.543	1.806
Men	0.159 (0.198)	0.423	1.172	1.949 (1.134)	0.086	7.024

−2 log likelihood = 934.9
χ^2 = 34.7; significance < 0.010
Nagelkerke R^2 = 0.071

Notes: See table 6.2. Multinomial logistic regression results, in which the reference category is those who said pensions should be provided "mainly by the state." Response category "other" is not shown. Values in parentheses are standard errors. Values in boldface are significant coefficients ($p < 0.05$). Response categories were coded: 1 = mainly by the state; 2 = mainly by contributions from employers and employees; 3 = mainly by individuals purchasing commercial insurance.

TABLE 6A.3
Confidence in the future of pensions

Variables	β	Significance
Age	−0.004 (0.007)	0.599
Education	0.002 (0.017)	0.927
Income	0.000 (0.000)	0.841
Men	−0.112 (0.107)	0.297
Retirees	**−0.355** (0.146)	0.015

−2 log likelihood=981.5
χ^2=14.2
significance=0.014

Notes: See table 6.3. Ordered probit regression results. Values in parentheses are standard errors. Values in boldface are significant coefficients ($p < 0.05$). Response categories were coded: 1=very confident; 2=not very confident; 3=not too confident; 4=not at all confident.

TABLE 6A.4
Trust in government agencies and commercial insurers

Variables	Local government β	Significance	Central government β	Significance	Commercial insurance β	Significance
Age	**0.021** (0.007)	0.001	0.009 (0.007)	0.190	−0.004 (0.006)	0.560
Education	0.023 (0.016)	0.166	−0.008 (0.016)	0.622	0.022 (0.016)	0.151
Income	0.000 (0.000)	0.849	0.000 (0.000)	0.897	0.000 (0.000)	0.520
Men	−0.103 (0.101)	0.305	0.022 (0.101)	0.829	**−0.249** (0.096)	0.010
Unemployed	−0.106 (0.137)	0.439	−0.176 (0.137)	0.199	−0.137 (0.131)	0.292
Retirees	**−0.292** (0.144)	0.043	−0.129 (0.144)	0.371	−0.037 (0.137)	0.790

−2 log likelihood=1,297.7   −2 log likelihood=1,276.0   −2 log likelihood=1,531.:
χ^2=12.0 χ^2=3.7 χ^2=12.2
significance=0.061   significance=0.719   significance=0.057

Notes: See table 6.4. Ordered probit regression results shown for each category. Values in parentheses are standar errors. Values in boldface are significant coefficients ($p < 0.05$). Response categories coded: 1=very much mistrus 2=trust not very much; 3=neutral; 4=trust somewhat; 5=trust very much.

TABLE 6A.5
Pension rights for farmers and migrants

Variables	Migrants		Farmers	
	β	Significance	β	Significance
Age	**0.019** (0.007)	0.008	**0.026** (0.007)	0.000
Education	**0.044** (0.017)	0.011	**0.046** (0.017)	0.007
Income	0.000 (0.000)	0.862	0.000 (0.000)	0.653
Men	0.155 (0.109)	0.157	−0.095 (0.106)	0.371
Retirees	**−0.300** (0.147)	0.041	−0.272 (0.142)	0.056
	−2 log likelihood=904.9 χ^2=12.9 significance=0.025		−2 log likelihood=986.6 χ^2=18.1 significance=0.003	

Notes: See table 6.6. Ordered probit regression results. Values in parentheses are standard errors. Values in boldface are significant coefficients ($p < 0.05$). Response categories were coded: 1=more; 2=same; 3=less.

TABLE 6A.6
Views on raising retirement ages

Variables	β	Significance
Age	0.012 (0.007)	0.068
Education	0.015 (0.016)	0.359
Income	0.000 (0.000)	0.824
Men	0.004 (0.099)	0.971
Retirees	−0.157 (0.133)	0.238
	−2 log likelihood=1,369.3 χ^2=3.99 significance=0.551	

Notes: See table 6.7. Ordered probit regression results. Values in parentheses are standard errors. Response categories were coded: 1=strongly agree; 2=somewhat agree; 3=somewhat disagree; 4=strongly disagree.

TABLE 6A.7
Views on equalizing retirement ages for men
and women

Variables	β	Significance
Age	0.008 (0.006)	0.178
Education	**0.039** (0.016)	0.012
Income	0.000 (0.000)	0.256
Men	0.061 (0.097)	0.528
Retirees	−0.171 (0.129)	0.184
	−2 log likelihood=1,339.2 χ^2=9.9; significance=0.078	

Notes: See table 6.8. Ordered probit regression
results. Values in parentheses are standard errors. Values in boldface are significant coefficients ($p < 0.05$).
Response categories were coded: 1=strongly agree;
2=somewhat agree; 3=somewhat disagree; 4=strongly
disagree.

TABLE 6A.8
Perceived gains and losses from pension reforms

Variables	Gains exceed losses			Gains and losses are the same			Don't know		
	β	Significance	exp(β)	β	Significance	exp(β)	β	Significance	exp(β)
Intercept	3.315 (2.094)	0.113		3.073 (1.767)	0.082		-0.305 (2.114)	0.885	
Age	-0.048 (0.033)	0.142	0.953	**-0.057** (0.027)	0.038	0.945	-0.045 (0.031)	0.156	0.956
Education	-0.006 (0.075)	0.938	0.994	0.118 (0.064)	0.065	1.125	**0.187** (0.078)	0.017	1.206
Income	0.000 (0.000)	0.229	1	0.000 (0.000)	0.226	1	0.000 (0.000)	0.669	1
Men	0.159 (0.449)	0.723	1.173	0.187 (0.378)	0.620	1.206	0.250 (0.461)	0.587	1.284
Retirees	**1.933** (0.637)	0.002	6.910	**1.415** (0.534)	0.008	4.116	0.020 (0.682)	0.976	1.020

-2 log likelihood=686.5
χ^2=45.6; significance < 0.000
Nagelkerke R^2=0.15

Notes: See tables 6.10 and 6.11. Multinomial logistic regression results, in which the reference category is "losses exceed gains" from pension reforms. Values in parentheses are standard errors. Values in boldface are significant coefficients ($p < 0.05$). Response categories were coded: 1=gains exceed losses; 2=gains and losses equal; 3=losses exceed gains; 4=don't know.

TABLE 6A.9
Focus group composition

Beijing private enterprises March 13, 2005		Beijing state enterprises March 13, 2005	
#1	Retired, age 38, female	#1	Production worker, age 46, male
#2	Staff, age 47, male	#2	Production worker, age 47, female
#3	Staff, age 40, male	#3	Production worker, age 32, male
#4	Production worker , age 53, male	#4	Production worker, age 51, female
#5	Retired, age 50, female	#5	Production worker, age 46, male
#6	Staff, age 45, female	#6	Production worker, age 37, male
#7	Production worker, age 47, female	#7	Skilled worker, age 46, female
#8	Production worker, age 30, male	#8	Skilled worker, age 36, male

Nanjing state enterprises March 12, 2005		Nanjing private enterprises March 12, 2005	
#1	Skilled worker, age 35, female	#1	Staff, age 41, female
#2	Skilled worker, age 36, male	#2	Production worker, age 38, female
#3	Skilled worker, age 38, female	#3	Skilled worker, age 40, male
#4	Skilled worker, age 42, male	#4	Staff, age 45, female
#5	Production worker, age 41, female	#5	Production worker, age 45, female
#6	Production worker, age 44, male	#6	Production worker, age 51, male
#7	Production worker, age 52, female	#7	Production worker, age 53, male
#8	Staff, age 54, male	#8	Production worker, age 54, male

Nanjing state enterprises March 12, 2005		Nanjing private enterprises March 12, 2005	
#1	Skilled worker, age 33, female	#1	Production worker, age 31, female
#2	Retired, age 52, female	#2	Skilled worker, age 38, male
#3	Skilled worker, age 37, male	#3	Skilled worker, age 38, female
#4	Production worker, age 35, male	#4	Staff, age 42, male
#5	Production worker, age 30, male	#5	Production worker, age 43, female
#6	Staff, age 41, female	#6	Staff, age 49, male
#7	Retired, age 53, female	#7	Retired, age 56, female
#8	Production worker, age 43, male	#8	Retired, age 53, male

Conclusion

After sixty years in power, the CCP faces a crucial choice about how to rebalance an economy whose rapid growth had been based on high savings, low consumption, and limited public welfare provision. As the United States and other economies on which China had relied so heavily for exports entered recessions in 2008, debate intensified over how best to allocate funds from the Chinese central government. One option was to revisit the strategy used in the slowdown of the late 1990s—injecting local governments with funds to expand infrastructure and to subsidize industries. In contrast to this producer-friendly stimulus, another policy option was to use government funds to directly target households by making large-scale transfer payments to spur domestic consumption. A Xinhua special report in December 2008 proclaimed "Economic Stimulus Package to Improve People's Livelihood" and noted that the central government had pledged a 10 percent increase in pensions starting in January 2009 (Wang and Jiang 2008). Yet other news reports were skeptical. For example, one report, citing Chinese policy analysts, pointed out that only 1 percent of the supposed 4 trillion yuan ($586 billion) in stimulus spending was to go toward increased social services (Batson 2008). How the Chinese government uses welfare spending as it responds to the global economic crisis carries significant implications for the future of Chinese politics and society.

One negative scenario involves what some have called the "Latin Americanization" of China, in which a ruling party manages a state that is increasingly corrupt and incapable of addressing problems of injustice and inequality (Gilboy and Heginbotham 2004; Lam 2007). At the other end of the spectrum is an optimistic scenario in which the CCP pursues policies that rebalance growth toward greater domestic consumption through income taxes and transfers to the poor, along with more effective and equitable spending on education, health care, and environmental protection. Scenarios anywhere in between these two extremes are also possible. In any event, the type of welfare policies that emerge in China over the short run will serve as an important indicator of the broader domestic political scenario that is likely to prevail. For example, the continued growth in pension benefits for urbanites and officials without the provision of basic health care and pensions for rural residents would lead to a greater likelihood of a "Latin Americanization" scenario. By contrast, the broader development of basic social assistance programs along with well-established social insurance institutions could bring about reductions in inequality measures and possibly even greater representation of disadvantaged groups within the ranks of the CCP.

As we have seen in the preceding chapters, urban governments, in their ability to undermine central regulations and to prioritize pensions over other social insurance programs, have become decisive actors in the new welfare regime of China. A decade ago, their preferences for pension policy led to the formation of a social insurance–based model in which individual and employer savings created large pools of pension funds, as well as pension debt. Then, as now, the sources of the new Chinese welfare state lie less with the policy designs of national policymakers than with the political incentives and constraints of local, especially urban, officials.

Those incentives and constraints stem largely from the ambiguous and contradictory functions that local governments perform as both regulators and in some cases shareholders or owners of local firms. Even if they do not have outright ownership stakes in such firms, local governments enjoy rights to revenues from local firms. The Chinese macroeconomic reforms beginning in the 1980s first exposed the state sector and local state enterprises to competition from foreign and private firms and allowed state enterprises to retain profits. State enterprise managers—and crucially, the urban governments that relied on state enterprises as their main source of revenue—demanded flexibility in labor policies. As many SOEs became unprofitable, and thus a drain on local finances, pressures for dismantling the state sector grew stronger. This broad pattern of economic reform was accompanied by a political realignment that drove the policy content of pension reforms. Urban governments and SOE managers agreed to enact bankruptcy and mergers that would enrich both parties while paying a minimum compensation to those left jobless by restructuring. They also agreed that firms would remit payroll taxes to get state-sector workers out of the labor market with pensions and to get migrant workers into the labor market with minimal protections.

Urban officials and SOE managers strengthened their alliance by pursuing local regulations that transferred the responsibility for welfare benefits, especially pensions, from state firms to local social insurance agencies. Pensions emerged as the largest component of social insurance, in part because of the revenue potential and in part because urban governments had to deal directly with the problem of unemployed workers. Pension regulations varied considerably by locality, thus undermining attempts to create standard national regulations for pensions and other benefits. When national regulations did emerge by the late 1990s, they reflected the often contradictory preferences of urban governments regarding social insurance.

National regulations made all employees of urban enterprises eligible for social insurance coverage. This eligibility standard for welfare rights both expanded the number of contributors and complicated the tasks of enforcement. The regulations attempted to cover all employees of any firm (be it state-owned, private, or otherwise), provided that the firm was located in a city or urban township. With the migration of millions of rural workers to cities and the conversion of rural townships to urban status, the number of contributors to social insurance funds increased rapidly, from 52 million in 1990 to 152 million by 2007 (State Statistics Bureau [SSB] and Ministry of Labor and Social Security [MOLSS] 2005, 574; Ministry of Human Resources and Social Security [MOHRSS] 2008a). Because the national regulations limited pension coverage to employees of urban enterprises, rural residents and workers in township and village enterprises were not technically eligible. Moreover, the ambiguous status of part-time or temporary workers in urban enterprises, along with the relative ease with which enterprise managers of smaller firms could evade social insurance regulations, meant that between 30 and 50 percent of urban workers remained without various forms of health and pension coverage, despite their being legally entitled to such coverage.

The evolution of the pension-dominant Chinese welfare regime thus reflected a political conflict in which institutions shaped the preferences, interests, and strategies of urban officials, SOE managers, and SOE workers and retirees. The cooperation between urban officials and SOE managers to dismantle much of the state sector and to use pensions as partial compensation to those left jobless in the process appears on the surface to be a straightforward pursuit of profit, much of it through corrupt means. But as the discussion in chapter 3 and elsewhere noted, this coalition and its strategies would not have been possible without the existence of two crucial institutions: the property rights claims that urban governments enjoyed over SOEs and the revenue rights that they had over extra-budgetary funds, such as those for pension and other social insurance funds. This finding shows that decentralized administration or multilevel governance in China helps us understand welfare politics, but only up to a point. More specifically, the institution of revenue rights enjoyed by local governments provides the best explanation for the direction that the new Chinese welfare regime has taken. This is what sets China off from other large uneven developers that also have decentralized administration (even formally federal systems) but nothing resembling the revenue-raising and expenditure assignments that are found at local levels in China.

In further support of the historical institutionalist approach outlined in chapter 3, the preferences and behavior of workers and retirees toward pensions can be explained by the legacies of work unit socialism and its dismantling during the 1990s. The apparent acceptance of what Marc Blecher (2002) labels as market hegemony among state-sector workers did not mean that this group also accepted the retreat of the state from its obligations to provide some form of welfare spending to the victims of mass layoffs. Those left jobless and classified by state policies as "retired" or "laid-off," mobilized on the basis of their work units to make effective subsistence claims to the public and the central government authorities. They succeeded in pressuring urban officials to deliver compensation in the form of pensions, and they also fueled the rapid growth in pension spending. Workers who remained in the labor force, a diverse group ranging from state-sector workers to migrants, experienced the transformation in welfare policies in a different way, and they articulated demands and pursued strategies based on the new legal and regulatory provisions governing pensions and other welfare measures. In the sections that follow, I situate pensions and the welfare regime of China within the broader framework of welfare politics in two other large uneven developers and within the context of politics in contemporary China. The Chinese case sheds light on the constraints and the possibilities for welfare policies in large economies with high levels of inequality. The findings here also offer insight into debates over the present and future of Chinese politics and policymaking.

WELFARE POLITICS IN LARGE UNEVEN DEVELOPERS

Studies of welfare spending in developing countries have noted a puzzling, and troubling, pattern in which higher levels of social spending are associated with a worsening of income distribution (Weyland 1996; McGuire 1999; World Bank 2001; Rudra 2002). Spending on programs such as health, education, and pensions turns out to be regressive because, according to one explanation, the beneficiaries are concentrated in privileged sectors of the labor force such as public-sector unions and other politically influential groups. Some have argued that this positive association between increased social spending and inequality is related to the fact that many developing country governments distribute benefits not to the median voter to ensure electoral success but in a clientelist fashion to unionized and public sector workers at the expense of those employed in unorganized and informal sectors. For example, James McGuire (1999), in a study of sixteen Latin American and East Asian cases, finds that labor union strength (measured in terms of union membership, collective bargaining levels, and other factors) had a negative impact on human development indicators such as life expectancy and infant mortality between 1960 and the 1990s. Labor union strength also had a weak but still negative effect on income inequality over the same period. Rudra (2002) finds, in a study of forty-six developing and developed countries between 1972 and 1996, that, although education and health spending showed a slightly positive effect on income inequality for globalizing developing countries, social security (pensions and unemployment) had a regressive effect on income inequality. In Rudra's account, the failure of social security spending to alleviate poverty and income inequality lies with the political interests and influence of businesses and formal-sector workers rather than with labor union strength. As she concludes, "Even [equity-promoting] reform-oriented governments would ultimately find it politically advantageous to maintain the existing regressive pension programs and sustain their longstanding ties with privileged labor groups" (Rudra 2002, 701).

Researchers infer from the findings of these large-*n* statistical studies that organized groups, including formal- and public-sector employees, in developing countries have successfully persuaded their governments to concentrate social spending in a narrow range that does little to alleviate poverty and inequality in the economy as a whole. This reasoning relies on the logic of collective action, in which governments respond to the demands of concentrated groups rather than the preferences of the diffuse, unorganized majority. A closer look at pensions in China and two other comparably uneven developers—Brazil and South Africa—suggests some refinement to this explanation. Governments in all three cases responded to growing inequalities with substantial increases in pension spending and pension commitments. In expanding new pension rights to substantial portions of the workforce, governments nonetheless reproduced or locked-in existing inequalities in income and in pension benefits. Pensions, which are usually tied to past earnings, gave the governments in question a path of least political resistance by allowing them to claim new programs that in fact did little to redistribute income or to reduce inequalities. Pensions also helped perpetuate the clientelism that existed between politicians and narrow groups of favored constituents (Lynch 2006). Highly fragmented pension systems such as those found in China and Brazil provided crucial, divisible resources to local politicians, and strengthened their opposition to centralized, universal pension benefits that would be more difficult to parcel out to a narrow group of supporters.

Brazil and South Africa have notoriously high measures of income inequality, with Gini coefficients of close to 58, according to the United Nations Development Programme ([UNDP] 2006). China has a less extreme Gini coefficient of 44.7, but this represents a significant increase over estimates in the low 30s during the late 1970s. In all three cases, the ruling parties that engineered growth faced pressures created by the salience of the inequalities and specifically by rural-to-urban migration. These pressures presented the ruling parties with the political choice of how to expand welfare coverage beyond politically influential occupations that were already receiving coverage. The authoritarian regimes in Brazil and South Africa adopted universal coverage (including noncontributory pensions for some or most of the population) while maintaining high levels of benefits and labor market protections for the public-sector workforce. This strategy placed increased debt burdens on the state and maintained inequality in welfare benefits, even while it extended welfare rights to all citizens. By contrast, the Chinese approach relied on dismantling the labor market protections for the state-sector workforce while introducing employment-based social insurance programs for urban workers.

What led politicians in China to take apart socialist labor regulations and provide urban-based social insurance coverage but those in Brazil and South Africa to choose to preserve corporatist arrangements for the elite segments of the workforce while universalizing coverage for welfare programs? This divergence in outcomes cannot be explained by the fact that Brazil and South Africa democratized—both attained nearly universal coverage for pensions under authoritarian or highly illiberal regimes. What best accounts for the separate evolutionary paths in welfare regimes is the fact that in China local governments had such large spending responsibilities as well as rights to locally raised revenues. At the same time, what makes China similar to these two cases is the primacy of pensions in their welfare regimes, an outcome reflected in the political choice to build popular welfare programs with a minimum of redistribution from rich to poor. In all three cases, high levels of pension spending achieved under such programs may have relieved poverty (especially among the rural populations in South Africa and Brazil), but pensions did little to reduce income inequalities.

Welfare expansion in South Africa took place over several decades in the twentieth century. In the 1920s, in response to labor unrest, a coalition government of rival parties passed legislation to create noncontributory pensions and disability grants. This legislation, passed in 1928, excluded black South Africans, but it also made provisions to include the landless poor, designated as "colored" or white, who had been driven off their farms by the commercialization of agriculture (Seekings 2005, 23–24). In 1944, the South African government enacted laws to extend social insurance coverage to all white and colored citizens, and to provide social assistance payments to black South Africans in rural and urban areas (Seekings 2005, 27). According to Jeremy Seekings, the wide extent of rural poverty in South Africa and the inability of the rural poor to support themselves on agricultural production motivated politicians to introduce this expansion in welfare coverage. Because this safety net for rural migrants also had the benefit of alleviating labor shortages and keeping wages down, employers supported these steps toward universal coverage for pensions and disabilities (Seekings 2005, 28).

By 2002, there were 1.9 million South Africans who received the social pension, which was funded from general tax revenues and represented approximately 60 percent of social expenditures, or 1.4 percent of GDP (Barrientos 2005, 3). Because these pensions are funded through taxation and because average white incomes are ten times those of black South Africans, pensions have introduced a significant element of redistribution (Lloyd-Sherlock 2002, 700–701). Yet spending on pension benefits overwhelms expenditures in other crucial areas. For example, in 1993, the government spent 9 billion rand on pensions but only 183 million rand between 1992 and 1997 on national AIDS programs (Lloyd-Sherlock 2002, 688–89). Moreover, in parts of the country, poor roads prevented many pensioners from reaching post offices where they were supposed to collect their benefits (Economist 2000).

The Brazilian military dictatorship in the 1970s, after nearly a decade of fast-paced growth, used welfare policy as a way to bolster its legitimacy and to be seen as responsive to glaring social inequalities. The Brazilian strategy of incorporation through welfare policies took the form of the universal provision for health care and pensions. In response to the mobilization of rural workers and pressures for land reform, the Brazilian government expanded this program during the 1970s. By the end of this decade, social security programs covered most of the population, including the rural sector and domestic servants (Malloy 1979, 129). Although not without financial problems and inequalities, the social security program in Brazil covered 87–93 percent of the population between the late 1970s and early 1980s (Malloy 1979, 134; Madrid 2003, 140).

With democratization in the mid-1980s, the Brazilian government expanded the foundations for welfare provision laid down by its predecessors and gave local governments substantial fiscal authority. The 1988 Constitution formalized welfare rights for rural workers and those in the informal sector. The government introduced a rural pension in 1991 that lowered the retirement age from sixty-five to sixty for men and to fifty-five for women. Workers in agriculture, fishing and mining, and informal employment received old age, disability and survivor pensions under the same legislation. These laws also provided rural women workers with various social protections. The Brazilian government introduced a pension for low-income urban residents in 1993, also with no contributions from the beneficiaries. Critics at the time noted how clientelism eroded the goals of such programs to better represent the interests of the poor. As Weyland (1996, 15) observed, "Social security policy has continued to sustain conservative elites, rather than contributed to the democratization of Brazilian society."

During the 1990s, programs such as the national health system were turned over to cities, along with responsibilities for spending on education and transportation (Baiocchi 2006, 57). Despite this de-centralization, pension expenditures remained the exception, and continued to be funded by the central government. Brazil spent approximately 1 percent of GDP on 5 million retirees in three noncontributory programs by 2000 (Barrientos 2005, 4). By another estimate, 65 percent of the central government's social spending in 2000 was for pensions, with the central government being responsible for nearly 80 percent of social insurance and social assistance expenditures and the states and municipalities assuming the remainder (Baiocchi 2006, 60–61). Brazilian expenditures on pensions remains among the highest, at more than 12 percent of GDP. As one study of federalism in Brazil concludes, "[decentralization] has not improved regional inequalities and sometimes has exacerbated them" (Baiocchi 2006, 54).

In Brazil and South Africa, democratization may have brought decentralization and improved service delivery across a range of programs, but the problem of inequality in welfare provision remains. Even though both countries have what amounts to universal coverage for pensions and social assistance programs, these programs have done little to reduce inequalities. In Brazil, civil servants, the military, and private-sector employees receive lucrative benefits dating back to Brazilian industrialization in the early decades of the twentieth century (Malloy 1979, 107–13). Although over 90 percent of the population was covered by the 1970s, rural workers received only flat-rate payments, whereas workers in the formal sector received extensive benefits from various welfare measures. More recently, the Lula administration in Brazil has enjoyed some success in raising the incomes of the poor through the introduction of a means-tested conditional cash transfer program (Bolsa Familia) that gives incentives to poor households to keep children in school (Llana 2008). The South African pension system has shown some evidence of reducing income inequality, but the government has failed to enact a proposed Basic Income Grant that could provide direct transfers to the poor. As Nattrass (2005, 3) has noted, "social assistance is provided only for those too old to work (the pension), too young to work (the child support grant), or too sick/disabled to work (the disability grant)."

Although Brazil and South Africa are both federal systems and China is unitary, these formal constitutional arrangements between central and local governments matter less than the practical fiscal relationships between central and local governments. As the preceding chapters have shown, the fiscal responsibilities assigned to local governments in China had a strong influence on the direction of welfare policy. The combination of revenue-raising incentives and welfare burdens that local administrations in China encounter stands in stark contrast to other cases in which local governments receive grants or other forms of funding from the central government to implement national welfare programs. Even in Brazil, where fiscal administration is highly decentralized, especially following the 1988 Constitution, local expenditures as a proportion of total government expenditures stand at 41.7 percent of GDP (Afonso and de Mello 2002, 268). As noted in chapter 1, local government spending in China represents 75 percent of total government expenditures, including formal budgetary and off-budget expenditures (Organisation for Economic Cooperation and Development [OECD] 2006, 27–28). In another crucial distinction, social security revenues (for pensions and other programs) are not shared with subnational governments in Brazil, and the federal government funds over 80 percent of social security spending (Afonso and de Mello 2002, 266). This relative centralization of social security spending and universal coverage for pensions stands in contrast to China, where the institution of de facto fiscal federalism has placed constraints on universal coverage and limited eligibility to urban workers.

Despite differences in coverage and in the level of administration responsible for funding social policies, in China, as in Brazil and South Africa, pensions took primacy in welfare policy because they offered in many respects the path of least political resistance. Pensions are primarily intergenerational transfers of wealth and do much less to create interregional or interclass transfers from the wealthy to the poor. Thus, they do little to alleviate the plight of low-income populations or regions. Unless the poor are predominately found among the elderly, pensions cannot be expected to remedy income inequality. Especially for large uneven developers that face structural inequalities even while they enjoy sustained growth, pensions are only a "quick fix" solution that politicians can use to demonstrate their commitment to resolving inequalities.

PENSIONS AND CHINESE POLITICS

As the preceding discussion suggests, the emergence of a new welfare regime in China can advance our understanding of how authoritarian ruling parties adapt to changing social and economic environments. The expansion of welfare provision shows that authoritarian parties do not have to choose between liberal versus illiberal strategies of adaptation, as is often portrayed in the democratization literature (Huntington 1991). Authoritarian ruling parties can use welfare policies to bolster their claims to look after the livelihoods of the population. China's new welfare regime thus has an important political rationale.

The expansion of welfare rights through pension and other social insurance coverage is a crucial part of a broader attempt by the CCP leadership under Hu Jintao to realign itself with mass constituencies that it had abandoned during the 1990s. In seeking a quasi-alliance with business owners during the 1990s, the CCP subordinated the interests of its erstwhile supporters in the urban working class and the rural sector (Lee 2002; Chen 2003; Solinger 2006; Dickson 2008). SOE reform during the late 1990s and early 2000s represented a grand retreat by the CCP from its socialist commitments to provide urban workers with employment guarantees and benefits. Urban officials and owners of state enterprises have also colluded to expropriate land from suburban rural villages at heavily discounted prices and to arrange favorable real estate deals that allowed developers to take over urban residential buildings. The collaboration of party cadres and crony capitalists moved toward a more formal alliance as the CCP successfully incorporated business owners into its ranks. In surveys, business owners expressed relatively strong support for the CCP as a ruling party, and they also opposed democratization on the grounds that it would bring instability (Pearson 1998; Tsai 2007; Dickson 2008). Some have argued that this alignment of the CCP and business interests is an explosive combination in which the demands of the excluded classes, namely workers and peasants, will be met with higher levels of repression (Chen 2003, 149).

The populist orientation of Hu Jintao represents an effort to realign the CCP with the interests of workers and peasants. As several studies of Chinese public opinion have argued, citizens appear to support the current regime in broad terms, although when asked about specific policy areas, such as providing job security, dealing with income inequality, and combating corruption, the public evaluation of government performance is negative. This dissatisfaction in terms of specific or policy-based support could eventually lead to an erosion of diffuse support, or legitimacy.[1] Because pensions are one of the most important and, certainly, the costliest programs that the Chinese government has introduced, public views about the effectiveness of pensions are very important measures for how Chinese citizens evaluate their government. The results of the urban survey discussed in chapter 6 show that urban residents maintained strong support for public pensions and pension rights to be expanded to farmers and migrant workers. With the passage of laws such as Labor Contract Law in 2007 and the likely passage of the SIL, the leadership team under Hu Jintao brought the state and the CCP into closer alignment with the preferences of the public over those of business interests.

The coalition of urban officials and SOE managers (referred to in earlier chapters as "the coalition of local cadres and crony capitalists") is likely to come under greater pressure in the future as urban officials have to extract higher levels of revenues from local firms to provide pension benefits for the swelling ranks of retirees. Even if urban officials expand coverage to gain new sources of social insurance revenues, governments in most areas of China will have to turn to the central government for additional subsidies to cover pension expenditures. Efforts to cope with rising pension costs are likely to constrain the ability of local governments to pursue broader public welfare measures in the future. As illustrated by the episodes of migrant workers lining up to cash out their pension savings (see chapter 3), urban governments face the prospect of mass withdrawals of accumulated pension funds.

With the manic swing in the PRC economy from a sharp increase in prices and inflationary pressures in 2007–2008 to an equally sudden decline in

---

[1] Chen (2004) has found that the CCP enjoys relatively high levels of broad (diffuse) support in terms of the basic political institutions through which the regime rules but a mixed level of specific support for its policies and performance. In Chen's surveys, conducted in 1995, 1997, and 1999, respondents were most satisfied with the ability of the PRC government to fight inflation and to "provide for the needy." They were least satisfied with corruption and income inequality. Shi (2000) also finds high levels of political trust and diffuse support for the regime. Tang (2005, 121–40) argues that public opinion influences decision making and political change in China and that citizens select from several different channels to express their opinions on political issues.

production and exports in the second half of 2008, pension expenditures increased rapidly. In January 2008, the central government announced its intention to subsidize further pension benefit increases for the next three years and committed to providing 15 billion yuan ($2.2 billion) for pensions to poor areas in the interior (Xinhuanet 2008). Average pensions in 2007 rose to 11,500 yuan ($1,573), up from 7,728 yuan in 2003. The SIL draft moved toward formal enactment in 2009 or 2010, and the expansion in pension coverage that will ensue if the law is seriously implemented suggests that the CCP has moved China toward a new phase of pension financing and possibly toward more centralized administration. The critical question will be whether the renewal of welfare programs and expenditures will do anything to remedy the persistent economic inequalities in China.

Under the political slogan "scientific development," or otherwise, the future of the welfare regime in China will be strongly constrained by the promises made and the implicit blank checks issued by local governments during the 1990s and 2000s as they restructured the state sector and paid for mass layoffs with the promises of early pensions. As the politics of pensions in virtually every other country has shown, once benefits are established and retirement ages fixed, it becomes politically very difficult, if not impossible, to scale back on what the state has promised to society. China will be no different, and if anything, the evidence points to an eventual expansion of pension rights that will bring a vastly larger financial commitment than the Chinese government faces today. Regardless of whether CCP rule continues under a resilient authoritarian regime or gives way to inter-party competition, debates over the costs of pensions and welfare provision will remain a central issue in Chinese politics.

APPENDIX

List of Interviews

Interview number	Informant	Date
#012005	administrator, international organization	January 20, 2005
#012505	executive, insurance company	January 25, 2005
#021805	municipal government policy analyst	February 18, 2005
#021905	benefits consultant	February 19, 2005
#022105	municipal official	February 21, 2005
#022105A	rural county resident of urban area	February 21, 2005
#022305	academic policy analyst	February 23, 2005
#022405	lawyer	February 24, 2005
#030705	municipal official	March 7, 2005
#030805A	provincial official	March 8, 2005
#030805B	state enterprise manager	March 8, 2005
#030905A	provincial official	March 9, 2005
#030905B	enterprise manager	March 9, 2005
#030905C	academic policy analyst	March 9, 2005
#031205	rural county resident of urban area	March 12, 2005
#031605	private enterprise manager	March 16, 2005
#031905	state enterprise manager	March 18, 2005
#032105A	benefits consultant	March 21, 2005
#032105B	former provincial official	March 21, 2005
#040405A	provincial official	April 4, 2005
#040605	municipal official	April 6, 2005
#052801	central government policy analyst	May 28, 2001
#053001	provincial official	May 30, 2001
#053101	provincial official	May 31, 2001
#060101A	provincial official	June 1, 2001
#060101B	manager, state enterprise	June 1, 2001

Interview number	Informant	Date
#060401	manager, state enterprise	June 4, 2001
#060501	provincial official	June 5, 2001
#060601A	municipal official	June 6, 2001
#060601B	manager, state enterprise	June 6, 2001
#062602	central government policy analyst	June 26, 2002
#062802A	policy analyst, international organization	June 28, 2002
#062802B	central government official	June 28, 2002
#070202	central government policy analyst	July 2, 2002
#070302	municipal government policy analyst	July 3, 2002
#102604	central government policy analyst	October 26, 2004
#110604	municipal official	November 6, 2004
#110904	benefits consultant	November 9, 2004
#120604	urban resident	December 4, 2004
#120904	laid-off worker	December 9, 2004
#121304	financial corporation executive	December 13, 2004

References

Afonso, José Roberto R., and Luiz de Mello. 2002. "Brazil: An Evolving Federation." In *Managing Fiscal Decentralization*, edited by Ehtisham Ahmad and Vito Tanzi, 265–85. London: Routledge.

All-China Federation of Trade Unions (ACFTU). 2002. *Zhongguo gonghui tongji nianjian 2001* [China Trade Union statistical yearbook 2001]. Beijing: Zhongguo tongji chubanshe.

Anderlini, Jamil. 2006. "Sasac Opposes Transfer of State Shares." *South China Morning Post*, November 20, p. 1.

Areddy, James T. 2006. "Shanghai Pension Probe Raises Ire." *Wall Street Journal*, September 18, p. A4.

Baiocchi, Gianpaolo. 2006. "Inequality and Innovation: Decentralization as an Opportunity Structure in Brazil." In *Decentralization and Local Governance in Developing Countries*, edited by Pranab Bardhan and Dilip Mookherjee, 53–80. Cambridge: MIT Press.

Banting, Keith G. 1995. "The Welfare State as Statecraft: Territorial Politics and Canadian Social Policy." In *European Social Policy: Between Fragmentation and Integration*, edited by Stephan Leibfried and Paul Pierson, 269–300. Washington, D.C.: Brookings Institution Press.

Barrientos, Armando. 2005. "Non-contributory Pensions and Poverty Reduction in Brazil and South Africa." Institute for Development Policy and Management Working Paper, University of Manchester.

——. 2006. "Poverty Reduction: The Missing Piece of Pension Reform in Latin America." *Social Policy and Administration* 4(4): 369–84.

Batson, Andrew. 2008. "China's Stimulus Slights Human Capital." *Wall Street Journal*, December 8, p. A2.

Béland, Daniel, and Ka Man Yu. 2004. "A Long Financial March: Pension Reform in China." *Journal of Social Policy* 33(2): 267–88.

Blecher, Marc, 2002. "Hegemony and Workers' Politics in China." *China Quarterly* 170: 283–303.

Bradsher, Keith. 2002. "Factory Dispute Tests China's Loyalty to Workers' Rights." *New York Times*, July 18, p. A3.

Brandes, Stuart D. 1976. *Welfare Capitalism, 1880–1940*. Chicago: University of Chicago Press.

British Broadcasting Corporation (BBC). 2003. "Liaoning Secretary Says Urban Social Security Scheme Successful." October 17. BBC Monitoring Asia-Pacific.

Brooks, Sarah M. 2005. "Interdependent and Domestic Foundations of Policy Change: The Diffusion of Pension Privatization around the World." *International Studies Quarterly* 49(2): 273–94.

Cai, Hongbin, and Daniel Treisman. 2006. "Did Government Decentralization Cause China's Economic Miracle?" *World Politics* 58: 505–35.

Cai, Yongshun. 2002. "The Resistance of Chinese Laid-off Workers in the Reform Period." *China Quarterly* 170: 327–44.

———. 2005. *State and Laid-Off Workers in Reform China: The Silence and Collective Action of the Retrenched*. New York: Routledge Press.

Caijing. 2004. "Investigation into the Diversion of 800 million RMB in Social Insurance Funds in Guangzhou." No. 105, April 15. Available at: http://www.caijing.com.cn/mag/preview.aspx?ArtID=5325 (accessed June 9, 2004).

Chandler, Andrea. 2004. *Shocking Mother Russia: Democratization, Social Rights, and Pension Reform in Russia, 1990–2001*. Toronto: University of Toronto Press.

Chen, An. 2003. "Rising Class Politics and Its Impact on China's Path to Democracy." *Democratization* 10(2): 141–62.

Chen Fang. 2008. "Shenji: Shanghai shebao heimu" [The audit: Behind the scenes of the Shanghai Social Insurance Agency]. *21st Century Business Herald*, March 26. Available at http://www.21cbh.com/print.asp?NewsId=30916 (accessed March 28, 2008).

Chen, Hengming. 2002. "Dangqian qiye canbao jiaofei renshu chengfu zengzhang de yuanyin ji duice" [Causes and countermeasures of the negative growth in the number of enterprise participants in insurance and contributors of fees]. *Zhongguo shehui baozhang, lunwen zhuanji* [China Social Security, special collection]: 174–75.

Chen, Jie. 2004. *Popular Political Support in Urban China*. Washington, D.C., and Stanford: Woodrow Wilson Center Press and Stanford University Press.

Chen, Lydia. 2007. "Pension-Scandal Trials Start in Jilin." *Shanghai Daily*, December 28. Available at http://www.shanghaidaily.com (accessed December 28, 2007).

Chen Tiangeng. 2002. "Chechu fanli: Dui feigongyouzhi jingji quanmian shishi shehui baoxian" [Demolishing the barrier: Social insurance comprehensive economic measures toward the non-state sector]. *Zhongguo shehui baozhang, lunwen zhuanji* [China Social Security, special collection]: 181–86.

China Daily. 2006. "China's Health Care System Search for Remedy." October 6. Available at http://www.chinadaily.com.cn/china/2006-10/06/content_702313_2.htm (accessed December 15, 2008).

——. 2007. "Embezzled Pension Fund Recovered: Mayor." January 28. Available at http://www.chinadaily.com.cn/china/2007-01/28/content_794667.htm (accessed February 1, 2007).

China Economic Review. 2005. "Closing the Pension Gap." September. Available at http://www.chinaeconomicreview.com/cer/2005_09/Closing_the_pension_gap .html (accessed October 28, 2007).

China Labor Bulletin. 2002. "Oil Workers in Sichuan Get Organized to Fight for Pensions and Employment." September 14. Available at http://www.china-labour .org.hk/en/mode/2146 (accessed February 17, 2003).

——. 2004. "Tieshu Textile Workers['] Historic First Hearing of Workers['] Collective Lawsuit against the Suizhou Social Insurance Bureau." Available at http:// www.china-labour.org.hk/en (accessed March 3, 2008).

——. 2006. "Half of Women Migrant Workers are in Irregular Employment." Report cited from *China Youth Daily*, November 22. Available at http://www.clb .org.hk/en/node/40216 (accessed March 3, 2008).

China Labor News. 2008. "Migrant Workers Leaving Shenzhen Queue All Night to Cash in Their Pensions." Available at http://www.clntranslations.org/article. Translated from *Southern Metropolitan Daily (Nanfang dushibao)*, January 15. Available at http://news.sina.com.cn/c/2008-01-15/030113258863s.shtml (accessed September 20, 2008).

China Labor Security Report. 2002a. "Qiye qianjiao yanglao baoxianfei yuanyin fenxi" [Analyis of reasons that enterprises owe pension insurance fees]. No. 2522.

——. 2002b. "Wode gongzi wo gaina; ni bujiaofei ni fanfa: shisan mei yifa weiquan" [I should draw my wages; If you don't remit fees then you break the law: 13 sisters protect their rights in accordance with the law]. No. 2629.

China Labor Watch. 2001. "Dongguan Elegant Top Shoes Co., Ltd." Available at http://www.chinalaborwatch.org/en/web/article.php?article_id=50007 (accessed October 29, 2007).

——. 2003. "China Releases Labor Activist Di Tiangui." Available at http://www .chinalaborwatch.org/en/web/article.php?article_id=50028 (accessed April 13, 2009).

——. 2004. "Kingmaker Footwear [Timberland Made in China]." Available at http://www.chinalaborwatch.org/en/web/article.php?article_id=50234 (accessed October 29, 2007).

——. 2005. "Procter & Gamble in China: Workers Fall through the Cracks." Available at http://www.chinalaborwatch.org/en/web/article.php?article_id=50296 (accessed October 29, 2007).

Chow, Nelson W. S. 2001. *Socialist Welfare with Chinese Characteristics: The Reform of the Social Security System in China*. Hong Kong: Centre of Asian Studies, University of Hong Kong.

Collier, David, and Richard E. Messick. 1975. "Prerequisites versus Diffusion: Testing Alternative Explanations of Social Security Adoption." *American Political Science Review* 69(4): 1299–315.

Cook, Linda. 2007. "Negotiating Welfare in Post-Communist States." *Comparative Politics* 40(1): 41–62.

Cook, Sarah, and Margaret Maurer-Fazio, eds. 1999. *The Workers' State Meets the Market: Labor in China's Transition.* London: Frank Cass.

Crane, Keith, Roger Cliff, Evan Medeiros, James Mulvenon, and William Overholt. 2005. *Modernizing China's Military: Opportunities and Constraints.* Santa Monica, Calif.: Rand Corporation.

Dickson, Bruce J. 2003. *Red Capitalists in China: The Party, Private Entrepreneurs, and Prospects for Political Change.* New York: Cambridge University Press.

———. 2008. *Wealth into Power: The Communist Party's Embrace of China's Private Sector.* New York: Cambridge University Press.

Duckett, Jane. 2003. "Bureaucratic Interests and Institutions in the Making of China's Social Policy." *Public Administration Quarterly* 27(1–2): 210–37.

———. 2004. "State, Collectivism and Worker Privilege: A Study of Urban Health Insurance Reform." *China Quarterly* 177: 155–73.

Dunaway, Steven, and Vivek B. Arora. 2007. "Pension Reform in China: The Need for a New Approach." IMF Working Paper. International Monetary Fund, Washington, D.C.

Economist. 2000. "From Apartheid to Welfare State." April 1, p. 42–43.

Esping-Andersen, Gosta. 1990. *The Three Worlds of Welfare Capitalism.* Princeton: Princeton University Press.

Fan, C. Simon, Chen Lin, and Daniel Treisman. 2009. "Political Decentralization and Corruption: Evidence from around the World." *Journal of Public Economics* 93: 14–34.

Fan, Jun. 2001. "Shaobao manbao: Rechu shifei duoshao" [Underreporting and falsely reporting: How much trouble is stirred up?]. *Zhongguo shehui baozhang* [China Social Security Magazine] 81: 10.

Feng Lanrui. 2001. "Cengceng fenjie jinpozhe xian chutai" [Resolving things level by level, first address what is most pressing]. *Zhongguo shehui baozhang, lunwen zhuanji* [China Social Security, special collection]: 205–7.

Fewsmith, Joseph. 2008. *China since Tiananmen.* New York: Cambridge University Press.

Frazier, Mark W. 2004a. "After Pension Reform: Navigating the 'Third Rail' in China." *Studies in Comparative International Development* 39(2): 43–68.

———. 2004b. "China's Pension Reform and Its Discontents." *China Journal* 51: 97–114.

Frieden, Jeffry, and Ronald Rogowski. 1996. "The Impact of the International Economy on National Policies: An Analytic Overview." In *Internationalization and Domestic Politics,* edited by Robert Keohane and Helen Milner, 25–47. New York: Cambridge University Press.

Gallagher, Mary E. 2005. *Contagious Capitalism: Globalization and the Politics of Labor in China.* Princeton: Princeton University Press.

Gao, Qin. 2008. "The Chinese Benefit System in Transition: Reform and Impacts on Income Inequality." *Annals of New York Academy of Sciences* 1136: 342–47.

Gelissen, John 2001. "Old-Age Pensions: Individual or Collective Responsibility?: An Investigation of Public Opinion across European Welfare States." *European Societies* 3(4): 500–501.

Gilboy, George J., and Eric Heginbotham. 2004. "The Latin Americanization of China?" *Current History* 103(674): 256–61.

Giles, John, Albert Park, and Fang Cai. 2006. "How Has Economic Restructuring Affected China's Urban Workers?" *China Quarterly* 185: 61–95.

Gilley, Bruce. 2004. *China's Democratic Future: How It Will Happen and Where It Will Lead?* New York: Columbia University Press.

Gold, Thomas B., William J. Hurst, Jaeyoun Won, and Li Qiang, eds. 2009. *Laid-Off Workers in a Workers' State: Unemployment with Chinese Characteristics.* New York: Palgrave MacMillan.

Gordon, Colin. 1991. "New Deal, Old Deck: Business and the Origins of Social Security, 1920–1935." *Politics and Society* 19: 165–207.

Guangdong Statistics Bureau (GSB). 2005. *Guangdong tongji nianjian* [Guangdong Statistical Yearbook]. Available at http://www.gdstats.gov.cn/tjkw/gdtjnj/2005/table/05/5_c.htm (accessed March 3, 2008).

Haggard, Stephan, and Robert R. Kaufman. 2008. *Development, Democracy, and Welfare States: Latin America, East Asia, and Eastern Europe.* Princeton: Princeton University Press.

Han Liangcheng and Jiao Kaiping, eds. 1997. *Qiye yanglao baoxian zhidu de tongyi yu shishi* [Unification and implementation of the enterprise old-age insurance system]. Beijing: Zhongguo renshi chubanshe.

Heclo, Hugh. 1974. *Modern Social Politics in Britain and Sweden.* New Haven: Yale University Press.

Hu, Shanlian, Shenglan Tang, Yuanli Liu, Yuxin Zhao, Maria-Luisa Escobar, and David de Ferranti. 2008. "Reform of How Health Care Is Paid for in China: Challenges and Opportunities." Available at http://www.thelancet.com (accessed October 20, 2008).

Hu Xiaoyi. 1999. "Yanglao baoxian, '98 pandian" [Overview of pension insurance in 1998]. *Zhongguo Shehui baozhang* [China Social Security Magazine] 55: 14–15.

Huang, Yanzhong. 2004. "Bringing the Local State Back In: The Political Economy of Public Health in Rural China." *Journal of Contemporary China* 13(39): 367–90.

Huang, Yasheng, 1996. *Inflation and Investment Controls in China: The Political Economy of Central-Local Relations During the Reform Era.* New York: Cambridge University Press

———. 2003. *Selling China: Foreign Direct Investment during the Reform Era.* New York: Cambridge University Press.

Huntington, Samuel P. 1991. *The Third Wave: Democratization in the Late Twentieth Century.* Norman: University of Oklahoma Press.

Hurst, William. 2004. "Understanding Contentious Collective Action by Chinese Laid-Off Workers: The Importance of Regional Political Economy." *Studies in Comparative International Development* 39(2): 94–120.

———. 2009. *The Chinese Worker after Socialism.* New York: Cambridge University Press.

Hurst, William, and Kevin O'Brien. 2002. "China's Contentious Pensioners." *China Quarterly* 170: 344–60.

Inglot, Tomasz. 2003. "Historical Legacies, Institutions, and the Politics of Social Policy in Hungary and Poland, 1989–1999." In *Capitalism and Democracy in Central and Eastern Europe: Assessing the Legacy of Communist Rule*, edited by Grzegorz Ekiert and Stephen E. Hanson, 210–47. New York: Cambridge University Press.

Jackson, Richard, and Neil Howe. 2004. *The Graying of the Middle Kingdom: The Demographics and Economics of Retirement Policy in China*. Washington, D.C.: Center for Strategic and International Studies.

James, Estelle. 2002. "How Can China Solve Its Old Age Security Problem?: The Interaction between Pension, SOE and Financial Market Reform." *Journal of Pension Economics and Finance* 1(1): 53–75.

Janky, Bela, and Robert Gal. 2007. "Public Opinion on Pension Systems in Europe." ENEPRI Research Report No. 36. Available at http://shop.ceps.eu/BookDetail .php?item_id=1519 (accessed August 19, 2008).

Jiang Chunze and Li Nanwe (Peter N. S. Lee). 1999. "Zhongguo Yanglao baoxian shengji tongchou yihou de maodun: fenxi yu duice yanjiu" [Contradictions in China's pension insurance after provincial-level pooling: Analysis and research on countermeasures]. Working paper, China Center for Economic Research (CCER). Available at http://old.ccer.edu.cn/workingpaper/workingpaper99c.htm (accessed May 15, 2002).

Jiang Deli. 2000. "Bu jinjin shi yi ge 'qian' zi: Ningxia jijia qianfei baoguang qiye zhuifang" [It's Not Simply the 'Money:' In Pursuit of the Exposure of Several Ningxia Delinquent Enterprises]. *Zhongguo shehui baozhang* [China Social Security] 12:4–5.

Jiao Kaiping, ed. 2001. *Yanglao baoxian* [Pension insurance]. Beijing: Zhongguo laodong shehui baozhang chubanshe.

Johnson, M. Francis. 2002. "Elites and Agencies: Forging Labor Policy at China's Central Level." *Modern China* 28(2): 147–76.

Kahler, Miles, and David A. Lake, eds. 2003. *Governance in a Global Economy: Political Authority in Transition*. Princeton: Princeton University Press.

Kasza, Gregory J. 2006. *One World of Welfare: Japan in Comparative Perspective*. Ithaca: Cornell University Press.

Katzenstein, Peter J. 1985. *Small States in World Markets*. Ithaca: Cornell University Press.

Kay, Stephen J. 1999. "Unexpected Privatizations: Politics and Social Security Reform in the Southern Cone." *Comparative Politics* 31(4): 403–22.

Kennedy, Scott. 2005. *The Business of Lobbying in China*. Cambridge, Mass.: Harvard University Press.

Khan, Azizur Rahman, and Carl Riskin. 2005. "China's Household Income and Its Distribution, 1995 and 2002." *China Quarterly* 182: 356–84.

Kornai, Janos, Stephan Haggard, and Robert Kaufman, eds. 2001. *Reforming the State: Fiscal and Welfare Reform in Post-Socialist Countries*. New York: Cambridge University Press.

Kramer, Mark. 1996. "Social Protection Policies and Safety Nets in East-Central Europe: Dilemmas of the Postcommunist Transformation." In *Sustaining the Transition: The Social Safety Net in Postcommunist Europe*, edited by Ethan B.

Kapstein and Michael Mandelbaum, 46–123. New York: Council on Foreign Relations.

Kwong, Julia, and Yulin Qui. 2003. "China's Social Security Reforms under Market Socialism." *Public Administration Quarterly* 27(1–2): 188–209.

Kynge, James. 2000. "Chinese Miners Riot over Severance Pay." *Financial Times*, April 3, p. 9.

Kynge, James, and Joe Leahy. 2002. "Beijing Backs Away from State Shares Sell-Off." *Financial Times*, June 25, p. 17.

Lam, Willy Wo-Lap. 2007. "The Latin-Americanization of China's Domestic Politics." *China Brief* 6(21). Available at http://www.jamestown.org (accessed January 15, 2009).

Landry, Pierre. 2008. *Decentralized Authoritarianism in China: The Communist Party's Control of Local Elites in the Post-Mao Era*. New York: Cambridge University Press.

Leckie, Stuart, and Yasue Pai. 2005. *Pension Funds in China: A New Look*. Hong Kong: ISI Publications.

Lee, Ching Kwan. 2002. "From the Specter of Mao to the Spirit of the Law: Labor Insurgency in China." *Theory and Society* 31(2): 189–228.

———. 2007. "The Unmaking of the Chinese Working Class in the Northeastern Rustbelt." In *Working in China: Ethnographies of Labor and Workplace Transformation*, edited by Ching Kwan Lee, 15–37. New York: Routledge.

———. 2008. *Against the Law: Labor Protest in China's Rustbelt and Sunbelt*. Berkeley: University of California.

Lee, Grace O. M., and Malcolm Warner. 2004. "The Shanghai Re-employment Model: From Local Experiment to Nation-wide Labor Market Policy." *China Quarterly* 177:174–89.

Lee, Peter Nan-Shong, and Chack-Kie Wong. 2001. "The Tale of Two Cities: Rolling Back the Boundary of the Welfare State during the Reform Era." In *Remaking China's Public Management*, edited by Peter Nan-Shong Lee and Carlos Wing-Hung Lo, 67–95. Westport, Conn.: Quorum Books.

Leisering, Lutz, Gong Sen, and Athar Hussain. 2002. *People's Republic of China: Old-Age Pensions for the Rural Areas: From Land Reform to Globalization*. Manila: Asian Development Bank.

Liao Yihai. 2002. "Qingli qiye qianfei renzhong daoyuan" [Shouldering heavy responsibilities in clearing up enterprise fee arrears]. *Zhongguo shehui baozhang, lunwen zhuanji* [China Social Security, special collection]: 161–63.

Lieberthal, Kenneth G. 1992. "Introduction: The 'Fragmented Authoritarianism' Model and Its Limitations." In *Bureaucracy, Politics, and Decision Making in Post-Mao China*, edited by Kenneth G. Lieberthal and David M. Lampton, 1–30. Berkeley: University of California Press.

Lieberthal, Kenneth G., and Michel Oksenberg. 1988. *Policymaking in China: Leaders, Structures, and Processes*. Princeton: Princeton University Press.

Lin, Kun-Chin. 2009. "Class Formation or Fragmentation?: Allegiances and Divisions among Managers and Workers in State-Owned Enterprises." In *Laid-Off Workers in a Workers' State: Unemployment with Chinese Characteristics*, edited by Thomas B. Gold, William J. Hurst, Jaeyoun Won, and Li Qiang. New York: Palgrave Macmillan, p. 61–92.

Lin, Yi-min, and Tian Zhu. 2001. "Ownership Restructuring in Chinese State Industry: An Analysis of Evidence on Initial Organizational Changes." *China Quarterly* 166: 305–41.

Lipsmeyer, Christine S. 2002. "Parties and Policy: Evaluating Economic and Partisan Influences on Welfare Policy Spending during the European Post-Communist Transition." *British Journal of Political Science* 32(4): 641–61.

Llana, Sara Miller. 2008. "Brazil becomes Antipoverty Showcase." *Christian Science Monitor*. November 13, p. 1.

Lloyd-Sherlock, Peter. 2002. "Formal Social Protection for Older People in Developing Countries: Three Different Approaches." *Journal of Social Policy* 31(4): 695–713.

Lü, Xiaobo. 2000. *Cadres and Corruption: The Organizational Involution of the Chinese Communist Party.* Stanford: Stanford University Press.

Lynch, Julia. 2006. *Age in the Welfare State: The Origins of Social Spending on Pensioners, Workers, and Children.* New York: Cambridge University Press.

Madrid, Raúl L. 2003. *Retiring the State: The Politics of Pension Privatization in Latin America and Beyond.* Stanford: Stanford University Press.

Malloy, James M. 1979. *The Politics of Social Security in Brazil.* Pittsburgh: University of Pittsburgh Press.

Mandelbaum, Michael. 1996. "Introduction." In *Sustaining the Transition: The Social Safety Net in Postcommunist Europe*, edited by Ethan B. Kapstein and Michael Mandelbaum, 1–9. New York: Council on Foreign Relations.

Mares, Isabela. 2003. "The Sources of Business Interest in Social Insurance: Sectoral versus National Differences." *World Politics* 55(2): 229–58.

McGuire, James W. 1999. "Labor Union Strength and Human Development in East Asia and Latin America." *Studies in Comparative International Development* 33(4): 3–34.

Mehrtens, F. John III. 2004. "Three Worlds of Public Opinion: Values, Variation, and the Effect on Social Policy." *International Journal of Public Opinion Research* 16(2): 115–43.

Mertha, Andrew C. 2005. *The Politics of Piracy: Intellectual Property in Contemporary China.* Ithaca: Cornell University Press.

Ministry of Civil Affairs. 2008. "2007nian minzheng shiye fazhan tongji gongbao" [Ministry of Civil Affairs developments and statistics report, 2007]. Available at http://cws.mca.gov.cn/article/tjkb (accessed December 1, 2008).

Ministry of Finance. 2003. *Difang caizheng tongji ziliao* [Local finance statistical materials]. Beijing: Zhongguo caizheng jingji chubanshe.

Ministry of Human Resources and Social Security (MOHRSS). 2008a. "2007nian laodong he shehui baozhang shiye fazhan tongji gongbao" [Report on labor and social security developments, 2007]. Available at http://w1.mohrss.gov.cn/gb/zwxx/2008-06/05/content_240415.htm (accessed August 9, 2008).

———. 2008b. "2007 nian quanguo shehui baoxian qingkuang" [National social insurance conditions, 2007]. Available at http://www.molss.gov.cn/gb/zwxx/2008-06/12/content_241248.htm (accessed January 15, 2009).

Ministry of Labor, Social Insurance Bureau. 1997. *Zhongguo shehui baoxian nianjian 1997* [China social insurance yearbook, 1997]. Beijing: Zhongguo renshichubanshe.

Ministry of Labor and Social Security (MOLSS). 2000. "Laodong he shehui bao-zhangbu guanyu jiakuai shixing yanglaojin shehuihua fafang de tongzhi" [MOLSS notice on speeding the implementation of the socialization of pension distributions]. Notice No. 9. Available at http://www.molss.gov.cn/correlate/lsbf20009.htm (Accessed Oct. 29, 2001).

———. 2001–2002. *Zhongguo laodong he shehui baozhang nianjian* [China labor and social security yearbook]. Beijing: Zhongguo laodong he shehui baozhang chubanshe.

———. 2002. "Laodong he shehui baozhangbu gongbu: qianjiao jiben yanglao ba-oxian fei qian wan yuan yishang qiye mingdan" [Ministry of Labor and Social Security announces list of enterprises that owe more than 10 million yuan]. January 8. Available at http://www.molss.gov.cn/news/2002/1081.htm (accessed August 10, 2002).

———. 2005. "Guanyu kaifa quanguo shehui baoxian jingban jigou renyuan peixun gongzuo de tongzhi" [Notice on development of training for National Social Insurance Agency staff]. Available at http://www.ln.lss.gov.cn/zcfg/user/note.asp ?LawId=1813 (accessed July 10, 2008).

Ministry of Labor and Social Security (MOLSS) Legal Department. 2002. *La-odong he shehui baozhang zhengce fagui huibian, 2001* [Compendium of labor and social security policies and regulations, 2001]. Beijing: Zhongguo laodong shehui baozhang chubanshe.

Ministry of Labor and Social Security (MOLSS) Social Insurance Management Center (SIMC). 2000. *Zhongguo shehui baoxian nianjian 2000* [China social insurance yearbook, 2000]. Beijing: Zhongguo renshichubanshe.

Ministry of Labor and Social Security (MOLSS) and Ministry of Finance. 1999. "La-odong he shehui baozhangbu caizhengbu guanyu jianli jiben yanglao baoxian shengji tongchou zhidu youguan wenti de tongzhi" [Ministry of Labor and Social Security and Ministry of Finance notice on the relevant problems in establishing provincial level pools for basic pension insurance]. Document No. 37. Available at http://www.molss.gov.cn/correlate/lsbf20009.htm (accessed October 29, 2001).

Montinola, Gabriella, Yingyi Qian, and Barry R. Weingast. 1995. "Federalism, Chinese Style: The Political Basis for Economic Success in China." *World Politics* 48(1): 50–81.

Müller, Katharina. 1999. *The Political Economy of Pension Reform in Central-Eastern Europe.* Northampton, UK: Edward Elgar.

———. 2003. *Privatizing Old-Age Security: Latin America and Eastern Europe Compared.* Northampton, UK: Edward Elgar.

Nanfang Zhoumo [Southern Weekend]. 2005. "Siying qiyejia chuzi zuo 'nongmin-gong yanglao baoxian wenti diaocha' " [An entrepreneur does an "investigation into the problem of migrant labor pensions"]. February 24. Available at: http://www.cnss.cn (accessed February 27, 2008).

National Audit Office. 2006. "Qiye zhigong jiben yanglao baoxian jijin, chengzhen zhigong jiben yiliao baoxian jijin he shiye baoxian jijin shenji jieguo" [Audit results for enterprise employees basic pension insurance funds, urban employees basic medical insurance funds, and unemployment insurance funds]. November 24. Available at http://www.audit.gov.cn/cysite/docpage/c516/200611/1123_516_17913.htm (accessed January 2, 2008).

National Committee on Aging. 2002. "Quanguo laoling gongzuo weiyuanhui fachu tongzhi yaoqiu shenru kaifa yu 'Falungong' xiejiao zuzhi de douzheng" [National Committee on Aging issues notice demanding the deepening of the struggle against the evil cult "Falungong"]. In *Laoling gongzuo wenjian xuanbian* [Selected documents from work on aging], edited by the National Committee on Aging, Vol. 1, 53–54. Beijing: Geming chubanshe.

National Council for the Social Security Fund (NCSSF), People's Republic of China. 2006. *2006 Annual Report* [Quanguo Shehui baozang jijin lishehui 2006nian gongbao]. Available at http://www.ssf.gov.cn/web/index.asp (accessed November 13, 2007).

National People's Congress (NPC). 2008. "Shehui baoxian fa shi goujian zheng ge shehui baozhang zhidu de hexin" [Social insurance law is the core for establishing a social security system]. January 3. Available at http://www.npc.gov.cn/npc/zt/2008-01/03/content_1388092.htm (accessed January 3, 2008).

——. 2009. "Guanyu shehui baoxianfa caoan zhengqiu yijian de qingkuang" [On the solicitation of comments on the draft Social Insurance Law]. February 23. Available at http://www.npc.gov.cn (accessed February 27, 2009).

Nattrass, Nicoli. 2005. "Trading Off Income and Health? AIDS and the Disability Grant in South Africa." *Journal of Social Policy* 35(1): 3–19.

Nelson, Joan M. 2001. "Pension and Health Reforms in Hungary and Poland." In *Reforming the State: Fiscal and Welfare Reform in Post-Socialist Countries*, edited by János Kornai, Stephan Haggard, and Robert R. Kaufman, 235–66. New York: Cambridge University Press.

O'Brien, Kevin, and Lianjiang Li. 1999. "Selective Policy Implementation in Rural China." *Comparative Politics* 31(2): 167–86.

Oi, Jean. 1999. *Rural China Takes Off: Institutional Foundations of Economic Reform*. Berkeley: University of California Press.

Orenstein, Mitchell A. 2000. "How Politics and Institutions Affect Pension Reform in Three Postcommunist Countries." World Bank Development Research Group, Policy Research Working Paper, No. 2310, World Bank, Washington, D.C.

——. 2005. "The New Pension Reform as Global Policy." *Global Social Policy* 5(2): 175–202.

——. 2008. *Privatizing Pensions: The Transnational Campaign for Social Security Reform*. Princeton: Princeton University Press.

Organisation for Economic Co-Operation and Development (OECD). 2006. *Challenges for China's Public Spending: Toward Greater Effectiveness and Equity*. Paris: OECD Publishing.

Orszag, Peter R., and Joseph Stiglitz. 1999. "Rethinking Pension Reform: Ten Myths about Social Security Systems." Paper presented at the World Bank conference on New Ideas about Old Age Security, Washington, D.C.

Pan, Philip P. 2002. "Chinese Workers' Rights Stop at Courtroom Door." *Washington Post*, June 28, p. A1.

Pearson, Margaret M. 1998. *China's New Business Elite: The Political Consequences of Economic Reform.* Berkeley: University of California Press.

Peerenboom, Randall. 2007. *China Modernizes: Threat to the West or Model for the Rest?* New York: Oxford University Press.

Pei, Minxin. 2006. *China's Trapped Transition: The Limits of Developmental Autocracy.* Cambridge, Mass.: Harvard University Press.

Pierson, Paul. 1994. *Dismantling the Welfare State?: Reagan, Thatcher, and the Politics of Retrenchment.* New York: Cambridge University Press.

———. 1995. "Fragmented Welfare States: Federal Institutions and the Development of Social Policy." *Governance* 8(4): 449–78.

Pierson, Paul, and Stephan Leibfried. 1995. "Multitiered Institutions and the Making of Social Policy." In *European Social Policy: Between Fragmentation and Integration,* edited by Stephan Leibfried and Paul Pierson, 1–40. Washington, D.C.: Brookings Institution Press.

Pierson, Paul, and Theda Skocpol. 2002. "Historical Institutionalism in Contemporary Political Science." In *Political Science: The State of the Discipline,* edited by Ira Katznelson and Helen V. Milner, 693–721. New York: W. W. Norton.

Polanyi, Karl. 1957/2001. *The Great Transformation.* Boston: Beacon Hill.

Pomfret, John. 2002. "China Cracks Down on Worker Protests." *Washington Post,* March 21, p. A21.

Rudra, Nita. 2002. "Globalization and the Decline of the Welfare State in Less-Developed Countries." *International Organization* 56(2): 411–45.

———. 2005. "Globalization and the Strengthening of Democracy in the Developing World." *American Journal of Political Science* 49(4): 704–30.

Rutkowski, Jan J. 1998. "Welfare and the Labor Market in Poland: Social Policy during Economic Transition." World Bank Technical Paper no. 417. World Bank, Washington, D.C.

Salditt, Felix, Peter Whiteford, and Willem Adema. 2007. "Pension Reform in China: Progress and Prospects." OECD Social, Employment and Migration Working Paper, no. 53. OECD, Paris.

Scharpf, Fritz W. 1988. "The Joint-Decision Trap: Lessons from German Federalism and European Integration." *Public Administration* 66(3): 239–78.

Seekings, Jeremy. 2005. "Prospects for Basic Income in Developing Countries: A Comparative Analysis of Welfare Regimes in the South." Centre for Social Science Research Working Paper no. 104. Cape Town, South Africa: Centre for Social Science Research, University of Cape Town.

Seekings, Jeremy, and Nicoli Nattrass. 2005. *Class, Race, and Inequality in South Africa.* New Haven: Yale University Press.

Segal, Adam, and Eric Thun. 2001. "Thinking Globally, Acting Locally: Local Governments, Industrial Sectors, and Development in China." *Politics & Society* 29(4): 557–88.

Sellers, Jeffrey M., and Andres Lidström. 2007. "Decentralization, Local Government, and the Welfare State." *Governance* 20(4): 609–32.

Shi Bainian. 1999. *Zhongguo shehui yanglao baoxian zhidu yanjiu* [Research on China's social old-age insurance system]. Beijing: Jingji guanli chubanshe.

Shi, Tianjian. 2000. "Cultural Values and Democracy in the People's Republic of China." *China Quarterly* 162: 540–59.

Shirk, Susan L. 1993. *The Political Logic of Economic Reform in China.* Berkeley: University of California Press.

Shliefer, Andrei, and Robert W. Vishny. 1993. "Corruption." *Quarterly Journal of Economics* 108(3): 599–618.

Shue, Vivienne. 1988. *The Reach of the State: Sketches of the Chinese Body Politic.* Stanford: Stanford University Press.

——. 2004. "Legitimacy Crisis in China?" In *State and Society in 21st-Century China: Crisis, Contention, and Legitimation,* edited by Peter Hays Gries and Stanley Rosen, 1–49. New York: RoutledgeCurzon.

Sin, Yvonne. 2005. "Pension Liabilities and Reform Options for Old Age Insurance." Working Paper Series on China. World Bank, Washington, D.C.

Solinger, Dorothy J. 2002. "Labor Market Reform and the Plight of the Laid-off Proletariat." *China Quarterly* 170: 304–26.

——. 2005. "Path Dependency Reexamined: Chinese Welfare Policy in the Transition to Unemployment." *Comparative Politics* 38(1): 83–101.

——. 2006. "The Creation of a New Underclass in China and Its Implications." *Environment and Urbanization* 18(1): 177–93.

Song Houzhen. 1999. "Yanglao baoxianfei zhengjiao nanti zenyang jie" [Resolving Difficulties in the Collection of Pension Insurance Fees]. *Zhongguo shehui baozhang* [China Social Security] 59:11–13.

State Council. 1991. "Guowuyuan guanyu qiye zhigong yanglao baoxian zhidu gaige de jueding" [State Council decision on pension system reform for enterprises employees]. Document No. 33. Available at http://www.molss.gov.cn/correlate/lsbf20009.htm (accessed October 29, 2001).

——. 1995. "Guowuyuan guanyu shenhua qiye zhigong yanglao baoxian zhidu gaige de tongzhi" [State Council notice on deepening enterprise employees pension system reform]. Document No. 6. Available at http://www.molss.gov.cn/correlate/lsbf20009.htm (accessed October 29, 2001).

——. 1997. "Guowuyuan guanyu jianli tongyi de qiye zhigong jiben yanglao baoxian zhidu de jueding" [State Council decision on establishing a unified basic pension insurance system for enterprise workers and staff]. Document No. 26. Available at http://www.molss.gov.cn/correlate/lsbf20009.htm (accessed October 29, 2001).

State Council Development Research Center, Research Group. 2001. "Zhongguo yanglao baozhang zhidu gaige" [Reform of China's pension system]. In *Zhongguo shehui baozhang tizhi gaige* [Restructuring China's social security system], edited by Wang Mengkui, 3–32. Beijing: Zhongguo fazhan chubanshe.

State Statistics Bureau (SSB). 1985. *Zhongguo laodong gongzi tongji ziliao, 1949–1985* [China labor and wage statistics, 1949–1985]. Beijing: Zhongguo tongji chubanshe.

——. 2004–2008. *Zhongguo tongji nianjian* [China statistics yearbook]. Available at: http://www.stats.gov.cn/tjsj/ndsj.

State Statistics Bureau (SSB) and Ministry of Labor and Social Security (MOLSS). 1998–2006. *Zhongguo laodong tongji nianjian* [China labor statistics yearbook]. Beijing: Zhongguo tongji chubanshe.

Steinfeld, Edward. 1998. *Forging Reform in China: The Fate of State-Owned Industry*. New York: Cambridge University Press.

Stockmann, Daniela. 2009. "One Size Doesn't Fit All: Measuring News Reception East and West." *Chinese Journal of Communication* 2(2): 167–77.

Tang, Wenfang. 2005. *Public Opinion and Political Change in China*. Stanford: Stanford University Press.

Thelen, Kathleen. 1999. "Historical Institutionalism in Comparative Politics." *Annual Review of Political Science* 2: 369–404.

———. 2003. "How Institutions Evolve: Insights from Comparative-Historical Analysis." In *Comparative Historical Analysis in the Social Sciences*, edited by James Mahoney and Dietrich Rueschemeyer, 208–40. Cambridge, UK: Cambridge University Press.

Thelen, Kathleen, and Sven Steinmo. 1992. "Historical Institutionalism in Comparative Politics." In *Structuring Politics: Historical Institutionalism in Comparative Analysis*, edited by Sven Steinmo, Kathleen Thelen, and Frank Longstreth, 1–32. Cambridge, UK: Cambridge University Press.

Tsai, Kellee S. 2007. *Capitalism without Democracy: The Private Sector in Contemporary China*. Ithaca: Cornell University Press.

United Nations Development Programme (UNDP). 2006. *Human Development Report*. Available at http://hdr.undp.org/en/reports/global/hdr2006 (accessed July 20, 2008).

U.S. Social Security Administration (SSA). 2008. "Social Security Programs throughout the World." Available at http://www.socialsecurity.gov/policy/docs/progdesc/ssptw (accessed July 18, 2008).

Wang Fayun and Yang Jianmei. 2004. "2003nian shehui baozhang tixi fazhan yu fawang" [2003 Social Security System developments and prospects]. In *Shehui lanpishu: 2004nian Zhongguo shehui xingshi fenxi yu ceyan* [Blue book of China's society: Analysis and forecast of China's social development, 2004], edited by Ru Xin, Lu Xueyi, and Li Peilin, 104–16. Beijing: Shehui kexue wenxian chubanshe.

Wang Heyan, Zhao Hejuan, and Ji Minhua. 2008. "End of the Line for the Shanghai Scandal" *Caijing*, April 1. Available at http://www.caijing.com.cn/English/Cover/2008–04–01/54869.shtml (accessed April 2, 2008).

Wang, Shaoguang. 2004. "China's Health System: From Crisis to Opportunity." *Yale-China Health Journal* 3:5–49.

Wang Yaguang, and Jiang Xufeng. 2008. "Economic Stimulus Package to Improve People's Livelihood." December 8. Available at http://www.xinhuanet.com (accessed December 6, 2008).

Wang, Yan, Dianqing Xu, Zhi Wang, and Fan Zhai. 2000. "Implicit Pension Debt, Transition Cost, Options and Impact on China's Pension Reform: A Computable General Equilibrium Analysis." World Bank Policy Research Working Paper Series. World Bank, Washington, D.C.

Wang Zeying 2004. "Empirical Analysis of Retirement Timing of Urban Workers in China: Suggestions for Policy Adjustments." Presentation slides, China Insurance and Social Security Research Center, Beijing University, November 12.

Waterbury, John. 1993. *Exposed to Innumerable Delusions: Public Enterprise and State Power in Egypt, India, Mexico, and Turkey.* New York: Cambridge University Press.

Wedeman, Andrew. 2001. "Incompetence, Noise, and Fear in Central-Local Relations in China." *Studies in Comparative International Development* 35(4): 59–83.

Wei Wenzhong. 2005. "Fei gongyouzhi jingji shehui baozhang zhidu jidai wanshan" [Needed completion of social security for the non-state economy]. *Jingji yu shehui fazhan* [Economic and Social Development] 3(6): 81–83.

Weissert, Will. 2009. "Cuba Boosts Retirement Age as Population Goes Gray." Associated Press, March 27.

Wenzhou Municipal Government. 2002. "Wenzhoushi renmin zhengfu guanyu fei gongyou qiye yanglao baoxian kuomian de tongzhi" [Wenzhou Municipal People's Government Office notice regarding the expansion of pension insurance in non-state enterprises]. Available at http://www.hngm.gov.cn/gb/wz/citizen/smbs/welfare/yanglao/zcfg/userobject10ai1329.html (accessed February 15, 2005).

West, Loraine A. 1999. "Pension Reform in China: Preparing for the Future." *Journal of Development Studies* 35: 153–83.

Weyland, Kurt. 1996. "Obstacles to Social Reform in Brazil." *Comparative Politics* 29: 1–22.

——. 2005. "Theories of Policy Diffusion: Lessons from Latin American Pension Reform." *World Politics* 57(2): 262–95.

White, Gordon. 1998. "Social Security Reforms in China: Towards an East Asian Model?" In *The East Asian Welfare Model: Welfare Orientalism and the State,* edited by Roger Goodman, Gordon White, and Huck-ju Kwon, 175–97. London: Routledge.

Whiteford, Peter. 2003. "From Enterprise Protection to Social Protection: Pension Reform in China." *Global Social Policy* 3(1): 45–77.

Whiting, Susan H. 2001. *Power and Wealth in Rural China: The Political Economy of Institutional Change.* New York: Cambridge University Press.

Wibbels, Erik. 2001. "Federal Politics and Market Reform in the Developing World." *Studies in Comparative International Development* 36(2): 27–53.

——. 2005. *Federalism and the Market: Intergovernmental Conflict and Economic Reform in the Developing World.* New York: Cambridge University Press.

Won, Jaeyoun. 2004. "Withering Away of the Iron Rice Bowl? The Reemployment Project of Post-Socialist China." *Studies in Comparative International Development* 39(2): 71–93.

Wong, Christine P. W., and Richard M. Bird. 2008. "China's Fiscal System: A Work in Progress." In *China's Great Economic Transformation,* edited by Loren Brandt and Thomas G. Rawski, 429–66. New York: Cambridge University Press.

World Bank. 1994. *Averting the Old Age Crisis: Polices to Protect the Old and Promote Growth.* New York: Oxford University Press.

——. 1997. *Old Age Security: Pension Reform in China.* Washington, D.C.: World Bank.

——. 2001. *Attacking Poverty: World Development Report 2000/2001.* Oxford: Oxford University Press.

———. 2006. *World Bank Development Indicators, 2006.* Washington, D.C.: World Bank.

———. 2008. *World Bank Development Indicators, 2008.* Washington, D.C.: World Bank.

World Health Organization (WHO). 2000. *The World Health Report 2000.* Geneva: WHO.

Xiang Huaicheng. 2002. "Zengjia shehui baozhang touru; wanshan shebao tixi" [Increase social security spending; perfect social security system]. *Renmin ribao* [People's Daily], December 23. Available at http://www.china.org.cn (accessed March 30, 2003).

Xiao Shuchen. 2004. "Henan Zhengzhou feiguoqi zhigong yanglao baoxian canbaolü" [Pension insurance participation rates of employees in nonstate enterprises in Zhengzhou, Henan]. *Gongren ribao* [Workers' Daily], June 22. Available at http://news.sina.com.cn/c/2004-06-22/0919287272718s.shtml (accessed November 15, 2007).

Xie Ai. 2002. "Woguo shehui baoxian lifa qushi" [Legislative trends in China's social insurance]. In *Zhongguo shehui baozhang, lunwen zhuanji* [China Social Security, special collection]: 208–11.

Xie Jianhua and Ba Feng. 1999. *Shehui baoxian faxue* [Social insurance legal studies]. Beijing: Beijing daxue chubanshe.

Xinhua. 1999a. "400,000 in Shanghai Pick Up Pensions without Leaving the Residence Committee." In *Zhongguo shehui baozhang* [China Social Security] 55: 41.

———. 1999b. "Liaoning Takes a Step Forward in the Legalization of Pension Insurance." In *Zhongguo shehui baozhang* [China Social Security] 63: 40.

———. 1999c. "Qingdao Issues Warning to 26 Enterprises Owing Fees without Cause." In *Zhongguo shehui baozhang* [China Social Security] 55: 41.

———. 2000a. "News Analysis on Socialized Distribution of Pensions in China." Foreign Broadcast Information Service, China. FBIS-CHI-2000–0823.

———. 2000b. "PRC State Council Premier Zhu Rongji at Forum on Improving Social Security System." Foreign Broadcast Information Service, China. FBIS-CHI-2000–0529.

———. 2000c. "PRC's Zhu Rongji Addresses Social Security Conference." Foreign Broadcast Information Service, China. FBIS-CHI-2000–1227.

———. 2001. "MOLSS Announces 20 Enterprises That Owe More than 10 Million Yuan." September 23. Available at: http://www.molss.gov.cn (accessed November 8, 2001).

———. 2002. "China Basically Fulfills Pension Distributions." February 26. Available at http://www.xinhua.com (accessed March 5, 2002).

———. 2007. "Official on Trial over Vanished Pension Funds." Available at http://www.chinadaily.com.cn/china/2007-10/30/content_6217416.htm (accessed October 30, 2007).

Xinhua Economic News Service. 2006 "Chinese SOEs Refuse to Transfer State-Owned Shares to Social Security Funds." Available at http://english.people.com/cn200612/19/eng20061219_334044.html (accessed April 21, 2007).

Xinhuanet. 2002. "Zouchu huise didai shebaojijin fengyu qianxing" [Out among the ashen land: Trials and hardships of social insurance funds]. In *Guoji jinrong*

bao [International Financial Report], August 9, 2002. Available at http://news
.xinhuanet.com/fortune/2002-08/09/content_517974.htm (accessed March 15,
2005).
——. 2008. "China Earmarks [U.S.] $2 Billion for Raising Retirement Pension
This Year." January 18. Available at http://news.xinhuanet.com/english/2008-01/
16/content_7433109.htm (accessed January 18, 2008).
Yang, Dali L. 2004. *Remaking the Chinese Leviathan: Market Transition and the
Politics of Governance in China*. Stanford: Stanford University Press.
Ye Xiangqun. 2004. *Zhongguo shehui yanglao baozhang: Kunjing yu jueze* [China's social pension security: Dilemmas and choices]. Beijing: Shehui kexue wenxian chubanshe.
Yuan Lunqu. 1990. *Zhongguo laodong jingji shi* [Labor economics history of China]. Beijing: Beijing jingji xueyuan chubanshe.
Zhao Yaohui, and Xu Jianguo. 1999. "Zhongguo chengzhen yanglao baoxian tixi de zhuangui wenti" [Transition problems in China's urban pension system].
Working paper, China Center for Economic Research (CCER). Available at http://old.ccer.edu.cn/workingpaper/workingpaper99c.htm (accessed June 1, 2002).
——. 2002. "China's Urban Pension System: Reforms and Problems." *Cato Journal*
21(3): 395–414.
Zhao Zhuoya. 2002. "Dui zhenan shanqu kuoda yanglao baoxian fugaimian de sikao" [Ideas for expanding pension coverage for the southern Zhejiang's mountainous region]. *Jiaxing xueyuan xuebao* [Journal of Jiaxing College] 14(2): 10–16.

Index